Critical Data Studies

Critical Data Studies

An A to Z Guide to Concepts and Methods

Rob Kitchin

polity

Polity Press
65 Bridge Street
Cambridge CB2 1UR, UK

Polity Press
111 River Street
Hoboken, NJ 07030, USA

ISBN-13: 978-1-5095-6652-5
ISBN-13: 978-1-5095-6653-2(pb)

A catalogue record for this book is available from the British Library.

Library of Congress Control Number: 2024942683

Typeset in 11 on 13pt Plantin
by Cheshire Typesetting Ltd, Cuddington, Cheshire
Printed and bound in Great Britain by CPI Group (UK) Ltd, Croydon

The publisher has used its best endeavours to ensure that the URLs for external websites referred to in this book are correct and active at the time of going to press. However, the publisher has no responsibility for the websites and can make no guarantee that a site will remain live or that the content is or will remain appropriate.

Every effort has been made to trace all copyright holders, but if any have been overlooked the publisher will be pleased to include any necessary credits in any subsequent reprint or edition.

For further information on Polity, visit our website:
politybooks.com

Contents

Acknowledgements

The writing of this book was conducted as part of the 'Data Stories: Telling Stories About and With Planning and Property Data' project, funded by a European Research Council grant (101052998). The text draws on a wide, interdisciplinary literature, as well as the various books (e.g., *The Data Revolution*, *Data Lives*, *Researching Digital Life*) and the numerous papers I have (co)written relating to data. With respect to my own sources, I have rewritten any material included. The open access publication of the book has been funded by the European Research Council and Maynooth University Library. Many thanks to Hugh Murphy, the Deputy University Librarian, for his support. I am grateful for members of the Data Stories project research team – Juliette Davret, Oliver Dawkins, Danielle Hynes, Carla Maria Kayanan and Sam Mutter – as well as an anonymous reviewer for reading and providing feedback on the initial draft manuscript. Many thanks to Mary Savigar, Stephanie Homer and Neil de Cort at Polity Books for commissioning the book and shepherding it through review and publication, and to Tim Clark for copyediting the manuscript. I am grateful to Laurie Frick for providing permission to use her data art 'Earth' from the Imagined Time series (2009) for the book cover. To view more of her work visit www.lauriefrick.com and @lauriefrick on Instagram.

Introduction

Data are incredibly important in today's contemporary world. They form the basis for scientific progress, constitute the evidence for social policy and business decisions, underpin the workings of management and governance, and have become a major economic asset, with *data markets* and *data services* forming a significant component of the world's economy. Yet, until recently, data received relatively little scrutiny. Traditionally, data have been treated as neutral, unproblematic measures that form the building blocks for *information* and *knowledge* or form the input for computation. While data were critical for answering scientific questions and essential for digital systems to work, attention was focused on what the data were being used for, and rarely the data themselves. If data were the focus of attention, it was usually in relation to *data quality*, *data access* or some technical aspect of their production, management, and use. This started to change two decades ago. Increasing *datafication*, the rise of *big data* and *open data*, and the proliferation of *data infrastructures* and data-driven systems and their mediation of all aspects of everyday life, led to data becoming the central focus of analysis for scholars across a number of disciplines (e.g., Media Studies, Science and Technology Studies, Sociology, Geography, Anthropology, Philosophy, Library and Archive Studies, and Data Science). Importantly, these studies did not treat data in a commonsensical way, but rather sought to critically interrogate their nature and the politics, praxes, and implications of their production and use.

In 2014, these studies were identified as a new field of academic enquiry and labelled as *Critical Data Studies* (CDS) (Dalton and Thatcher, 2014). CDS is an umbrella term to describe the collection of scholars and their work that take *data* as their primary research object (Iliadis and Russo, 2016; Richterich, 2018; Hepp et al., 2022; Kitchin, 2022). CDS theorises the nature of data, how they are produced and shared, the institutional and infrastructural apparatus assembled to manage and govern the *data lifecycle*, how data are used to make sense of the world and to perform practical action, and examines whose agenda data and data-driven systems serve. CDS never takes data and their use at face value, but actively reflects on and questions data forms, processes, and purposes, and considers what is at stake when data are produced and deployed to create knowledge, manage society, derive business value, and perform numerous other tasks.

Philosophically, CDS is rooted in a number of schools of thought that sit under the umbrella of critical social theory, such as feminism, poststructuralism, structuralism, and critical realism. These ways of thinking actively question the *epistemology* and *methodology* of the *scientific method* and centre questions of politics and power in the production of knowledge, and in understanding how social and technical processes work in practice to create the world in which we live. Methodologically, CDS most often uses *qualitative methods* to examine the politics and praxes of data work, but it also uses *quantitative methods*, though it does so using a post-positivist framing, such as those adopted within *feminist data science, critical GIS* or *radical statistics*. The aim is to produce *reflexive* and *situated knowledges* about and with data.

CDS has expanded rapidly since being named as a new field. Thousands of papers and dozens of books that take data as their core focus have now been published across disciplines. A new journal, *Big Data & Society* was founded in 2014, which acts as a key site of dissemination, and there are regularly organised international conferences such as *Data Power* and *Data Justice*, along with dozens of other singular, themed conferences and workshops. Numerous concepts have been developed to make sense of the nature of data and the contemporary data-driven world, and a diverse set of methods have been created and utilised. Intellectually, through its unique constellation of new, borrowed and adapted concepts and methods, and institutionally, through its academic endeavours, CDS has come of age as a vibrant, interdisciplinary field.

The principal aims of this book are threefold. First, to produce a comprehensive (but not exhaustive) mapping of the conceptual and methodological terrain of CDS. To that end, the book identifies the present state-of-play, providing succinct definitions and descriptions of 413 key terms, along with suggested further reading. Second, to provide a pedagogic resource that enables students and researchers to look up terms that might be used in the classroom or in publications but in a way shorn of a detailed explanation of their meaning. The entries are designed to quickly orientate and improve the reader's comprehension of a term and to point to sources that provide more information. Third, the book acts as a guide for discovering ideas, concepts, and methods that might be of value for students and researchers in their own studies and analysis. By browsing or following the trail of cross-references, the reader is introduced to new ways to think about and approach data-related phenomena and issues.

Many of the concepts discussed in the book are still in their infancy, and the methods in an experimental phase: they are far from being fully developed and grounded on a strong empirical basis. In part then, a number of concepts that hold promise for sense-making, but require further theoretical and empirical exploration and explication, are identified. As such, the book hints at a potential roadmap for CDS research for the next decade and beyond. No doubt, some of the concepts will prove to be stickier than others, becoming a key means through which to understand data and their uses, and adopted as a fundamental part of the CDS lexicon, whereas others will fail to gain traction and be discarded and replaced with new terms or ideas. Many of the concepts and methods detailed have a wider usage across other fields and disciplines and their inclusion reveals how interdisciplinary and porous CDS is conceptually and methodologically; here, they are discussed specifically in relation to their definition and use within CDS.

Hopefully the book provides a useful guide to how data and our present data-driven world are being made sense of and researched, and the entries will enrich your knowledge, inform your own data practices, and aid your studies.

References

Dalton, C. and Thatcher, J. (2014) 'What does a critical data studies look like and why do we care?', *Society & Space blog*, 19 May, www.societyandspace.org/articles/what-does-acritical-data studies-look-like-and-why-do-we-care

Hepp, A., Jarke, J. and Kramp, L. (2022) 'New perspectives in Critical Data Studies: The ambivalences of data power – An introduction', in Hepp, A., Jarke, J. and Kramp, L. (eds), *New Perspectives in Critical Data Studies*. Palgrave Macmillan, Cham, Switzerland, pp. 1–23.

Iliadis, A. and Russo, F. (2016) 'Critical data studies: An introduction', *Big Data & Society*, 3(2): 1–7.

Kitchin, R. (2022) *The Data Revolution: A Critical Approach to Big Data, Open Data, and Data Infrastructures*. Second edition. Sage, London.

Richterich, A. (2018) *The Big Data Agenda: Data Ethics and Critical Data Studies*. University of Westminster Press, London.

How to use this book

Rather than consisting of a narrative overview of Critical Data Studies (CDS), with the discussion organised in a set of related chapters, this book adopts a dictionary-style format and is structured alphabetically as 413 separate entries. Each entry provides a definition and description of a concept or method that is employed within CDS, along with cross-references to other entries (marked in *italics*) that detail related information. Following the established practice for dictionary-style entries, the source material used is not extensively cited. Instead, readers are pointed to key reference texts that will expand their comprehension of the term and its focus. Further reading is only suggested for entries where there is active debate and/or a much more extensive literature related to the issue or topic. Beyond the 413 full entries, a number of the headwords simply cross-reference to other synonymous terms; they have been included as a headword as they are common terms that a reader might search for.

It is not expected that a reader will work their way through the book from A to Z. Rather, the reader can dip in-and-out of the text, searching for specific terms as required, or they can browse to discover ideas, concepts, methods, issues, and phenomena they might not otherwise encounter. Whether dipping in-and-out or browsing, the cross-referencing in each entry can be followed, enabling the reader to create their own path through the material. Meandering along a trail of cross-references allows related additional insights to be gained and facilitates the widening and deepening of the reader's knowledge of the field. A small number of the cross-references do not exactly match the target headword; for example, *aggregated* might be italicised to point to aggregation or *preserve* to point to preservation. This has been done to avoid constructing convoluted sentences to ensure that the exact headword is used; hopefully, the headwords that these non-exact cross-references point to are obvious. Another mode of navigation is to use the index to find all entries that discuss particular terms.

A–Z of Critical Data Studies

A

abduction   A mode of logical inference and reasoning that seeks a conclusion that makes logical and credible sense based on established knowledge and already available evidence. Abduction is commonly used to devise *hypotheses* based on assessing the *veracity* of previous findings and conclusions to determine what might logically be the answer to a yet unanswered question or constitute a missing piece of a theory. This hypothesis is then tested through a *deductive* approach to determine if the initial abducted inference holds true. The same process can be applied to prospecting the most suitable approaches and methods to empirically answer questions and provide new insights. See also *induction*.

Further reading

Miller, H.J. (2010) 'The data avalanche is here: Shouldn't we be digging?', *Journal of Regional Science*, 50(1): 181–201.

access, see *data access*

accountability   Being held responsible for ensuring that data generation, *data sharing*, and data use are compliant with ethical expectations. Accountability is one of the core tenets of *Fair Information Practice Principles*. To be effective, accountability has to be encoded into *data regulations* and legislation (see *law and data*), be enforced, and be accompanied by a redress system.

Accountability is also a key principle for *open data*, though in this context the availability of open data provides an evidence base for holding its producers to account with respect to their policies and actions (see *disclosure data*, *transparency*).

accuracy and precision   Accuracy is how close a set of measurements are to their true value. Precision is the variance in error, and the degree of *repeatability*, *reproducibility*, *and replicability* in a measurement. The more fine-grained a measurement, the more accurate it potentially becomes (e.g., measuring in millimetres rather than centimetres). Similarly, a low degree of variance in measurement error increases precision (the confidence in a statistical result expressed as a standard deviation). The repetition of a study is precise when the findings across repetitions are the same or very closely grouped. In the context of a political poll, accuracy is how closely the poll results match the actual outcomes, and precision is the standard deviation in relation to the poll results (e.g., political party A will receive 21 per cent of the vote, +/– 2 per cent). A dataset can be accurate, precise, both, or neither. Ideally, a dataset is both. Accuracy can be improved through *calibration*, and precision through improvements to the measurement technique that reduce variance.

administrative data   Data that are collected by organisations for the purpose of managing their operations and activities. In the context of government and public bodies, administrative data are used for monitoring populations and services. Administrative data are essential for state *bureaucracy* and include registrations, applications, transactions, and general record keeping. The rise of e-government and e-governance has expanded the volume of administrative data and also how they are processed and value extracted from them. They are increasingly used as evidence to inform policy, to produce *metrics* to monitor the effectiveness of state work, and to produce *official statistics*. Most *open data* published by government bodies are administrative data transformed by *aggregation* and *anonymisation*; they also constitute the *indicator data* displayed in open *dashboards*. Nonetheless, a large proportion of public administrative data remains closed, especially *personal data*, used solely for the work of government. In businesses, administrative data are used to record and manage operations, transactions and interactions with customers and suppliers, and for general corporate bureaucracy. There is a *data politics* to what data are captured for the purposes of administration, as well as who/what is counted or *uncounted*. Common concerns include *data quality* and data being used to practise *social sorting*.

Further reading

Cobham, A. (2020) *The Uncounted*. Polity Press, Cambridge.

Cole, S., Dhaliwal, I., Saulmann, A., and Lilhuber, L. (eds) (2020), *Handbook on Using Administrative Data for Research and Evidence-Based Policy*. Abdul Latif Jameel Poverty Action Lab, Cambridge, MA.

affect The various ways in which people make sense of and emotively experience the world in response to a particular set of conditions, including feelings, emotions, moods, intuition, imagination, predispositions, and pre-cognitive thoughts. How people engage with data is experiential and affective in nature, sparking a range of feelings, emotions, and moods that can shape their sense of themselves and influence well-being. Undertaking data work can be frustrating and provoke feelings of uncertainty and *data anxieties*; it can also be tedious and boring, or stimulating and exciting. The decisions and recommendations made by data-driven systems can incite anger or delight, and the pressures of multitasking across devices and *platforms* can create stresses. Anthropological and phenomenological forms of *Critical Data Studies* identify and document how interfacing with data produces affective responses, and examine how data work is shaped by how people feel and act. See also *data performativity, datafied agency, embodiment*.

Further reading

Lupton, D. (2020) *Data Selves*. Polity Press, Cambridge.

aggregation The conversion of individual data points into a single composite data point. Aggregation can be performed in a number of ways, usually statistical in nature. For example, the aggregate age of a population can be calculated as its mean, median or mode. Typically, aggregation is used to compare groups of samples (e.g., to compare the population characteristics of neighbouring districts). Aggregation enables standardisation that is independent of population size (e.g., number of people per square kilometre). It is also used as a means of anonymising data and circumventing *data protection* and *privacy* laws, which are generally targeted at individual-level data (see also *data minimisation principle*). It should be noted that aggregation can produce *ecological fallacies* in interpretation (i.e., assuming that an aggregate value is reflective of the underlying individual data points) as variance within a dataset is removed. For example, the mean of a sample of scores (95, 90, 10, 5) is 50, yet no member of the sample has a score reflective of the mean score.

algorithm   A set of defined steps structured to process instructions and data in order to produce a desired output. An algorithm can be analogue in nature, such as a written set of procedures for calculating a mathematical formula. More commonly, it is understood to refer to computer code that will computationally process data, perform calculations, and enact decisions. Fundamentally, software consists of interlinked sets of algorithms, each designed to perform a certain function. Since just about every aspect of society is now mediated by software, algorithms have become central to how everyday tasks are performed. Algorithms are key to: search, discovery, calculation, *automation*, optimisation, *profiling, prediction*, recommendations and decision-making. *Critical Data Studies* (CDS) recognises that algorithms are produced to perform specific tasks and their creation and operation is political in nature; that is, they serve particular interests. Algorithms are not neutral and value free, but embody and implement regimes of *power/knowledge* and they are used to manage and govern society and economy. As such, CDS focuses attention on the politics of algorithms and the secondary agency they enact. From this perspective, algorithms are understood to be *contingent*, their work shaped by wider *context*, and performative, influencing how a system functions and shapes the wider world. In particular, CDS highlights that algorithms are reliant on the data that they process, and poor *data quality* will affect how algorithms perform and their outcomes.

CDS also recognises that understanding the constitution and work of algorithms is not straightforward. Algorithms are often *black-boxed* given they embody important *intellectual property rights* and create competitive advantage for their developers. They generally do not work singularly, but are intertwined with hundreds of other algorithms, making it difficult to identify the effects of specific algorithms. Moreover, they are constantly being refined, reworked, and patched, and some are programmed to evolve as they self-learn from data and outcomes, meaning that they can be somewhat of a moving target. Since their work is contingent and contextual in nature, varying outcomes are produced in different circumstances. They can have *biases* and *glitches*, perform unintended acts, and produce *unanticipated consequences*. Researching algorithms then poses challenges. A number of methodological approaches have been adopted to make sense of algorithms, including examining source code where possible, reverse engineering an algorithm by running dummy data through a black-boxed system and building a model that replicates outcomes, interviewing programmers or conducting an ethnography of a coding team, or examining the effects of algorithms on a how a system works and performs.

Further reading

Amoore, L. (2020) *Cloud Ethics: Algorithms and the Attributes of Ourselves and Others.* Duke University Press, Durham, NC.

Kitchin, R. (2017) 'Thinking critically about and researching algorithms', *Information, Communication and Society*, 20(1): 14–29.

analogue data Data that are captured and stored in a non-digital form. Analogue data might be recorded on paper, captured on photos or microfilm, or be etched onto stone or vinyl, or recorded using other material forms. Processing and performing calculations on analogue data can be demanding and time consuming as they are undertaken by hand or using basic calculative instruments (e.g., abacuses, slide rules, calculators). In recent years, significant investment has been made in *digitising* analogue data (e.g., scanning or re-recording data sources) to enable *re-use* and analysis using *data analytics*. See also *digital data*.

anonymisation The process of hiding the identities of *data subjects*. Anonymisation protects the *personal data* and *privacy* of individuals by removing the means to connect their data to them. A range of techniques can be used to anonymise a dataset, including the use of *pseudonyms*, reducing precision through *generalisation*, removing sensitive fields, and *aggregation*. There are concerns relating to some of these techniques, especially the use of *pseudonyms*, as these are *indexical data* and are also vulnerable to reidentification by third parties.

Further reading

Green, B., Cunningham, G., Ekblaw, A., Kominers, P., Linzer, A., and Crawford, S. (2017) *Open Data Privacy*, The Berkman Klein Center for Internet & Society Research Publication No. 2017–1. Harvard University, Cambridge, MA, https://ssrn.com/abstract=2924751

API (application programming interface) A piece of software that enables two or more computer programs to communicate with one another. APIs provide tools and services for interfacing with other software and they are an important means of *data access* and *data sharing*. In most cases APIs are private, used internally within a company or with designated partners to construct, run, and interconnect systems. Open APIs allow others to also interface with those systems to access specific data and services, while at the same time hiding certain system details. In cases where there is no open API, it can be possible to create a bespoke API to perform *data scraping* on publicly accessible websites.

archive A formal collection of materials, including data, that are actively curated and preserved for future use. Long-standing archives have large collections of *analogue data* and materials. Many of these archives are in the process of *digitising* some of these collections and making them available online. A digital archive is not simply a *data holding* or backup system but is structured, documented, and managed by archivists who *curate* the data held and aid those accessing the archive. The data collections are accompanied by *metadata* that aids discovery and a *preservation* plan that prolongs their life, along with all supporting documents, *metadata*, records of *lineage* and *provenance*, and conditions of use. Some archives have a statutory obligation to archive collections and make them available to the public; for example, national archives, libraries, museums and galleries, and *national statistics organisations*, which are mandated to preserve nationally important and culturally significant material and data. Their digital collections are designed to extend the audience and use of archived material and to preserve *born-digital data* for future generations. Other archives are private endeavours and access might be limited; for example, company and personal archives.

Traditionally, what is archived has been skewed to elite interests, with materials relating to ordinary citizens less likely to be preserved, and those belonging to marginalised groups entirely absent or misrepresented. In addition, some archives store displaced materials; for example, records belonging to one country stored in another as a result of colonial relations and theft. By managing what gets archived, the state and elite interests get to control the past and what is known about it. Archives then are not a neutral, technical means of preserving records and artefacts. Instead, they are *socio-technical* systems; their focus, aims, and practices, and their choices about what to archive, who can access the materials, and what they can do with them, are all politically mediated and negotiated. Dissatisfaction with the strategies and policies of some archives has led to the formation of *community archives* and the practice of *counter-archiving*. See also *data infrastructure, data repository, trusted digital repository*.

Further reading

Featherstone, M. (2006) 'Archive', *Theory, Culture & Society*, 23(2–3): 591–6.

Lowry, J. (ed.) (2017) *Displaced Archives*. Routledge, London.

articulation   Identifying, assembling, scheduling, coordinating, and monitoring all the tasks – and the steps in these tasks – in order to complete a job. The process of articulation involves performatively joining together and building tasks to achieve a goal, such as performing *data entry, data cleaning* or compiling *metadata*. This includes organising the work and its delivery across individuals and institutions. Each stage might be separately articulated, with stages themselves then meshed together. A key component of articulation is working through a course of action to reach completion despite problems encountered, such as *glitches* and unanticipated events. Articulation reveals data work to be a situated, sometimes uncertain, activity composed of many tasks and steps that unfold *contingently* through individual and collective action, including changing procedures and direction if required. A poorly articulated process is less likely to succeed in its execution. *Standardised* processes seek to reduce articulation work by having a specified workflow, though they remain open to uncertainty and coordinated and improvised interventions. See also *scaffolding*.

Further reading

Nadim, T. (2016) 'Data labours: How the sequence databases GenBank and EMBL-Bank make data', *Science as Culture*, 25(4): 496–519.

Tanweer, A., Fiore-Gartland, B., and Aragon, C. (2016) 'Impediment to insight to innovation: Understanding data assemblages through the breakdown–repair process', *Information, Communication & Society*, 19(6): 736–52.

artificial intelligence   The ability of digital devices to computationally produce required information, to make informed decisions and to act on them, and to learn from their operation. Some definitions refer to artificial intelligence being computationally equivalent to, or an imitation of, human intelligence. Generally, however, the intelligence aspect is seen more as an analogy and its use signifies a degree of self-learning and that decisions and outcomes are autonomously derived by a digital device, enabling degrees of *automation* in systems. The degree of intelligence in AI systems varies substantially. Some systems perform a single task well, such as searching for information, recognising faces, or transcribing recorded interviews, based on a limited set of *training data* and fixed parameters. AI that utilises deep learning aims to be more generative and flexible, able to tackle a range of tasks and to self-adjust parameters and outcomes in relation to context and direction. While the programming of AI is undoubtedly paramount, the sourcing and quality of training data are also key as they can produce significant *bias* and *error*. See also *machine learning*.

Further reading

Elliott, A. (2022) *Making Sense of AI: Our Algorithmic World*. Polity Press, Cambridge.

McQuillan, D. (2022) *Resisting AI: An Anti-Fascist Approach to Artificial Intelligence*. Bristol University Press, Bristol.

arts-based methods   Methods that use creative practice and media to undertake and communicate research. Such creative practice and media include creative writing (e.g., fiction, poetry, and creative non-fiction), art and craft practices (e.g., painting, photography, sculpture, textiles), performance (e.g., theatre, film, music), and media and installation art (e.g., interactive video, digital media). Arts-based methods for engaging with audiences beyond academia have become increasingly popular because they present ideas and findings in ways that might be more engaging, illuminating, and impactful. More recently, arts-based methods have also been utilised for undertaking social sciences research (including *Critical Data Studies*), being the means through which data are generated and sense is made of phenomena. Termed *research-creation*, the affordances of creative practices are used to enable questions to be explored and answered in new ways.

Further reading

Ash, J., Kitchin, R., and Leszczynski, A. (2024) *Researching Digital Life: Orientations, Methods and Practice*. Chapter 7. Sage, London.

Kara, H. (2015) *Creative Research Methods in the Social Sciences*. Policy Press, Bristol.

attribute data   Data that record the attributes of a phenomenon, but do not uniquely identify it. For example, with respect to a house, attribute data might consist of the size of the property and plot, the number of rooms, the price, the property tax band, the energy rating, and so on. Attribute data are connected to the phenomena to which they refer by *indexical data*. Attribute data can be combined and analysed in order to compare grouped samples (see *aggregation*). The vast majority of data generated and stored are attribute data.

autoethnography, data, see *data autoethnography*

autographic data   Data that is inscribed in the materiality of the phenomenon being examined. Since objects, environments, and bodies bear the marks of past events, they actively record and process data. In some cases, this data inscription or embodiment can be quite explicit; for example, tree rings materially reveal the age of a tree. Often the data inscription is not so clear or is more elusive, yet nonetheless traces are present. Traditionally, these inscriptions have been captured and encoded as representative data (as abstract symbols – numbers, letters) and presented through various forms of statistics, models, and visualisations. An autographic approach to data instead focuses on the origins of data and how data are inscribed in phenomena, rather than their abstract representation. In so doing, it places attention on the materiality of data and the actual world, and not its symbolic representation, which is often confused with reality yet can also be a poor model of it. In other words, an autographic approach to data promotes a non-representational notion of data and examining and presenting data in ways that do not rely on statistics and visualisation; for example, exploring the physical qualities of self-inscribed data (e.g., tree rings or ice core layers) and using *data physicalisations*. See also *data materiality*.

Further reading

Offenhuber, D. (2024) *Autographic Design: The Matter of Data in a Self-Inscribing World.* MIT Press, Cambridge, MA.

automated data   The automatic generation and capture of data through algorithmic processes. An example of automated data generation is the use of weather sensors at selected sites to produce a range of related data (e.g., temperature, humidity, rainfall, wind speed and direction, barometric pressure), which are transferred in real-time via an internet connection to a central server for processing and analysis (see *sensor data*). Similarly, *APIs* can be used to automatically access and capture machine-readable data from *platforms* (see *data scraping*). Automated data processes typically produce data that are *machine-readable* and therefore are open to *automated* processes of handling and analysis.

automated management   The use of automated systems in the management and governance of society. For example, welfare systems are being increasingly automated, with peoples' entitlements automatically calculated and administered. Likewise, traffic management is automated, with speed cameras linked to machine-vision systems that can detect and read number plates, cross-reference them to a licensing database, and automatically impose fines or penalty points for detected infractions. The use of such automated systems raises ethical and political questions, especially since their decisions and actions can have a major impact on individual lives. Weak *algorithms*, biased *training data*, and poor *data quality* can all lead to erroneous or unfair decisions and actions. *Black-boxing* and a lack of *transparency* and oversight weakens *accountability*. The result is systems where automated decisions are made, but those affected by the decisions do not know the basis of the outcome and nor can they effectively argue against the decision.

Further reading

Eubanks, V. (2017) *Automating Inequality: How High-Tech Tools Profile, Police, and Punish The Poor.* St Martin's Press, New York.

automation Machines undertaking practices and processes that are usually performed by people. Automation is adopted in order to reduce labour costs and human error, and to increase efficiency and productivity. The first wave of automation occurred as electro-mechanical machines replaced manual labour; for example, in factories as the production line became mechanised. More recently, automation is taking place through the use of digital devices, such as digitally mediated machines and robots, and the use of computers. The power of computation and the use of *artificial intelligence* now means that it is not only manual labour that is being replaced by automation, but also knowledge-based labour that involves formalised rules, such as law, medicine, finance, and administration. People, though, are not entirely removed from the operation of most automated systems, with there being three levels of human participation. In human-in-the-loop systems, automation is used to undertake rote work, but people make and perform key decisions. In human-on-the-loop systems, automation is used to run all aspects of work and decision-making, but a human operator oversees the system and can intervene and override the automated process. In human-out-of-the-loop systems the automated system is autonomous, acting without human input or interaction. The level of automation raises important questions of *accountability* and redress, particularly when used to govern populations. Both the *algorithms* and the data employed are vital to how automation performs, with unsuitable or poor *data quality* undermining outcomes. Yet, since most automated systems are *black-boxed*, it is often difficult to assess the suitability and *veracity* of algorithms and data. A contention of *Critical Data Studies* is that most analyses of automation overly focus on its algorithmic aspects, with too little attention paid to the data used. See also *automated data*.

Further reading
Andrejevic, M. (2019) *Automated Media*. Routledge, London.

B

benchmarking The process of comparing the relative performance of *indicator data* across different entities such as individuals, organisations, and places. Benchmarking usually involves creating a scorecard by ranking entities in relation to their performance on a specific, or set of, indicator data, as well as noting whether the entity is rising or falling in the ranking over time. For example, the relative performance of different cities might be compared across a range of benchmarked indicators. Through such a process a city can evaluate how well it is performing against cities that are competing for the same inward investment, and consider policies to guide urban development and social and economic interventions. The data can also be used by citizens as means of holding local government to account for their decisions and actions if performance is falling. While a popular management tool of business and government, benchmarking is not universally endorsed. For example, university rankings have been critiqued for: failing to recognise differences in inputs and ambitions between institutions (e.g., universities have different student populations and resources and seek to realise varying outcomes) meaning a straight comparison of indicator data can be misleading; being biased towards and rewarding those institutions that already perform well, making it difficult for others to catch up; and encouraging competition between individuals and institutions that can be counterproductive by undermining collegiality and cooperation. See also *dashboards, key performance indicators, metrics*.

Further reading

Kitchin, R., Lauriault, T., and McArdle, G. (2015) 'Knowing and governing cities through urban indicators, city benchmarking and real-time dashboards', *Regional Studies, Regional Science* 2: 1–28.

bias   A consistent pattern of error within a dataset, or within a method of data processing and analysis, that skews findings and interpretation. Bias can be introduced into a dataset unintentionally or deliberately. It is usually caused by the *sampling* technique adopted or issues with a method (e.g., poorly constructed questions on a survey) or instrument (e.g., weak *calibration* of a measuring device). Many *platforms* have biases relating to the populations that use them along lines of age, *gender*, *race*, class, and political views (e.g., only a small percentage of people aged over sixty-five use Twitter/X), meaning that data harvested from such platforms inherently lack *representativeness*. Data processes such as *aggregation* can create bias by reducing the variance in a dataset. Bias in a dataset can cause *ecological fallacy* issues, wherein conclusions are not truly representative of the phenomenon under investigation (see *veracity*). Such ecological fallacies can have a marked impact, such as racist biases in the *training data* of predictive policing systems perpetuating the unjust targeting of black people. It is therefore important to try to establish if bias exists within a dataset and to perform *data cleaning* and *data wrangling* to remove it, or to account for its effects in the interpretation of findings.

Big Brother   An analogy that describes a condition of *surveillance* that renders populations highly visible and open to control by those that own the means of monitoring. The term was popularised by George Orwell's novel *1984*, published in 1949, which depicts a future society saturated with surveillance technologies that enable the state to closely monitor and control the actions of a population. The term is presently evoked to characterise the potential consequences of mass surveillance, *dataveillance*, and the use of algorithmic governance in contemporary society, particularly by government bodies (see *governmentality*). The routine use of indexical data, including *biometric data*, diverse streams of *big data*, *profiling* and *social sorting* makes a Big Brother situation seem a possibility. This is particularly the case in authoritarian regimes.

big data Data that are generated and processed in real-time and are exhaustive to a system; that is, they are continuously produced for an entire population rather than a sample (see *real-time data, exhaustivity*). The term was first used in the mid-1990s to refer to the handling and analysis of massive datasets, and was popularised in the late 2000s to refer to data that was characterised as having *volume, velocity,* and *variety*. Prior to this period, the production and handling of data were constrained across these three attributes, with it only being possible for two to exist simultaneously (volume and velocity; variety and velocity; volume and variety). Advances in computation, database design, storage capacity, and analytics, however, enabled datasets to possess all three.

The definition of big data has been much debated in the literature. In addition to volume, velocity, and variety, other characteristics have been identified, including: *exhaustivity* (wherein an entire population is captured (i.e., n = all), rather than being sampled); *granularity* (being fine-grained); *indexicality* (uniquely identifiable); *relationality* (easily conjoined to other datasets); *extensionality* (add/change new fields easily); and *scalability* (can expand in size rapidly). In reality, very few datasets that are commonly identified as big data possess all these traits. However, two in particular – velocity and exhaustivity – distinguish big data from what are now being called *small data*. Others contend that the definition of big data is less about the *ontological* characteristics of the data, and more about how they are processed using *automated* techniques and analysed using *data analytics* that employ *machine learning*.

Big data have been central to what has been termed the data revolution; that is, the increasing importance of data-driven systems in mediating all aspects of everyday life. Developments such as social media, online shopping, mobile computing, and *artificial intelligence* would be severely constrained without big data. Consequently, the production and use of big data have been a central concern of *Critical Data Studies* (CDS) and it is no coincidence that the premier CDS journal is named 'Big Data & Society'.

Further reading

boyd, d. and Crawford, K. (2012) 'Critical questions for big data', *Information, Communication and Society*, 15(5): 662–79.

Kitchin, R. and McArdle, G. (2016) 'What makes big data, big data? Exploring the ontological characteristics of 26 datasets', *Big Data & Society* 3: 1–10.

biometric data   Unique, *personal data* that can be used for identification, such as DNA, fingerprints, iris and facial patterns. Biometric data are *indexical data* in nature, enabling *attribute data* relating to a person to be linked together. Such data are becoming more commonly generated as a means to ensure that a person is correctly identified and to secure systems. For example, biometric data are used to access some state services and to cross state borders, and *surveillance* and policing systems are being extended through biometric tracing (e.g., CCTV enhanced with facial recognition capabilities and DNA databases). The use of such data, it is argued, reduces fraud and helps tackle crime. Biometric data are also becoming a means for securing and accessing personal digital devices (e.g., using a fingerprint or facial recognition to access a smartphone). The generation and use of biometric data raises a number of ethical issues, such as: *error* and *bias* in biometric *databases*; lack of safeguards for *data security*; unwarranted fine-grained surveillance, the spectre of *Big Brother*, and *social sorting*; the lack of redress and *accountability*; and the potential for *control creep* and inappropriate *data sharing* and *re-use*.

Further reading

Madianou, M. (2019) 'The biometric assemblage: Surveillance, experimentation, profit, and the measuring of refugee bodies', *Television & New Media*, 20(6): 581–99.

Nair, V. (2021) 'Becoming data: Biometric IDs and the individual in "Digital India"', *Journal of the Royal Anthropological Institute*, 27(S1): 26–42.

black-boxing   The occlusion of how a system works in practice. *Algorithms* and code encapsulate the key intellectual and business ideas at the heart of digital technologies. Those ideas are what produce the competitive advantage that allows companies to grow and develop. Not unsurprisingly then, their developers often want them to remain a secret. One way they achieve this is by denying access to the source code and sharing only the compiled app. For example, Google has black-boxed the workings of its PageRank algorithm used to sort search results. Similarly, companies and states will deny access to valuable data, only sharing what is necessary for the program/app to work and often in a fashion that cannot be *data scraped* (e.g., displaying data in a chart or map rather than sharing the underlying *database*). A key issue with black-boxing is when highly significant decisions (such as whether someone gets a loan or a job or a government benefit) are being made by algorithmic systems, but the means by which these decisions are made are not *transparent* and open to scrutiny, *accountability*, and redress. A counter to black-boxing has been the open source and *open data movements*, which enable all source code and data to be viewed and re-used.

Further reading

Pasquale, F. (2016) *The Black Box Society: The Secret Algorithms That Control Money and Information.* Harvard University Press, Cambridge, MA.

blockchain   A distributed *database* that enables the encrypted storage of data and anonymous and secure transactions. First introduced in 2009 as an alternative means of tracking financial transactions, a blockchain is a tamperproof public ledger where transactions are cryptographically verified by the entire network of peers. In traditional financial services, banks and other institutions act as trusted intermediaries that maintain a centralised database that records account transactions. In a cryptocurrency, such as Bitcoin, that utilises a blockchain ledger, transactions are shared among all owners of bitcoins who collectively verify the transaction and update the ledger. Since the ledger is public it cannot be amended without all participants knowing. In this sense, it is a trustless database in that the transaction is not dependent on a trust relationship with an intermediary; the integrity of the transaction is guaranteed by the technology. Given this transactional integrity, blockchain has been applied to a diverse range of activities that traditionally relied on social trust, such as *provenance* for artworks, supply chain management, legal and property contracts, and development aid. While blockchain seems like an ideal solution to *data integrity* and trust in transactions, it has also been critiqued with respect to the politics driving its introduction and implementation, as well as its environmental sustainability given the energy consumption required to maintain its architecture (see *political ecology of data*).

Further reading

Jutel, O. (2021) 'Blockchain imperialism in the Pacific', *Big Data & Society*, 8(1): 1–14.

born-digital data   Data that are produced through digital processes, rather than *analogue data* that has been *digitised*. A particular concern relating to born-digital data is *data loss* and long-term *preservation* for use by future generations, since digital data has a short lifespan without active maintenance. Public bodies, such as national *archives*, have started to create *trusted digital repositories* to ensure the preservation of born-digital data.

broken data   A concept that highlights how datasets are often incomplete, contain gaps, *errors*, *biases*, *gamed data* or *fake data*, and often require *data cleaning*, *data wrangling*, and *data maintenance and repair* to become useable. The concept was introduced by Pink et al. (2018) to highlight that data are often imperfectly produced and that over time, especially as they pass through numerous processes of handling, transformation, and storage, they can be disrupted, contaminated, and decay, becoming 'broken' to varying degrees. Data then have a fragility, and processes of data maintenance and repair need to be employed to ensure ongoing robustness and *data integrity*. Acknowledging the brokenness and need for maintenance of data highlights the contingency in their production and use. See also *stranded data*, *zombie data*.

Further reading

Pink, S., Ruckenstein, M., Willim, R., and Duque, M. (2018) 'Broken data: Conceptualising data in an emerging world', *Big Data & Society*, 5(2): 1–13.

bureaucracy   1. An administrative structure, usually composed of non-elected officials, that undertakes the management and policy tasks determined by its governing institution. 2. The use of administrative systems to manage and govern society. Since the Enlightenment, the state has sought to implement a more systematic way to manage and govern populations, businesses, and its own operations. A key means of doing this has been through formalised processes of capturing data about people, institutions, and activities. Registers, censuses, book-keeping, application procedures, and other types of record-keeping and form-filling enable states to produce detailed knowledge of their jurisdictions. They can then use this information to determine individual rights, entitlements, obligations, and duties with respect to domains such as welfare, education, health, finance, and taxation, and to detect non-compliance, evasion, and fraud. Other organisations, such as businesses, developed their own bureaucracies for managing suppliers, customers, and their own operations. Bureaucracy is a vital component of a *calculative regime* relating to a domain. *Datafication*, and the adoption of e-government and e-governance systems that generate *big data*, have expanded the scope, extent, and *timeliness* of bureaucracy by extending the production of *indexical data*, enabling the capture of *real-time data* with a finer *granularity*, and increasing the value that can be extracted from these data through improved *data management*, *data analytics*, and *profiling*.

Further reading

Kitchin, R. (2022) *The Data Revolution: A Critical Approach to Big Data, Open Data, and Data Infrastructures.* Chapter 10. Second edition. Sage, London.

C

calculative regime   The use of an interlocking set of measurement and monitoring procedures and technologies to enact a certain mode of thinking and behaviour. Calculative regimes are institutionalised by the state through *bureaucratic* systems that capture and monitor data about citizens, using these data to provide services and to reward and punish them. Individual sites, such as a school, enact a calculative regime that tracks student performance and discipline, as well as the work of staff, and the school itself might be subject to site-inspections and be compared against other schools (see *benchmarking*). Businesses have calculative regimes composed of the use of in-person supervision and evaluations, targets and *key performance indicators*, and *surveillance* technologies within a workplace (e.g., cameras, keystroke monitoring). A calculative regime is the means by which a mode of *governmentality* is expressed and implemented. Its aim is to produce a particular kind of social, economic, and moral arrangement whereby people are compelled to think and act in a desired manner, with penalties accruing to those who fail to comply. The *big data* age has had a pronounced effect on the constitution and operation of calculative regimes by increasing the scope, range, and *granularity* of measurement and monitoring, and shifting the mode of governmentality from discipline to control. See also *data regime*, *discursive regime*.

Further reading

Crooks, R. (2021) 'Productive myopia: Racialized organizations and edtech', *Big Data & Society*, 8(2): 1–16.

calibration   The comparison and adjustment of the performance of a measurement device in relation to a standard of known *accuracy*. The accuracy of a measurement instrument can alter over time, especially if its conditions alter, such as it being moved or damaged, or if it has been modified or repaired. Sometimes an instrument's performance can just gradually degrade. It is therefore necessary to periodically check and retune its measurement accuracy. For example, displayed time might be checked against a known accurate clock, or a thermometer calibrated against the true temperature. A calibration standard is usually set by a national or international *metrology* body (e.g., the International Bureau of Weights and Measures). Failure to calibrate an instrument can lead to systematic *bias* in a measurement sample.

capta   Units of *data* selected and harvested from the sum of all potential data. Etymologically, what we commonly refer to as data should technically be termed capta. Data is derived from the Latin word 'dare', meaning to give, whereas capta is derived from the Latin word 'capere', meaning to take. Data in its Latin root are all the potential data that can be sourced from a phenomenon, and capta are all those data that are actually captured. As such, to be etymologically correct, this book should be retitled 'Critical Capta Studies'. However, the use of data to mean that which is taken is so firmly embedded in science and popular use that correcting it to capta is all but impossible.

CARE data principles A set of people- and purpose-orientated principles designed to enable *data sovereignty*. Developed by the Global Indigenous Data Alliance, the CARE principles are: collective benefit (the data benefits those it concerns, improving governance and citizen engagement, and creating equitable outcomes); authority to control (those the data concern have a leadership role in *data governance*); responsibility (the data are handled and used responsibly); and *ethics* (the data are not used to cause harm and are used to create justice). The CARE principles aim to extend the *FAIR principles* (findable, accessible, interoperable, re-usable) commonly applied to *open data*. They are designed to protect and enhance the *data rights* of Indigenous and other marginalised communities with regards to the data related to them, and to counter data extraction, *biases*, misrepresentations and forms of *data power* that work against their interests. See also *decolonising data, Indigenous data*.

Further reading

Carroll, S.R., Herczog, E., Hudson, M., Russell, K., and Stall, S. (2021) 'Operationalizing the CARE and FAIR Principles for Indigenous data futures', *Nature: Scientific Data*, 8: 108.

categorisation and classification The process of organising data about phenomena by allocating them to categories/classes based on their characteristics. Categorisation is often used synonymously with classification; however, categorisation is the general practice of assigning data based on shared characteristics to separate informal categories as determined by the categoriser, whereas classification involves assigning data to classes using formal, established criteria. For example, books might be categorised by genre (e.g., fiction/non-fiction, or crime, science fiction, romance) where these categories are not formally defined, or they can be classified using the Dewey decimal system that has established *taxonomies* of standardised criteria. Categorisation and classification can involve different levels of abstraction. For example, a book could be identified with a high level of abstraction as 'non-fiction', which has a high degree of generality. A medium level of abstraction might identify the book as a social science text (Dewey class 300), whereas a low level of abstraction describes it as about 'social groups' (Dewey class 305), and a fine level of abstraction, which has a high degree of specificity and within-category similarity, as about 'racial, ethnic and national groups' (Dewey class 305.8) (see *ethnic data*, *Indigenous data*, *race and racist data*).

From a *Critical Data Studies* perspective, the processes of creating categories and classes, and of allocating entities to them, are not *objective*, neutral and value-free tasks. They involve evaluations and choices as to the category/class parameters and allocations. Different decisions will lead to varying taxonomies, which in turn will shape subsequent analysis and interpretation and potentially create *ecological fallacies*. In other words, categorisation and classification can be the outcome of explicit *data politics* (designed to enable discrimination) or create such data politics through their use. See also *data ontologies*.

Further reading

Bowker, G.C. and Star, S.L. (2000) *Sorting Things Out: Classification and its Consequences*. MIT Press, Cambridge, MA.

census   A *survey* of the population within a specified area. Censuses are typically conducted at the national scale. They are designed to count the number of people living in a country, their characteristics (e.g., age, *gender*, *race*, *ethnicity*, marital status, household composition), and aspects of their lives (e.g., their residence, education, work, health). Given the scale and cost of the task of surveying an entire population, and producing associated *tertiary data*, a census is usually taken once every ten years. The data are published in an *aggregated* form in order to protect confidentiality; in many countries, the *primary data* are only released after 100 years. Despite the effort and costs required to conduct a census, they are undertaken because the data generated provide important insights into a population and how it is changing over time, and they are used extensively in formulating social and economic policy. While maintaining the longitudinal aspect of a census is considered paramount (see *longitudinal data*), census questions do not remain static and questions are tweaked to try to improve *data quality* or replaced in order to capture data on new specific areas of interest. Similarly, the underlying *statistical geography* of the data can also be altered through boundary changes. There is therefore a tension between maintaining stability and allowing change, and the process of deciding on questions for each new census is full of *data politics* as different stakeholders argue their case. Many countries are examining the possibility of replacing their census with *administrative data* captured by state agencies.

chief data officer (CDO) An executive level post that has responsibility for an organisation's *data infrastructure, data management, data governance, data strategy* and data use. Prior to the *big data* age, these responsibilities usually lay with the chief information officer or head of IT, or with specific business units. A CDO oversees what data are generated, how they are processed and stored, what value are extracted from them, if and how they are shared, and ensures that *data standards* and *data regulations* are adhered to. They seek to maximise the value and use of data, identifying data assets and gaps, breaking down internal *data silos*, and driving change management towards being a more data-driven enterprise. A CDO takes the lead role in data innovation, *data maturity frameworks*, and the development and implementation of a data strategy. CDOs with varying education, work experiences, and business philosophies will approach and perform the role in different ways, shaping the data culture, *data practices*, and *data policies* within an organisation.

Further reading

Carruthers, C. and Jackson, P. (2020) *The Chief Data Officer's Playbook*. Second edition. Facet Publishing, London.

choice In the context of *data protection* and *privacy* regulations, choice concerns the ability of a *data subject* to opt in or out with regards to how their data are used or disclosed. Choice is a core principle of the *Fair Information Practice Principles*. Choice is linked to *consent* and *notice*. In practice, the choices regarding what data are generated, whom they are shared with, and how they are used, is constrained by difficulties in understanding the choices on offer, or by being presented with confusing options. For example, while it may be possible to make choices regarding the privacy settings in an app, it is often not intuitive to do so without technical knowledge. Restrictions and confusion in choice have partially driven the calls for *privacy by design*.

citizen science   Scientific research undertaken on a voluntary basis by members of the general public, usually in collaboration with professional scientists. Activities undertaken by citizens can include the generation, processing, analysis, and interpretation of data. In some cases, it might include contributing to the *research design*, running the project, and disseminating the findings. Citizen science endeavours are generally divided into three operational types: contributory, where the research design is undertaken and controlled by scientists and citizens simply contribute data; collaborative, where citizens might provide feedback on the research design and undertake analysis and interpretation; and co-created, where citizens are involved in all stages of the research, including leadership and research design. In some cases, a citizen science project is entirely conceived and operated by citizens and is designed to meet the same standards as professional research, but has limited or no involvement of professional scientists. Such projects are usually seeking to address a local issue by filling a knowledge gap or by providing *counter-data* to a dominant narrative.

Citizen science is viewed as being of great benefit to 'proper' science as it enables the mobilisation of a large body of labour and resources (such as local computing power, personal devices, and skilled knowledge) to contribute to solving scientific and social problems that would be difficult to achieve otherwise. From a data generation perspective, citizen science can provide an embedded, geographically distributed flow of data over time, where it would be costly to place professional staff in these locations. For example, observations from meteorological stations in remote areas are often collected and communicated to national weather bodies by trained farmers and other local citizens, who perform this role over many years (these roles are gradually being replaced with *automated* stations). While citizen science aims to produce data and analysis that meet the standards of professional research, there are some concerns over *data quality* and the continued commitment of contributors, though these are considered less of an issue than in bottom-up, citizen-organised *crowdsourcing* initiatives. See also *civic hacking, hackathons*.

Further reading

Hecker, S., Haklay, M., Bowser, A., Makuch, Z., Vogel, J., and Bonn, A. (eds) (2018) *Citizen Science: Innovation in Open Science, Society and Policy*. UCL Press, London.

citizenship, see *data citizenship*

civic hacking   The creation by citizens of apps, hardware, and data resources that are designed to address a social issue. The issues to be tackled and the potential solutions are determined by those participating. The solutions can involve the hacking together of software and apps, the creation and building of hardware (e.g., sensor arrays or community-owned internet infrastructure), and the production of datasets and *data analytics* tools (e.g., interactive *dashboards* and *data stories*). The hacking together of data resources is often a key activity. Unlike *hackathons*, civic hacking usually lasts months or even years. Initiatives can be either located in a particular place, addressing local issues, or be geographically dispersed with participants collaborating online. An example of the former is Code for America, where chapters are based in individual cities and meet regularly to progress their projects. Examples of the latter include open source software initiatives (e.g., Linux), and data initiatives on issues such as gun violence (e.g., Gun Violence Archive, Mapping Police Violence) and discrimination against Black people (e.g., Data for Black Lives). In some cases, civic hacking initiatives are run in conjunction with universities or with state bodies, who can provide resources such as data and equipment, meet-up space and skilled advice. See also *citizen science, crowdsourcing*.

Further reading

Gordon, E. and Mihailidis, P. (eds) (2016) *Civic Media: Technology, Design, Practice*. MIT Press, Cambridge, MA.

classification, see *categorisation*

cleanliness   In the context of *data quality*, cleanliness is a measure of how clean the data are (i.e., free of errors, gaps, biases, formatting, and structural issues). The cleaner the data, the less effort is necessary to address any shortcomings and to wrangle it into serviceable data (see *data cleaning, data wrangling*). While it can be relatively easy to spot gaps and formatting issues, errors and mis-coding are not always obvious. As such, it can sometimes be tricky to assess the level of data cleanliness. Nonetheless, it is important to always check the data and to run *exploratory data analysis* that might reveal cleanliness issues in order to increase the *veracity* of the analysis and the conclusions drawn.

cloud, the   The distributed storage of data and software services that can be accessed via an internet connection. Rather than storing data or software on a local or external hard drive, they are stored on servers that can be physically located anywhere on the planet, with any device with permission rights able to access them in *real-time*. Cloud storage providers enable users to buy or lease *data storage*, with some companies providing free hosting for a set amount of data with a fee accruing for additional data or services. Benefits to businesses include: the reduction of capital, energy, maintenance, and staff costs; they only pay for the storage they use; and the creation of new internet-accessed products and services. Along with NoSQL databases, the cloud has been a key enabler of *big data*, mobile apps, and *platforms*. It is thus central to the operations of networked computation and the services that are reliant on the internet. The development of the cloud has raised environmental sustainability concerns given the energy and water demands of *data centres* (see *political ecology of data*). In addition, since data can be physically stored anywhere, there have been concerns regarding *data protection* and *data security*, with some countries (e.g., Germany) mandating that state data cannot be hosted on servers located outside of the jurisdiction.

Further reading

Mosco, V. (2015) *To the Cloud: Big Data in a Turbulent World.* Routledge, London.

commons, see *data commons*

community archives   *Archives* that are created and managed by local communities. Community archives seek to preserve records and artefacts that are typically not being collected and curated by state bodies or companies. Their collections generally relate to ordinary citizens in a particular place, or to a local activity or marginalised identity, and seek to preserve collective memories and reveal history from below. These collections might complement, or form a counterpoint to, institutional archives, which typically reflect elite interests (see *counter-archiving*). The archive might be run by volunteers rather than professional paid staff, though they seek to undertake all the functions, practices, and governance structures of institutional archives. Some run training programmes to upskill citizens to be able to become active in the archive as curators or in other roles.

Further reading

Caswell, M., Migoni, A., Geraci, N., and Cifor, M. (2017) '"To be able to imagine otherwise": Community archives and the importance of representation', *Archives and Records*, 38(1): 5–26.

community of practice A group of people who share, learn, and interact around a common interest or endeavour. With respect to data, a community of practice might be a *civic hacking* initiative where people meet regularly to share knowledge, experience, and ideas, and learn through discussion and peer-to-peer support, with respect to their common practice of using data-driven technologies to try to solve a local issue. Within a work place, it might be a group of workers who meet over coffee or lunch to discuss common issues of interest, such as how to improve *data practices* or *data governance*. A community of practice can also be virtual, such as groups on social media or mailing lists. Civic hacking is a relatively formal type of community of practice given that there is an organisational structure and scheduled meetings. Through a community of practice members gain knowledge, a social identity, and personal development, and the community as a whole benefits through social learning and improvements with respect to their shared interest. The views and politics of members shape how a community of practice approaches an issue, and in turn the dialogue and learning within the community fosters shared dispositions and habits. Communities of practice can play an important role in mediating the structure, governance, and performance of data work in different contexts and settings.

Further reading

Blanc, S., Christman, J.B., Liu, R., Mitchell, C., Travers, E., and Bulkley, K.E. (2010) 'Learning to learn from data: Benchmarks and instructional communities', *Peabody Journal of Education* 85(2): 205–25.

completeness   The extent to which a dataset is complete in terms of the range and extent of its records and *coverage*. Many datasets are incomplete, missing data records, or have gaps in the coverage, or only relate to a sub-sample of a population. For example, some questions on a census form may have been left unanswered, or some households might not fill out a form at all. Sometimes a regular survey might be cancelled, or a sensor loses power for a while, leaving a gap in a time-series. Incomplete data might be caused accidentally, or be a deliberate effect of non-response, or be an artefact of how a system is designed. Incomplete data are often analysed as is, but care needs to be taken in interpreting results. Sometimes incomplete records can be addressed by filling gaps with *synthetic data*. See also *representativeness*.

composite indices   *Indicators* that are an amalgam of multiple *attribute data*. For example, a social deprivation index reports a single score for each locale (usually out of 100), with the score calculated by combining related attribute data in a weighted formula. These attribute data generally consist of income, employment status, education level, health status, crime levels, and housing conditions, with income and employment being more heavily weighted than the other variables. Composite indicators are useful when there is no single variable that adequately represents a phenomenon (see *veracity*). There are issues, however, with using composite indicators. The relative significance of each attribute is hidden within a composite score, and the allocation of weightings can have a significant effect on the score, meaning that changes to the weightings can radically alter the relative position of locales if the scores are ranked (and potentially cause *ecological fallacy* issues) (see *benchmarking*). This can have significant effects; for example, in jurisdictions where social deprivation indices are used to decide on area-targeted interventions to address deprivation, how the score is composed can make a difference as to whether an area is allocated funding.

computational social sciences A form of social science research that uses *machine learning* and *data analytics* to undertake statistical analysis and modelling of social phenomena. The approach builds on a much longer history of the use of the *scientific method* and *quantitative analysis* in social science research. It differs in that it leverages the massively increased computational power and sophisticated algorithmic and *modelling* techniques now available to undertake analysis that would have been all but impossible in the pre-digital era. In so doing, it is contended that the approach addresses a number of the shortcomings that attracted criticism of the quantitative social sciences, such as the charges of reductionism, generalisation, and universalism due to relatively small and static samples. Now, *big data* and data analytics enable wider-scale, finer-grained, dynamic, and nuanced analysis of large, *exhaustive* datasets. Nonetheless, the approach is still critiqued by critical social sciences for its *positivistic* logics and applying the scientific method to social issues, failing to acknowledge that human behaviour is often not rational and is inflected by culture, politics, power, and history that are open, contested, and often contradictory. Moreover, it largely fails to take into consideration metaphysical issues, such as opinions, values, and beliefs. Human societies, the detractors contend, are too complex, contingent, and messy to be explained meaningfully by formulae and laws. As a consequence, the computational social sciences are seen as being mechanistic, reductionist, and determinist. At the same time, a number of post-positivists use the same methods as computational social scientists, but do so within a different *epistemological* frame that seeks to leverage their insights while acknowledging their shortcomings (see *feminist data science, critical GIS, radical statistics*).

Further reading

Alvarez, R.M. (ed.) (2016) *Computational Social Science*. Cambridge University Press, Cambridge.

Engel, U., Quan-Haase, A., Lin, S.X., and Lyberg, L. (eds) (2021) *Handbook of Computational Social Sciences*. Routledge, London.

consent   Data are only generated and disclosed with the permission of the individuals to whom the data refer. Consent is a core principle of the *Fair Information Practice Principles*. Consent stipulates that data should be generated openly, be processed and used fairly and lawfully, and where possible this should be with the knowledge and permission of the *data subject*. Information regarding what consent involves should be communicated to the data subject through a *notice* and the response should involve a *choice*. A common critique of consent is that users often have little knowledge as to what they are consenting to, and that it is either implicitly assumed (through downloading, installing, and opening an app) a user has de facto consented to its terms and conditions of data extraction, or there is little to no ability to negotiate the rights being sought (with the user presented with either an 'accept' or 'decline' choice). Often, not agreeing to the terms and conditions of use means a service is denied, yet it might be the only means of performing a task, meaning that consent on the terms of the service provider is mandatory. Consent then can be an empty exercise.

Further reading

Andreotta, A.J., Kirkham, N., and Rizzi, M. (2022) 'AI, big data, and the future of consent', *AI & Society* 37(4): 1715–28.

Sexton, A., Shepherd, E., Duke-Williams, O., and Eveleigh, A. (2018) 'The role and nature of consent in government administrative data', *Big Data & Society*, 5(2): 1–17.

consistency   Stability and comparability in how data are generated, stored, and shared. Ideally, how data are produced over time, or between different jurisdictions or studies, are consistent in nature, making them directly comparable. While consistency is desirable, the way a measurement is undertaken may change due to alterations in how questions are phrased, or an instrument may be replaced or lose *accuracy* and *precision*. Different studies might use different questions, instruments or methods of data *categorisation and classification*. For example, national censuses are altered for each *census*, with amendments to questions and some questions being dropped. In addition, censuses in different countries might ask different questions or classify the data in different ways. A means of ensuring consistency is *standardisation*.

context   The situation in which a phenomenon or process takes places makes a difference to how it unfolds and to the outcome. A key assertion of *Critical Data Studies* is that context matters to the form and operations of data-driven systems. *Epistemologies* and *methodologies*, interpersonal and social relations, resourcing and capacities, organisational governance, policies and strategies, finance, institutional politics, the wider political, legal, and economic situation, and other factors influence choices, decisions, practices, and processes, shape *articulation*, and cause *data frictions* and *unanticipated consequences*. Data work is thus a situated, *contingent, socio-technical* activity, not one that takes place in a hermetically sealed vacuum of perfect, expected conditions. These contextual factors need to be documented and accounted for in any research focused on any aspect of the *data lifecycle* and how data are used.

Further reading

Loukissas, Y. (2019) *All Data Are Local: Thinking Critically in a Data-Driven Society*. MIT Press, Cambridge, MA.

contingency   A process or practice is never fixed in its application, but is always open to emerging and evolving in indeterminate ways depending on context, chance, and uncertainty. While the workings of a data system can be planned in detail, how it actually works will be full of contingencies: it might always be otherwise. One method can be chosen over another, a *glitch* can occur, individuals can make mistakes, a job is passed to another worker who uses a different approach, policy or governance arrangements are changed, and so on. Even small acts can change the course of how something is performed and the resulting outcomes. The *context* in which data work occurs can make a marked difference to the work undertaken. In other words, data and data work have a *liveliness* and are relational in nature. Recognising and accounting for contingency in the *data lifecycle* and the use of data is a key element of *Critical Data Studies* (CDS), highlighting how data are always cooked and never raw (see *cooked data, raw data*). For some, contingency shifts the *ontology* (what something is) of CDS to ontogenesis (how things become). Data from this perspective have no ontological security (are not fixed in nature and meaning), but are ontogenetic, continually produced through embodied, social, and technical practices and are put to work through situated, contextual activities. They are never, then, produced or used in the same way, but are always contingently remade every time they are engaged with.

Further reading

Kitchin, R. (2022) *The Data Revolution: A Critical Approach to Big Data, Open Data, and Data Infrastructures*. Second edition. Sage, London.

Tavmen, G. (2020) 'Data/infrastructure in the smart city: Understanding the infrastructural power of Citymapper app through technicity of data', *Big Data & Society*, 7(2): 1–15.

control creep   When a system designed for monitoring and managing a particular issue is *repurposed* to perform another function. Control creep particularly relates to systems designed to enact management and governance functions. For example, the technologies and data of traffic management systems might creep into being used in routine *surveillance*, policing, and security work. Covid-19 contact tracing apps were generally introduced with the promise that the data would not be used for other purposes, but in some jurisdictions data from the apps crept into legal cases (e.g., to prove location). Control creep typically violates the *data minimisation principle* of the *Fair Information Practice Principles* and undermines public trust in the uses of data-driven systems.

control room   A site from which a system or infrastructure is managed in real-time. *Sensor data* about present conditions and performance are communicated to a control room from measurement sites across a system or infrastructure, with these data used to modify how the system or infrastructure operates. With respect to a traffic system, *real-time data* from inductive loops and cameras at junctions are fed back to a control room, with the data then used to alter traffic light phasing across the city in an effort to avoid congestion and to keep traffic flowing. Within a city there are a plethora of control rooms, from small installations to manage a single site (e.g., CCTV in a shopping mall) or a technical system in a factory (e.g., a production line), to large control rooms for managing infrastructures such as bus and rail networks, air travel, water, energy, and communications. Control rooms have been in use since the 1930s, with early systems electro-mechanical in design. From the 1960s on they have progressively become digital in nature, and increasingly *automated* (though systems mainly remain human-on-the-loop, overseen by a human operator). In recent years, as part of the initiative to create smart cities, new integrative control rooms have been built that collapse *data silos*. Rather than controlling a single system or infrastructure, several are controlled from a single site, preferably from within a single management system. This merging of operational control aims to provide a more holistic, integrated, efficient, and productive form of operational governance. The use of control rooms raises a number of concerns with respect to cybersecurity, *data security*, *surveillance*, *privacy*, and *governmentality*.

Further reading

Luque-Ayala, A. and Marvin, S. (2020) *Urban Operating Systems: Producing the Computational City*. MIT Press, Cambridge, MA.

cooked data   A descriptive term used to signify that data are never raw, but are always cooked to some degree. That is, data do not pre-exist their collection, simply waiting to be harvested. Rather, all data are framed and produced through socio-technical processes and practices. Ideas, assumptions, protocols, and standards shape the methods used to produce data, instruments and techniques mediate how data are generated, and various means of *data cleaning* and *data wrangling* are applied to facilitate use. For example, altering the settings on an instrument will generate data that differs in its *accuracy and precision*. In other words, data are not independent of the framing, methods, and practices used to produce them, being cooked to some recipe. This is the case for all data even when supposed *objectivity* is applied.

Further reading

Gitelman, L. (ed.) (2013) *'Raw Data' is an Oxymoron*. MIT Press, Cambridge, MA.

copyright   An *intellectual property right* that bestows economic and moral rights to the creator of an original work (or another owner of the right such as a publisher) for a defined period of time. An original work can be a written document or a piece of art, music, film or other creative output. Copyright protection does not relate to an idea itself, but rather to the expression of that idea, which must meet a minimal threshold of originality. Copyright owners are granted the exclusive right to control how a work is used, distributed, and adapted. The associated economic rights enable the copyright owner to receive payment for the use of the work by others. The moral rights allow the creator or owner to be linked to a work and to object to any alterations or use that might harm their reputation. While the legal concept is used globally, the specific expression of rights within legislation varies across jurisdictions. Typically copyright protection terminates 50 or 100 years after the creator dies. Copyright protections might be waived in some contexts, such as fair use for educational purposes, and through the use of creative commons licensing that lets the copyright holder define gratis use. Copyright does not apply to *facts* and *data* (unless the data are original creative works, as with some *qualitative data*). However, copyright protection does apply to the original intellectual creation of a *database*, recognising the investment of time, labour, and capital in its production.

counter-archiving   The creation of an archive that parallels or counters an existing archive. In the case of paralleling, an attempt is made to capture the same data – usually through an *API* or using a process of *data scraping* from the original source – and to structure and store the data to enable analysis. For example, many researchers used Twitter/X's API (before access without payment was terminated) to create their own counter-archive in order to conduct research. After Facebook halted access to its API, some researchers used data scraping to create their own counter-archive of a selection of the same materials. Others have scraped data from government archives to produce counter-archives that enable them to expose and challenge state work. *Community archives* can act as counter-archives, challenging the *preservation* strategies of institutional archives, and archiving materials that provide counter-evidence to the official narratives and histories generated by them.

Further reading

Ben-David, A. (2020) 'Counter-archiving Facebook', *European Journal of Communication*, 35(3): 249–64.

counter-data action   The generation and use of data by citizens to challenge institutional *data regimes* and their data work. Counter-data actions enable citizens to resist dominant *data power* and to propose alternative approaches, and to claim *data rights* and *data sovereignty*. Counter-data actions include citizens producing their own datasets about an issue, either to fill an evidence gap or to counter official sources, or examining the *data politics* of official data and exposing their *error* and *bias*, or using official data to provide counter-analysis and interpretation. Other actions include providing training to local citizens with regards to *data literacy*. Undertaking a counter-data action is a core means of practising *data activism*. See also *civic hacking*.

Further reading

Currie, M., Paris, B.S., Pasquetto, I., and Pierre, J. (2016) 'The conundrum of police officer involved homicides: Counter-data in Los Angeles County', *Big Data & Society*, 3(2): 1–14.

coverage   The attribute, spatial or temporal extent of a dataset. Datasets are *sampled* and refer to selected phenomena, locales or time periods. Coverage denotes what data have been sampled and their range. For example, a dataset might relate only to a sub-sample of a population or to a single city rather than a whole nation, and might be for a single year rather than a longer period. Only a selection of *attribute data* might have been generated, rather than a larger set of variables. The coverage of datasets might reflect the deliberate choices of data producers, but could also be due to issues with a methodology or unknown omissions. Coverage shapes the analysis that can be undertaken using a dataset and needs to be considered in the interpretation of findings (see *ecological fallacies*).

critical data literacy, see *data literacy*

Critical Data Studies (CDS)   A field of study that focuses on the nature, production, and use of *data*. Until recently, data were largely ignored from a philosophical perspective, with conceptual attention instead directed to *information* and *knowledge*. If reflexive consideration was paid to data it was usually from a methodological or technical point of view. CDS centres data as the object of study. CDS is 'critical' in the sense that it does not conceive of data in an essentialist, commonsensical, taken-for-granted way, where data are understood as neutral, unproblematic measures that form the building blocks for information and knowledge, or the input values for computation. Instead, CDS understands data as being *contingent* and relational in nature; their generation, processing, and use *contextually* framed (conceptually, technically, socially, economically) and thoroughly infused by politics (personal, institutional, cultural). Data then are not merely a means for understanding the world, unworthy of critical analysis themselves. Rather data demand scholarly attention as contingent, mutable, *socio-technical* materials that are vital for producing knowledge, creating business value, and managing society.

CDS applies the concepts and methods of critical social theory (encompassing a number of schools of thought such as feminism, structuralism, poststructuralism, postcolonialism, political economy, and critical realism) to make sense of: the nature of data; the praxes and politics operating across the *data lifecycle*; *data mobilities*; *data imaginaries* and the discourses shaping data-driven endeavours and agendas; the socio-technical infrastructures supporting data-driven systems; the logics and practices of *data management* and *data governance*; the ways in which data are used, for what ends and for whose benefit, and the legal, *data ethics*, and *data justice* issues these raise; the consequences of *datafication* and data-driven systems for society, economy, and science; and how these all vary across time and space.

A relatively young interdisciplinary field, initial studies were first grouped together and labelled as CDS in 2014. Practitioners of CDS are typically located in social science disciplines that have long paid critical attention to the production of knowledge and to technology, such as Science and Technology Studies, Media Studies, Sociology, Geography, Anthropology, and Library and Archive Studies, as well as allied fields and approaches such as Software Studies, Surveillance Studies, and *critical GIS*. Since its inception, CDS scholars have undertaken numerous empirical studies, employing a range of approaches and methods, and created a rich set of concepts for making sense of data and how it is used.

Further reading

Hepp, A., Jarke, J., and Kramp, L. (2022) 'New perspectives in Critical Data Studies: The ambivalences of data power – An introduction', in Hepp, A., Jarke, J., and Kramp, L. (eds), *New Perspectives in Critical Data Studies*. Palgrave Macmillan, Cham, Switzerland, pp. 1–23.

Kitchin, R. (2022) *The Data Revolution: A Critical Approach to Big Data, Open Data, and Data Infrastructures*. Second edition. Sage, London.

Richterich, A. (2018) *The Big Data Agenda: Data Ethics and Critical Data Studies*. University of Westminster Press, London.

critical GIS   An approach to GIS (geographical information systems) that is mindful of its epistemological shortcomings, seeking to be more open with respect to *positionality*, power, and the production of *situated knowledges*, and using GIS as part of a *mixed methods* approach. GISs are used to collate and manage *spatial data*, to create bespoke maps, and to undertake *spatial analysis*. In the 1990s, GIS and its framing as an objective, neutral scientific method for spatial analysis was critiqued. Drawing in particular on feminist critiques of science, detractors argued that GIS produced a reductive, instrumental analysis of phenomena and did not provide an *objective* 'view from nowhere' as claimed. Moreover, this analysis largely reproduces the interests of those utilising the technology, which are mainly states and companies. While some rejected the use of GIS and quantitative methods more broadly, others argued for a reframing of GIS that was *reflexive*, open about its assumptions, methodological limitations, and the *data politics* inherent in the datasets used, and mindful of the power interests it might serve. In addition, critical GIS sought to change who performed spatial analysis by embracing participatory GIS in which local citizens are empowered to learn how to use a GIS to undertake counter-mapping projects to challenge state and corporate agendas. See also *feminist data science, positivism, radical statistics*.

Further reading

Wilson, M.W. (2017) *New Lines: Critical GIS and the Trouble of the Map*. University of Minnesota Press, Minneapolis.

crowdsourcing   The collective, voluntary effort of many people to produce a resource. The resource might be a dataset or a set of ideas. For example, OpenStreetMap is a crowdsourced project wherein tens of thousands of people have collaborated to produce an online map of the world; Wikipedia is a crowdsourced encyclopaedia with millions of entries written and edited by citizen volunteers. The benefit of crowdsourcing is that large and costly tasks can be subdivided across many people who provide their labour on a non-paid basis. The benefit to participants is that they produce an open resource that they can use freely. The critique of crowdsourcing is that: it can be difficult to create a crowd and to then keep them motivated so they continue to maintain and extend the resource; typically a small core group undertakes the bulk of the labour; those most active are not *representative* of the wider population (e.g., they are younger, wealthier, more tech-savvy), which can lead to biases in the resource; while labour is voluntary, projects do require some funding to pay for core technologies and services (e.g., servers/cloud hosting costs); and *data quality* can be highly variable depending on *data management* and *data governance*. The result is that many crowdsourced projects fail to generate a sufficient crowd to produce a useful resource and terminate shortly after starting. Those that do manage to operate over a number of years are often reliant on foundations to fund some costs. See also *citizen science, civic hacking*.

Further reading

Dodge, M. and Kitchin, R. (2013) 'Crowdsourced cartography: Mapping experience and knowledge', *Environment and Planning* A 45(1): 19–36.

curation   The practice of gathering, selecting, organising, preserving, and guiding the use and interpretation of data and information relating to a topic. Given the volume and range of data, information, and artefacts that exist, curation seeks to determine what is of most potential value and to then organise the items selected in a way that aids discoverability and sense-making. Curating content is a common practice in *archives*, museums, *data repositories*, and activities such as digital marketing. Curation might also involve directing the attention of audiences and users and providing interpretation of displayed materials. Curation is not a neutral practice and the choices and decisions that are made in selecting and organising materials, or providing interpretation, are inherently political despite any claims to *objectivity*.

Further reading

Bhaskar, M. (2016) *Curation: The Power of Selection in a World of Excess*. Piatkus, London.

D

dashboards A form of *visual analytics* for displaying indicator data. Just as a car dashboard displays critical information to operate a vehicle, analytical dashboards provide an overview of *key performance indicators* and other associated indicators relating to an operational system (e.g., the electricity grid) or a domain (e.g., social and economic activity in a city). Their utility is that they enable a large amount of information to be quickly viewed and interpreted and they are a common tool in *control rooms*. The indicator data displayed might be *administrative data* that is published monthly, quarterly or yearly, or *sensor data* that updates as *real-time data*. These data are typically shown as a time-series or in relation to a target using visual analytics, such as gauges, traffic light colours, meters, bar charts, graphs, and maps. These visual analytics are often interactive, enabling users to zoom in or out, turn layers on or off, and access additional data. Several visual analytics might be shown simultaneously, with the dashboard acting as a console for monitoring and making sense of several interconnected indicators. While dashboards supposedly possess *objectivity* and neutrality in what they display and how they are used, a common critique is that they are highly reductionist and instrumental, reducing a system or domain to just a handful of indicators and using these to make decisions outside of the wider context; there is also a politics to indicator selection and how the dashboards are used.

Further reading

Kitchin, R. and McArdle, G. (2017) 'Urban data and city dashboards: Six key issues', in Kitchin, R., McArdle, G., and Lauriault, T. (eds), *Data and the City*. Routledge, London, pp. 111–26.

Tkacz, N. (2022) *Being With Data: The Dashboarding of Everyday Life*. Polity Press, Cambridge.

data Representative measures of phenomena captured through some form of measurement or *observation*, or derived or inferred values produced through calculations such as *statistics* or *modelling*. Data form the building blocks from which *information*, *knowledge*, and value are produced, and constitute the input for and output from computational processes. Etymologically, data is derived from the Latin 'dare', meaning 'to give', wherein data are all aspects of a phenomenon that could potentially be measured. In practice, data refers to those aspects that are captured, processed, and used (see *capta*). The meaning of data has changed over time. It was first used in the seventeenth century in conjunction with the growth of science and *bureaucracy* to refer to factual information about the world that exists independently of the means of measurement and which can be captured and recorded. Data could take a number of representative forms – numbers, characters, symbols, words – possessing the qualities of being discrete and intelligible (each datum separately delineated and clearly defined), aggregative (can be built into datasets), and retaining their meaning independent of format, medium, language, and producer. By the eighteenth century, data was understood to be the measures produced and used in experiments, surveys, and administrative processes, and in the twentieth century data also described the input and output measures used in digital computing.

Up until relatively recently, data have been understood in realist, essentialist terms; that is, as pre-analytic (waiting to be captured or revealed through calculation) and benign (straightforwardly representative), revealing some inherent truth about the world, subject to the technical constraints of measurement and processing (see *veracity*). On this understanding, the key issue for producing good quality data and extracting insight and value from them is to ensure that a neutral, impartial approach (see *objectivity*) is adopted, using methods that minimise measurement-induced *error* and *bias*. This view of data has been countered in recent years. Data, it is contended, do not pre-exist their capture; rather they are produced using methods and processes that are inherently political and *contextual* in nature. That is, data are made not captured. How data are made is shaped by numerous decisions and choices framed by established knowledge and training, resourcing, practicalities, regulatory and legal requirements, as well as its intended purpose. From this perspective, data are never *raw data*, but are always cooked to some recipe (see *cooked data*). Data then are not captured in an objective, neutral fashion, but are produced in *contingent*, relational, and contextual ways. This contingent understanding of data is foundational to *Critical Data Studies*.

Further reading

Kitchin, R. (2021) *Data Lives: How Data Are Made and Shape Our World*. Chapters 1 and 2. Bristol University Press, Bristol.

data access   Whether data are available for use by third parties. In the past, given that data were time consuming and costly to produce and process, and they created competitive advantage for their owners, they were either kept secret or were expensively traded. The means of accessing and sharing was also limited given the need for physical movement and the cost of reproduction. The digital era has transformed the conditions for data access and *data sharing* by rendering data *non-rivalrous* and easily copied for marginal cost, and enabling remote access via the internet. The success of the *open data movement* has led to much public *administration data* becoming accessible for *re-use*, though the vast bulk of state data remains closed. Despite data being easier to share, accessing data is often not straightforward. Companies and civil society organisations are under no obligation to share data, and the state's obligation is partial. Data access might be limited so their value can be fully exploited by their owners, or because they want to restrict what the data might reveal, or because there is a legal obligation to protect personal and sensitive data. The data owner might also lack the skillset and resources to prepare data for sharing (e.g., *data cleaning*, adding *metadata* and *documentation*) or to build and operate a data *archive*, create and maintain *APIs*, or to undertake *data ingestion* to a *data repository*. Access to privately held data is usually negotiated and involves agreeing to terms and conditions regarding *intellectual property rights* and how the data can be used (see *licensing*). Even with an agreement in place, access might be limited to a sample of the overall dataset. Controlling data access is a political act, shaped by values and intent, and it has political effects by limiting how the data might be used as well as who benefits. See also *data philanthropy*.

data activism   The mobilisation of citizens to collectively challenge data injustices, reorder *data power*, and claim *data sovereignty*. Through the enactment of grassroots *data politics*, data activism seeks to resist, transgress, and reconfigure hegemonic *data regimes* and the uneven and unequal socio-economic relations they reproduce. It aims to produce *data citizenship* that provides strong *data rights*, ensures an *ethics of data care*, and creates *data justice*. While data activism is diverse in its aims, politics, and practices, in broad terms there are two main forms, as identified by Milan and van der Velden (2016). Reactive data activism works to oppose, dismantle, and replace asymmetrical arrangements of data power; for example, by conducting political protest, running social media and media campaigns, taking legal action, submitting counter-policy briefs, or refusing to participate in a data regime. Proactive data activism co-opts the data and tools of data power to conduct *counter-data actions* that challenge that power; for example, using open government datasets, employing *data analytics*, practising *citizen science*, and creating data tools such as *dashboards* to highlight data injustices and forward alternative visions. These two forms of data activism are not mutually exclusive: data activists can campaign for stronger data regulation and conduct counter-data actions. A potential paradoxical issue, however, is that proactively employing the data and tools of the hegemonic data regime works to reaffirm their status as the dominant mode of *power/knowledge* (that is, the data and tools used remain the ones introduced by those in power in order to retain their power). As such, proactive data activism needs to use these data and tools within a different epistemological framing that employs *reflexivity* and produces *situated knowledges*, using an approach such as *data feminism* or *critical GIS*. See also *civic hacking*, *crowdsourcing*, *data commons*.

Further reading

Gutiérrez, M. (2018) *Data Activism and Social Change*. Palgrave, Cham, Switzerland.

Milan, S. and van der Velden, L. (2016) 'The alternative epistemologies of data activism', *Digital Culture & Society*, 2(2): 57–74.

data affordance   A potential action that is made possible by the qualities or properties of data. Data, through its constitution, content, structure, *relationality*, presentation (e.g., table, visualisation, narrative) and other qualities (e.g., *coverage, timeliness*), affords certain uses and outcomes. Some of these affordances are designed and some emerge as unintended possibilities. Importantly, affordances are not simply an intrinsic property of data, but arise out of the relationship between users and data. Moreover, affordances need to be actualised to be realised and this process is contingent and contextual in its unfolding (see *contingency* and *context*). Nonetheless, specific affordances prompt and promote particular uses. The greater the range of affordances, the more utility data possess. Data affordance is weakened by poor *data quality* and frail *veracity*.

Further reading

Fjortoft, H. and Lai, M.K. (2021) 'Affordances of narrative and numerical data: A social-semiotic approach to data use', *Studies in Educational Evaluation* 69: 100846.

data amplification   Supplementing the analysis of a dataset with additional, related analysis and wider contextual framing. While *data enrichment* extends the value of data by combining it with other data, data amplification extends the insights that can be drawn by undertaking related analysis and placing the findings in context. For example, sentiment analysis of social media data might be complemented by mapping geo-referenced content, undertaking analysis of *administrative data*, plus conducting an analysis of the historical and policy context related to the phenomenon under investigation. Here, the insight gained from the original analysis is amplified through combining forms of analysis and sense-making.

data analytics   A set of computational analysis tools that utilise *machine learning* and the calculative power of computing to process and analyse *big data*. Data analytics can also be applied to large volumes of *small data*. Traditional methods of analysis for both *quantitative data* and *qualitative data* are designed to analyse relatively low quantities of sampled, small data. These traditional methods struggle to handle very large volumes of data without the aid of computing given the significant amount of calculations needed to perform the analysis (which would be all but impossible by hand). Data analytics solves this calculation problem by providing computational forms of traditional analysis and creating new tools and techniques. In some, but not all, cases, data analytics are *automated* and become self-learning through the application of machine learning. There are four broad categories of data analytics: *data mining* and *pattern recognition*; *data visualisation* and *visual analytics*; *statistics*; and *modelling* (including *prediction*, *simulation* and optimisation). The development and application of data analytics is a core competency of the new discipline of *Data Science*.

Further reading
Moreira, J., Carvalho, A., and Horvath, T. (2018) *A General Introduction to Data Analytics*. John Wiley & Sons, Hoboken, NJ.

data anxieties   The anxieties, uncertainties, and concerns experienced by those using data or those affected by data-driven processes (such as *surveillance* or *social sorting*), and how these anxieties affect trust and confidence. The concept was introduced by Pink et al. (2018) to capture how data are not experienced in a neutral, technical, practical way that evokes mechanical *objectivity* and is devoid of feelings and concerns; rather, engagements with data are *affective* encounters that are often riddled with doubts, concerns, and hopes. Data anxieties shape how people understand and act in their engagements with data. In order to fully understand *data labour* and how people react to and trust (or not) data-driven systems, identifying data anxieties needs to be an aspect of the analysis.

Further reading
Pink, S., Lanzeni, D., and Horst, H. (2018) 'Data anxieties: Finding trust in everyday digital mess', *Big Data & Society*, 5(1): 1–14.

data archaeology   Excavating the *lineage, provenance*, and development of *data infrastructures*, and their associated datasets, to chart how they have been constructed and operate. Whereas a *data ethnography* observes social interactions and talks to actors within a community of practice, a data archaeology focuses more on examining artefacts and infrastructures such as *documentation*, *metadata* records, *databases*, *software*, hardware, and policy briefs. It seeks to understand how datasets and *data assemblages* are formed, their nature (such as component technologies, *data formats*, *data standards*, *data quality*), how they work, and how they unfold over time through their discursive and material artefacts.

Further reading

Mackenzie, A. (2017) *Machine Learners: Archaeology of a Data Practice*. MIT Press, Cambridge, MA.

data architecture   The policies, rules, and standards that describe and govern how data are generated, processed, stored, and integrated within an IT system and how it connects with other systems. A data architecture is the blueprint for: how data are organised; the suite of expected data processes (including operational procedures, emergency measures, data backups, and *data security*); *data journeys* within and between systems; and the technologies, *software*, and standards used to ensure the system works as required.

Further reading

Henderson, D. and Earley, S. (eds) (2017) *DAMA-BMBOK: Data Management Body of Knowledge*. Second edition. Technics Publications, Basking Ridge, NJ.

data assemblage   The *socio-technical* amalgam of heterogeneous constituent elements, material and discursive practices and processes, and institutional arrangements that compose and shape a data formation. For example, a data infrastructure is constructed from a diverse set of technical elements (e.g., hardware, software, databases, networked infrastructure) whose assemblage and ongoing evolution, maintenance, and operation are materially and discursively produced through diverse social practices and processes, shaped by knowledge, experience, discourses, finance, politics, law, governance, institutional arrangements, markets, and other factors. Material practices and processes include a range of *data practices* (e.g., forms of *data management*, *data* *maintenance and repair*) and *data mobilities*. Data assemblages are discursively supported by *data imaginaries* and *discursive regimes*. How a data assemblage functions is guided by an evolving set of *data regulations, protocols*, and *data standards*, and *data governance* arrangements, as well as its *data habitus* that unconsciously shapes its unfolding nature. Data assemblages are never fixed, but rather ceaselessly evolve, mutate, coalesce, and collapse with technical, social, and business innovations, organisational and personnel change, new regulations and laws, changing aims and ambitions, and market conditions. They are also open to rupture by *glitches*, exploitation, and other factors. The inherent *contingency* and *contextual* relationality of data assemblages can produce *unanticipated consequences*. Comprehending a data infrastructure (or other data formation) then requires charting how they are continually being reassembled through complex, material, and discursive relationships between diverse socio-technical elements.

Further reading

Kitchin, R. (2022) *The Data Revolution: A Critical Approach to Big Data, Open Data, and Data Infrastructures.* Second edition. Sage, London.

Williamson, B. (2017) 'Learning in the "platform society": Disassembling an educational data assemblage', *Research in Education*, 98(1), 59–82.

data audit   A process of determining what data are being generated and stored, and their associated *metadata*, within an IT system. Conducting a data audit is a means of constructing a *data dictionary* if one is not already available (or it is not open access), and of charting the data *lineage* of a dataset. It might also be used to *validate* data and ensure *data integrity* by checking for discrepancies; for example, whether published data matches the source data. An audit to construct a data dictionary can be undertaken by inspecting the data/metadata and documenting what is held, or by observing how data are entered into a system. If access to the dataset or system is restricted it might be possible to perform an audit by examining documents published by an organisation or by examining their *data services*. For example, much of the data held by a real-estate consultancy can be identified by examining their market reports (which are rich in facts, tables, graphs) and by viewing what data are presented on their websites (such as displayed on the page for each property for sale). A comprehensive audit will document the associated metadata for each dataset variable, including its creator, source, date, description, format, spatial and temporal coverage, language, and rights.

data augmentation, see *data transformation*

data autoethnography   A form of *data ethnography* in which the researcher self-observes and reflects on their involvement in, engagement with, and experiences of data and data-driven systems. Autoethnography is a form of *observational* research, but one centred on the observer's own life, wherein they critically self-reflect on their own experiences in order to understand some aspect of the world. The critical self-reflection is important; data autoethnography is not simply seeking to document engagements with data, but rather to think through what they mean, or why a data-driven system works as it does, or to probe how it might work differently under other circumstances. For example, a researcher might critically self-reflect on how they curate their use of apps and what data they share on social media as a means to consider how people perform a personal *ethics of data care*.
    Further reading
    Fraser, A. (2019) 'Curating digital geographies in an era of data colonialism', *Geoforum* 104: 193–200.

data bounds   How data are used to form a boundary around, and provide limits to, how a phenomenon is understood. The term was introduced by Lawson (2022), who used it to explain how, during the Covid-19 pandemic, specific indicator data (e.g. cases, hospitalisations, deaths, vaccine rates) created data bounds that delimited what was a meaningful way to understand, discuss, and react to the crisis, with these data used to direct government response and shape media discourses. Other datasets are framed as being 'out of bounds', their legitimacy questioned, and excluded from official narratives. Identifying how data bounds are formed, maintained, and alter over time reveals how *data power* is constructed and wielded, as well as how it is resisted and challenged. In the context of Covid-19, mis- and dis-information that challenged official data bounds circulated widely on social media and media channels.

Further reading

Lawson, B. (2022) *The Life of a Number: Measurement, Meaning and the Media*. Bristol University Press, Bristol.

data breach   The breaching of security on an IT system leading to data being stolen or held to ransom. All IT systems are vulnerable to cyberattacks, wherein a malicious attempt is made to hack a closed system, and to other forms of breaches (e.g., unprotected *API*, lost/stolen media, leaking by a disgruntled employee, accidental publication). The majority of hacking attempts fail, repelled by *data security* measures. However, a number are successful. Many of these attacks target the data held, such as names, addresses, social security numbers, credit card details, and administrative records. These *personal data* constitute a valuable commodity as they enable identity theft and financial fraud. In the case of large administrative systems or *platforms*, millions of records might be stolen. The cost to a company whose system has been breached can be significant, including direct compensation to customers and credit card companies, payments in class-action lawsuits, loss in share price, and the costs of repair and system upgrades. Alternatively, companies or state bodies might be subject to a ransomware demand, wherein they are locked out of their systems and data unless they pay a substantial fee. Data breaches undermine trust in data-driven systems and are a major threat to *privacy* and individual assets.

Further reading

Fowler, K. (2016) *Data Breach Preparation and Response: Breaches are Certain, Impact is Not*. Syngress, Cambridge, MA.

Goodman, M. (2015) *Future Crimes*. Bantam Press, New York.

data brokers   Companies that collate data from various sources and rent/sell these data or use them to provide value-added data products or *data services*. Data brokers have been operating for more than a century, providing services such as direct marketing, credit checking, and voter lists by collating data from polls, surveys, newspaper and magazine subscriptions, mail-order retailers, product registration and warranties, and government records.

In the era of *big data* and mass *datafication*, the range and extent of the data that data brokers collate has increased enormously to include *real-time data* about consumer purchases, web browsing, social media, location and movement, as well as data relating to finances, logistics, business intelligence, real estate, private security, media, and open government data. Selling data to data brokers has become a significant stream of revenue for many companies. In addition, some companies enable data brokers to embed tracking code into their websites and apps to be able to capture user behaviour and to deliver targeted advertising. Linking all these data together, and using them to produce *derived data* and *inferred data*, enables the creation of detailed personal, group or place *profiles* (see *data doubles*) and to subject these to *social sorting* and other *data analytics*. These profiles are used for a number of purposes, including micro-targeted advertising and marketing, assessing creditworthiness and risk, conducting background checks, detecting fraud, producing business analytics, and undertaking bespoke data analysis and consultancy.

The scale and value of these operations has led to the observation that a new form of generating capital, one where data act as a type of capital and form the primary mode of production (rather than goods and business services), has emerged, termed *surveillance capitalism*. Indeed, given the value of data, profiles, products and services, the number and scale of data brokers has significantly expanded over the past twenty years. Some data brokers are global enterprises that consolidate a wide range of data and provide many services and products, others specialise in particular markets (e.g., crime, security). The largest brokers have extensive databases; for example, in 2019 Acxiom held records on 2.5 billion addressable consumers globally. The value of the global data broker market is worth hundreds of billions of dollars annually.

To a large degree, the work of these data brokers is not well known by the public. A situation that is cultivated by the industry, which is highly secretive in its operations. There is good reason for this given the various concerns about their business models and practices. The excessive intrusiveness of data brokers and their attempts to maximise value from collated data raise worries with respect to *privacy* and compliance with *Fair Information Practice Principles*. There are also ethical questions concerning how the data are used to profile and sort constituencies, discrimination in these processes, and their consequences (in terms of whether somebody gets a loan, tenancy, job, etc.) (see *data ethics*). Moreover, there is little *transparency* as to data brokers' operations, and limited *accountability* and redress (in part because it is difficult to know that they are responsible). Consequently, in recent years, the industry has attracted the attention of politicians and legislators who have sought stronger *data regulations* (such as GDPR in the European Union), but many would argue that these have not gone far enough to address concerns. See also *data colonialism, data footprints and shadows*.

Further reading

Christl, W. (2017) *Corporate Surveillance in Everyday Life*, Cracked Labs, Vienna, https://crackedlabs.org/dl/CrackedLabs_Christl_Cor porateSurveillance.pdf

Zuboff, S. (2019) *The Age of Surveillance Capitalism: The Fight for the Future at the New Frontier of Power*. Profile Books, New York.

data capitalism   A form of capitalism wherein data are a type of capital, rather than simply a commodity that can be converted into monetary value, and the accumulation of capital is derived from extracting value from data. In other words, data are the key driver of economic production and profit generation, with investments into IT being principally to enable data to be produced, circulated, traded and value to be derived from them, and to facilitate a data-driven economy. From this perspective, mass *datafication* is driven by capital's desire to capture weakly or non-commodified elements of trade, and other aspects of social and economic life, and to extract value from them. Within a business, all aspects of its operations (products, components, logistics, services, governance, staff, customers) are targets for datafication in order to create new products, identify new markets, reorganise operations, improve labour efficiencies, and increase productivity. Within a home, all kinds of activity become captured as data through smartification (e.g., smart TVs, meters, kettles, fridges, thermostats, doorbells), which are then leveraged into new payment streams and commoditised via *data brokers*. With respect to the state, all forms of *bureaucracy* have become highly data-driven, and the prevalent neoliberal political economy has strongly pushed state data work to the private sector, creating new markets for *data services*; at the same time, state data are being published as *open data* from which value can be extracted. Data-driven systems and *automation* seek to maximise value extraction from data, while also enhancing capital accumulation from more traditional sources such as property, infrastructure and labour through business intelligence. In this sense, data capitalism is much broader in its production of capital than *surveillance capitalism*, which is a form of data capitalism. Many of the most capitalised companies globally (e.g., Amazon, Apple, Facebook, Google, Microsoft) are now businesses centred on data in multiple ways (e.g., data-centred *platforms*, data capture, *data analytics* and services, data brokerage, *cloud* storage). See also *data colonialism, political economy of data*.

Further reading

Sadowski, J. (2019) 'When data is capital: Datafication, accumulation, and extraction', *Big Data & Society*, 5(1): 1–12.

data centre   A facility that houses servers, IT systems, and telecommunications infrastructure for the storage and distribution of data and software services (commonly known as the *cloud*). The facility is usually a dedicated building, or set of buildings, that has sufficient energy supply, cooling technologies (air or water-based), fire suppression, and data security. Given that they are accessed by networked infrastructure (e.g., the internet), data centres are somewhat geographically footloose, though they tend to cluster in places where costs can be saved in relation to energy, labour, and tax. This raises territorial and *data protection* issues given that the data stored might be located outside of the jurisdiction that is legally responsible for them. The short lifespan of the technologies used (usually a few years) and the energy demands of data centres have led to concerns regarding waste and environmental sustainability (see *political ecology of data*).

Further reading

Bresnihan, P. and Brodie, P. (2021) 'New extractive frontiers in Ireland and the moebius strip of wind/data', *Environment and Planning E: Nature and Space*, 4(4): 1645–64.

Rossiter, N. (2017) 'Imperial infrastructures and Asia beyond Asia: Data centres, state formation and the territoriality of logistical media', *Fibreculture Journal*, 29: 1–20.

data circulation The movement of data across *data ecosystems* and domains. Data circulation refers to the diversity of *data journeys* which data might take that are stretched out over time and space. Data circulates through *archives, data repositories,* and *data markets,* as well as its derived products (e.g., analytics, information, knowledge), to thousands or more users, being shared through various means and used in all kinds of ways. Key datasets on *open data* sites might be downloaded tens of thousands of times, being used to conduct a range of analyses, which then might feed into reports, with a portion (such as key *facts* or derived *data visualisations*) flowing into news media that are viewed by potentially millions of people. This circulation is difficult to track and trace and unfolds in diverse ways since the data are transformed into different forms as they pass along routes. *Data protection* and *privacy* legislation seeks to place limits on the circulation of *personal data.*

Further reading
Beer, D. (2016) *Metric Power*. Palgrave, London.

data citizenship The rights and entitlements of citizens conferred through data and available with respect to data. Traditionally, citizenship is defined as the rights, entitlements, and duties that delimit an individual's membership of a state. These typically relate to four domains: civil/legal (e.g., freedom of speech, right to justice, right to own property), political (e.g., right to vote or run for political office); social (e.g., right to welfare), and cultural/symbolic (e.g., right to recognition, respect, and protections with respect to identity such as gender, race, sexuality, faith). This notion of citizenship is evident in regulations around *data protection,* wherein there are rights to privacy and confidentiality (see *Fair Information Practice Principles*). With a shift to a neoliberal political economy, citizenship has shifted from inalienable rights and entitlements towards personal responsibilities, obligations, and the market, with services based on what people can afford or are seen to deserve. Citizens are recast as customers rather than sovereign subjects. From this perspective, privacy is something you buy or earn rather than a basic right. *Data capitalism* and data-driven governance favour a neoliberal notion of citizenship, requiring payment or compliant behaviour to receive certain services that previously might have been universal, and performing *social sorting* and *profiling* to determine who deserves what services based on measured performance against criteria. Political sovereignty is becoming data-defined, with citizenship rooted in a person's *data footprints and shadows* and algorithmic processing as opposed to parental lineage or birth certificate or passport (which are also rendered data points). As such, the social contract between state and citizens is being redefined through data-driven systems of *bureaucracy*. Claims by technology companies and states that their digitally mediated systems are citizen-centric often then ring hollow. Even so, rights and entitlements remain important and *data activism* often seeks to protect or reassert such rights and to claim some degree of *data sovereignty*.

Further reading

Hintz, A., Dencik, L., and Wahl-Jorgensen, K. (2019) *Digital Citizenship in a Datafied Society*. Polity Press, Cambridge.

data cleaning   The process of improving *data quality* by identifying and addressing *error*, *bias*, *noise*, poor *consistency* and *completeness*, and improving *accuracy and precision*. Data are cleaned by modifying, replacing, infilling or deleting records to produce a more complete, standardised, uniform dataset. Once cleaned, *data integrity* might be checked through data *validation*. In addition, a dataset might need further *data wrangling* to make it ready for use.

Further reading

Osbourne, J.W. (2013) *Best Practices in Data Cleaning*. Sage, London.

data colonialism   The colonisation of all aspects of everyday life by *datafication*, with data extracted in a predatory manner by capitalist interests. *Data capitalism* and *surveillance capitalism* seek to capture as much data as possible for as minimum cost as possible, and to extract the maximum value from these data while sharing as little of this value as feasible with *data subjects*. Some have likened this process to historical, imperialist projects in which territory and resources were colonised in a highly exploitative manner, with little reciprocal exchange, and enforced through asymmetric power relations. In the case of data, capital is accumulated through data dispossession, wherein data and the labour in their production are provided for free to those that control the means of production. For example, a social media *platform* captures the demographic and social data of those using the platform, which are then used to generate advertising revenue and sold to *data brokers*, with none of the profits from this trade shared with users. Social media users provide free labour and information, with their personal and communal resources enclosed within the platform, which are then monetised by the platform owner. These data are used to target users for further value extraction, either directly through the app/service, or indirectly through downstream use (e.g., by data brokers). Users have little recourse to challenge this exploitative economic relation, having to accept it if they want to continue to use the platform, which might be necessary for work or social purposes. From the platform company's perspective, data are the price for a free service (though the same data dispossession exists for paid subscription services); however, the profits generated far exceed that price. Data colonialism can be amplified for marginalised communities, as not only are they enrolled in a new form of exploitative practice, but their data can be used to deepen social and economic divides through *social sorting* and *redlining*. Some have argued that the term data colonialism is problematic, as while there is accumulation through data dispossession the use of platforms is largely a choice, whereas in territorial colonialism people are subjugated against their will through force.

Further reading

Mejias, U.A. and Couldry, N. (2024) *Data Grab: The New Colonialism of Big Tech (and How to Fight Back)*. Penguin, London.

Thatcher, J., O'Sullivan, D., and Mahmoudi, D. (2016) 'Data colonialism through accumulation by dispossession: New metaphors for daily data', *Environment and Planning D*, 34(6): 990–1006.

data commons   The view that data should be an open, collective, shared resource that benefits all. A commons is a resource that is accessible to all members of a society. A data commons applies this concept to data, with it being actualised by pooling and sharing data through an open repository. Unlike a *data trust*, a data commons does not set terms of access and use. The pooling and sharing of data can be centralised or decentralised in nature.

In a centralised commons, data are held in a resource managed by *data stewards* on behalf of the public, such as an *open data* repository. In a decentralised commons, the data resource is collectively managed by all members of the commons, such as a *blockchain* repository.

Further reading

Mills, S. (2019) *Who Owns the Future? Data Trusts, Data Commons, and the Future of Data Ownership*. SSRN, http://dx.doi.org/10.2139/ssrn.3437936

Prainsack, B. (2019) 'Logged out: Ownership, exclusion and public value in the digital data and information commons', *Big Data & Society*, 6(1): 1–15.

data controllers and processors The legal entities responsible for complying with *data protection* and *privacy* legislation. A data controller is any person or institution who determines the purposes for which, and the manner in which, any *personal data* are processed. In other words, they set the rules regarding the handling and use of personal data. A data processor is any person or institution who holds or processes data given to them by the data controller, who is required to comply with the defined rules. While data controllers and processors are specifically named roles in the European Union's GDPR legislation, their roles also apply in other jurisdictions. See also *Fair Information Practice Principles*.

data cooperatives, see *data trusts*

data derivatives The amalgamation of disaggregated fragments of data and *inferred data* into a reconstituted whole that is used to make decisions about *data subjects*. The term was introduced by Amoore (2011) to explain how border security agencies capture, derive, and infer data to assess and act on risk. In this case, a data derivative is a risk score for each individual derived from a variety of data sources, which are combined through *data fusion* and subjected to *data mining* and *data analytics* to calculate future scenarios of potential risk. Individuals are acted on in relation to this derivative data; in other words, governance is enacted on inferred, projected data rather than directly measured data. In this sense, border security is not centred on who an individual is, nor what their data says about them, but on what can be imagined and inferred about who they might be and what they might do (see *data determinism*). How a data derivative is calculated – what data are selected, how they are combined and calculated – then matters, yet this process is *black-boxed* and its *data power* rarely subject to *accountability* and redress. See also *data double*.

Further reading

Amoore, L. (2011) 'Data derivatives: On the emergence of a security risk calculus for our times', *Theory, Culture & Society*, 28 (6): 24–43.

data dérive An experimental type of *data walk* or data walk-through that utilises ideas from the Situationist movement and psychogeography to incorporate novel and creative methods that disrupt the usual means of understanding a phenomenon. The method was proposed by Thatcher and Dalton (2017). Situationism, an experimental art movement that gained prominence in 1950s France, developed methods to explore cities in novel ways (such as walks that take random paths, with prompts to make walkers reflect on what is encountered). A data dérive applies this kind of experimental practice to data walks, such as taking paths dictated by urban augmented reality apps to explore how the city is data-driven. The method can also be applied to a *database* or a *data infrastructure*, such as drifting through a data *archive* using a prompt protocol to explore the *data power* in its collection, construction, and operation. In this sense, the method uses feelings of estrangement (pushing a person outside of what they comfortably know) and defamiliarisation (making the familiar strange) created by the dérive to prompt critical reflection about data-related phenomena.

Further reading

Thatcher, J. and Dalton, C.M. (2017) 'Data derives: Confronting digital geographic information as spectacle', in Briziarelli, M. and Armano, E. (eds), *The Spectacle 2.0: Reading Debord in the Context of Digital Capitalism*. University of Westminster Press, London, pp. 135–50.

data determinism Data being the determinant of how an individual is treated. Rather than an individual being assessed, judged, and treated on the basis of social engagement (e.g., an interview) or personal testimony (e.g., a reference), data relating to them determines an evaluation and decision outcome. In cases where predictive *profiling* is undertaken, a person is not judged on the basis of what the data says they have done, but on a calculated inference of what they might do in the future (see *inferred data, social sorting*). Here, data determinism is operating in an anticipatory way, where people are treated and held accountable to data-derived *predictions* rather than actual actions (see *data derivative*). A key issue is that individuals are being reduced to their data, but these data might have poor *data quality* and in-built *bias*.

Further reading

Aizenberg, E. and van den Hoven, J. (2020) 'Designing for human rights in AI', *Big Data & Society*, 7(2): 1–14.

data dictionary   A *metadata* document that details all the data generated and held within a *database*, providing information about its meaning. Ideally a data dictionary will provide descriptions of attributes, definitions of terms, and detail other metadata relating to *data format*, *data standards*, and data *lineage*. A data dictionary enables a system user to understand what data should have been generated, their relationship to other data, how they might be used, and to assess whether they can sensibly be conjoined with other data. A data dictionary can be partial, or not well known or available to front-end users, limiting knowledge and stifling informed use.

data double   The assembled data about an individual, which is increasingly used to make decisions in relation to that *data subject*. The term was coined by Haggerty and Ericson (2000) to refer to the abstraction of data about individuals via processes of digital *surveillance* (see also *data footprints and shadows*) and their reconstitution in the form of personal *profiles*. These data doubles can be remarkably detailed, providing an intimate data portrait of a person's characteristics, behaviour, opinions, and attitudes. Data doubles circulate independently of individuals through the work of *data brokers*, yet the analytics performed on them by companies or states directly inform a host of decisions that shape people's everyday lives, from consumer recommendations to access to credit and employment. A number of other metaphors have been used to refer to the same phenomenon, such as digital persona and dividual. See also *data derivatives, dataveillance, personal data, personally identifiable information*.

Further reading

Cheney-Lippold, J. (2017) *We Are Data: Algorithms and the Making of Our Digital Selves*. New York University Press, New York.

Haggerty, K.D. and Ericson, R.V. (2000) 'The surveillant assemblage', *The British Journal of Sociology* 51(4): 605–22.

data doxa   The acceptance by the majority of society that the existing *data regime* is the natural, commonsensical state of affairs and that there is no realistic alternative. In other words, the imaginaries, operations, and *data power* of data-driven governance and economy have been normalised as necessary, logical, and legitimate (see *discursive regime, power/knowledge*). The power of a doxa is that those who are most discriminated against and exploited by it come to accept the logic of their own oppression. This is the doxa power of capitalism: that those who are least well-off accept a system that benefits the rich as it is difficult to imagine another political economic system. Gavin Smith (2018), who introduced the concept, contends that there are three types of data relation that maintain the present data doxa rooted in *data capitalism* and neoliberalism. Fetishisation, wherein data-driven systems are cast as the only viable means of addressing societal challenges and driving economic growth. Habituation, wherein *datafication* and data-driven systems are so central to everyday practices that it is difficult to imagine life without them. Enchantment, wherein people are seduced by the power of systems and *platforms* such that they are prepared to live with their downsides. These relations produce an orientation to the present hegemonic situation which suppresses alternative arrangements being sought, thus reproducing the status quo.

Further reading

Smith, G.J.D. (2018) 'Data doxa: The affective consequences of data practices', *Big Data & Society*, 5(1): 1–15.

data dredging   The practice of analysing a dataset in different ways to find a statistically significant result between variables without testing a specific *hypothesis*. In large datasets it is very likely that a statistically significant result will occur simply by chance rather than there being an actual relationship between the variables. If a hypothesis is then retrospectively applied to the finding, or it is not confirmed by repeating the finding in another independent dataset, then the finding is spurious. Data dredging creates an *ecological fallacy* in interpretation because, rather than attempting to analyse the data impartially, the researcher has sought to establish any kind of seemingly credible answer. Its use is considered to be poor research practice, though it is often used within *data mining* and *exploratory data analysis*.

Further reading

Smith, G. (2020) 'Data mining fool's gold', *Journal of Information Technology*, 35(3): 182–94.

data ecosystem   An interlinked collection of datasets and *data infrastructures* that share related *data services*, which are bound together through institutional and governance arrangements and working partnerships. For example, a set of health data infrastructures administered by health care sites (e.g., surgeries and hospitals) and by regional and national government bodies form a data ecosystem that shares data and resources, with decisions and actions in one system having potential consequences in another. The ecosystem metaphor denotes that these data infrastructures have co-determinate relationships and overlapping *epistemic communities*, with a multitude of interdependent actors seeking to co-exist through collaboration, competition, and exchange of data and resources. The data ecosystem is sustained by institutional (e.g., *licensing*, memorandums of understanding) and technical (e.g., *protocols*, *data standards*) arrangements, guided by regulations, values, and norms, as well as 'keystone species' such as *data intermediaries* that create enabling conditions (bridging between organisations, producing shared tools and services), and evolves through new actors, innovations, and relationships. A data ecosystem is full of *data politics* and *data power* and relationships can be precarious or conflictual, requiring mediation and active management. Charting a data ecosystem focuses on plotting the intersecting *data assemblages*, the nature and functioning of relationships, and the constituent *data mobilities*.

Further reading

Dawes, S.S., Vidiasova, L., and Parkhimovich, O. (2016) 'Planning and designing open government data programs: An ecosystem approach', *Government Information Quarterly*, 33(1): 15–27.

van Schalkwyk, F., Willmers, M., and McNaughton, M. (2016) 'Viscous open data: The roles of intermediaries in an open data ecosystem', *Information Technology for Development*, 22(S1): 68–83.

data enrichment The adding of data to a dataset from another source in order to address gaps or *error* and to extend the value that can be extracted. Usually data enrichment is the merging of third-party data, preferably from an authoritative source, with internally held first-party data, though it can involve merging first-party datasets held in different systems, or merging two or more third-party datasets. A dataset on its own might provide a certain degree of insight. Combining the dataset with other related data can enrich insight by revealing associations, relationships, and patterns not otherwise discernible. Where there are shared fields, data in one dataset can be used to validate and fix errors and missing fields, improving *data quality* and *data integrity*. By gathering together and combining a diverse range of datasets, *data brokers* use data enrichment to create rich composite datasets to provide powerful *data services*. See also *data amplification, data fusion*.

data entry The manual adding of new data to a system. Data entry is usually performed by typing data into fields in an interface or into a spreadsheet or database, or by scanning analogue records (see *digitisation*). Because data entry is a manual process it is subject to a number of issues that can reduce *data quality*. These include *errors* such as miscoding, misclassification, duplication, and omission, as well as the deliberate entering of *gamed data* or *fake data* by individuals. There might also be behavioural effects that limit data entry, such as operators only entering required fields and skipping optional fields or entering the minimal amount of *metadata*. See also *data ingestion*.

data erasure, see *deletion*

data ethics The consideration of what is ethical with respect to the production and use of data, identifying appropriate responses that would enact ethical practice, and the application of these responses in social settings. Ethics is essentially concerned with defining, recommending, and defending concepts of right and wrong. The era of *big data*, mass *datafication*, *data capitalism*, and data-driven government has raised a number of concerns with respect to the operations of *data power*, the uneven and unequal treatment of people, and the enactment of data-produced harms (e.g., *redlining*, *social sorting*). Data ethics focuses attention on *data politics* and data power and questions relating to equality, fairness, *accountability*, *transparency*, rights, entitlements, trust, and issues of *data citizenship* and *data justice*, as well as how ethical positions should be enacted in practice. Data ethics informs political debate and is embedded into *data policy*, *data rights*, *data governance*, *data regulation* and *laws* (e.g., *CARE principles*, *data citizenship*, *data protection*, *Fair Information Practice Principles*, *privacy*, *right to be forgotten*, and *right to information*).

Data ethics are contested in two main ways. First, there are different philosophical schools of thought as to how best to conceive and practice ethics. For example, with respect to normative ethics (moral standards and how things should be), ethics can be judged with respect to action, consequence, and intent. A deontological approach prioritises action and following agreed rules concerning what is right or wrong. A consequential approach judges the outcome of an action rather than whether it complies with rules. A virtue approach focuses on whether an attempt was made to do the right thing, rather than on rule-following or consequence. *Research ethics* tends to apply a deontological approach, enforced through *institutional review boards*. An *ethics of data care* is more rooted in virtue ethics. Second, different constituencies, such as civil society, government, and business, have varying agendas, political sensibilities, and views concerning appropriate levels of datafication, *privacy*, and fair use of data, as well as how ethical considerations should be translated into policy, regulations, and law, and applied in practice. Gaining consensus for applied ethics is therefore difficult given vested interests. Data ethics then is an ongoing and evolving debate.

Further reading
O'Keefe, K. and O'Brien, D. (2023) *Data Ethics: Practical Strategies for Implementing Ethical Information Management and Governance.* Kogan Page, London.
Taddeo, M. and Floridi, L. (eds) (2016) 'The ethical impact of data science', special issue, *Philosophical Transactions of the Royal Society A*, 374(2083).

data ethnography   A methodological approach to understanding how data are produced and used that involves an immersive and holistic analysis of *communities of practice*. Typically, an ethnographic approach consists of a sustained engagement with a community, documenting in detail their organisation, operation, governance, culture, practices, interpersonal relations, and external engagements in order to understand their lifeworld. This usually involves a mix of participant *observation*, in-depth *interviews*, and examining documentary sources. In the case of data ethnographies, the aim is to document the ways in which particular communities of practice are orientated towards, conduct, and resist data-related work (e.g., producing data, building and operating *data infrastructures*, conducting *civic hacking*). A data ethnography can be conducted at a single site (e.g., a workplace) or transversally across several sites, including being run as a virtual ethnography conducted online (e.g., via social media).
Further reading
Knox, H. and Nafus, D. (eds) (2018) *Ethnography for a Data-Saturated World.* Manchester University Press, Manchester.
Pink, S., Horst, H., Postill, J., Hjorth, L., Lewis, T., and Tacchi, J. (2015) *Digital Ethnography: Principles and Practice.* Sage, London.

data feminism   The application of feminist philosophy and ideals to understanding the nature of data and their production and use. On the one hand, data feminism focuses on the ways in which data are gendered (and intersectional, inflected with *race, ethnicity*, sexuality (see *queer data*), *disability*, class) and are used to reproduce patriarchal relations (and other forms of *data power* and associated discrimination), and how to challenge and reconfigure data-driven systems and data practices to produce a fairer, more just society (which may include *data activism*). Such work uncovers how sexism pervades how data are generated and interpreted, and the operations of data-driven systems (see *gender and gendered data*). On the other hand, data feminism critiques the dominant ontological understanding of the nature of data and the epistemology of the *scientific method* that underpins *Data Science* and the use of data by states and companies. From a feminist perspective the nature of data is produced rather than essentialist (natural and value free); data do not pre-exist their generation and are not collected neutrally and objectively; rather they are created using processes and systems riddled with *power/knowledge*. Similarly, epistemologically, making sense of the world through the analysis and interpretation of data is not an *objective* exercise, but rather is framed contextually and produces *situated knowledge*. Either an alternative methodological approach is required that is sensitive to the politics and ethics of analysis, or research using scientific principles needs to acknowledge its *positionality* and situatedness (see *feminist data science*).

Further reading

D'Ignazio, C. and Klein, L.F. (2020) *Data Feminism*. MIT Press, Cambridge, MA.

Leurs, K. (2017) 'Feminist data studies: Using digital methods for ethical, reflexive and situated socio-cultural research', *Feminist Review*, 115: 130–54.

data flow, see *data journeys*

data footprints and shadows Data footprints are the trail of data that people leave behind as they use digital technologies, whereas data shadows are the data captured by others about them, often without their knowledge. Footprints are volunteered data, such as filling out *surveys*, or adding posts, comments, and photos on social media. Data shadows include forms of *surveillance* and the capture of data as an essential aspect of interacting with a service. Data footprints and shadows are used to *profile* people and to make decisions in relation to them. Given mass *datafication*, *dataveillance* and surveillance, and the digital mediation of everyday life, producing data footprints is a necessary life practice, and it is all but impossible not to be captured in data shadows. While actual footprints and shadows are ephemeral, usually lasting a few moments, data footprints and shadows can be persistent, stored in databases indefinitely. Nonetheless, data footprints and shadows are fragmented and dispersed across the diverse entities that capture them, though organisations such as *data brokers* seek to join them together to produce detailed *data doubles*.

data format   The encoding scheme used to record and store data. Data can be recorded and stored using a number of different file formats, each of which uses a different encoding scheme. A spreadsheet, for example, can be stored using an open format such as .csv, or in a *proprietary data* format such as .xlsx (Microsoft Excel). A proprietary format is owned by a company or organisation and is linked to specific software, with details of the encoding scheme kept secret or subject to *intellectual property rights*. Since the data can only be accessed using the specific software (or other licensed software), the data owner is dependent on it, unlike an open data format which can be accessed via many software applications. Proprietary data formats limit use and the danger over time is that the data become inaccessible because the software is no longer produced. For example, data that in the past was compressed using the utility pkpak can no longer be readily accessed since the pkunpak utility is no longer maintained and does not work on modern computers. The data format used to record and store a dataset in large part depends on the nature of the data (text, image, numbers, etc.) and what system is going to be used to process and analyse them.

data fragmentation   The separation and dispersal of data about a phenomenon across a number of datasets. Data related to an individual or to an activity can be held across a number of different databases within an organisation or across organisations. These data might have different data structures, standards, formats, and management, which make it difficult to know the full extent of the data held and to conjoin and unify these data. Fragmentation reduces the value that can be extracted from data and creates *data quality* issues. See also *data enrichment, data fusion, data silos*.

Further reading
Gibbs, M.R., Shanks, G., and Lederman, R. (2005) 'Data quality,
database fragmentation and information privacy', *Surveillance &
Society* 3(1): 45–58.

data friction   Impediments or blockages that hinder the movement of data between different technologies, across *data infrastructures*, and between actors and organisations. Data frictions
can be caused by a number of issues, such as incompatible *data
formats*, refusal of actors to cooperate and share data, and regulatory and legal limitations. Data frictions slow down or limit what
can be done with data, including constraining data *re-use* and
repurposing. That said, frictions are not inherently a problem and
some exist for good reason; for example, to protect *privacy* or
proprietary knowledge and to ensure *data security*. Frictions then
are not always something to be overcome; depending on context
and risk, some may even be fostered. Data frictions are common
in *data ecosystems* and are tackled through: negotiation and the
practices of *data politics*; *data governance* and *data sharing* agreements; *data cleaning*, *data wrangling*, and *data standards* to improve
interoperability. Overcoming frictions can produce *unanticipated
consequences*, such as frictions being displaced to another site. See
also *data hugging, data journeys, data mobilities, data threads*.
Further reading
Bates, J. (2018) 'The politics of data friction', *Journal of Documentation*,
74: 412–29.
Edwards, P. (2010) *A Vast Machine: Computer Models, Climate Data,
and the Politics of Global Warming*. MIT Press, Cambridge, MA.

data fusion   The joining together of variously sourced data
to produce larger, richer, and more consistent data. While *data
enrichment* consists of adding data to a dataset from a different
source, data fusion involves integrating two or more datasets
within a unified framework in terms of organisation, format, and
standards. When datasets do not fully share *data standards* and
metadata then an *ETL (extract, transform, load)* process is used
to transform the data into a common, coherent, and consistent
format, and add *derived data*. Data fusion can improve *data quality*
and enhance analysis and its utility. Given the proliferation of data

across systems and the propensity to create *data silos*, data fusion is a means to integrate data and extract additional insights from them. See also *data ingestion*.

data futures   Consideration of the possible, plausible, probable, and desired future trajectories of data and their uses and the nature of the future relationship between data and society. We have moved from a data poor to a data-saturated world in just a handful of decades, with policy and legal responses trying to catch up. The fast pace of creative destruction, whereby new technologies are developed, rolled out, and then quickly rendered obsolete by the next wave of innovation, ensures ever-shifting data futures. The study of data futures seeks to forecast/predict how data-related developments might unfold and to think through normative futures (what should be) and how these might be achieved. The use of futures (plural) is deliberate given that there is no one future that unfolds teleologically, but there are many possible ways the future might occur. Consideration of futures is not simply about what lies ahead since the future is put to work in the present. For example, scenarios about how *automation* will alter the nature of future work are used to formulate present policy. This relationship between the present and future is captured by Adam and Groves' (2007) notions of the 'present future' (the future imagined and projected forward from the present) and the 'future present' (working back from an anticipated or desired future to map out a pathway to that future). Studies of the present future include anticipatory and foresight studies, forecasting, and *prediction*, with visioning, scenario building, and backcasting used to consider the future present. See also *temporalities of data*.

Further reading

Adam, B. and Groves, C. (2007) *Future Matters*. Leiden, Brill.

Selwyn, N. (2022) 'Critical Data Futures', in Housley, W., Edwards, A., Montagut, R., and Fitzgerald, R. (eds), *The Sage Handbook of Digital Society*. Sage, London, pp. 593–609.

data gaze, see *dataveillance, governmentality, surveillance*

data generalisation   A process of summarising and categorising data to reduce data volume or to protect *privacy* by masking information that might be used to identify individuals. In essence, a more general form of the data is produced. For example, a set of ages in a population of 100 adults might be generalised into a set of classes – 16–29 (12); 30–44 (28); 45–59 (27); 60–74 (23); 75+ (10) – where the number in brackets is how many people belong to each group (see *aggregation*). Generalisation reduces the precision in a dataset (see *accuracy and precision*) while ensuring that the data are still useful (e.g., one can still target anonymised individuals based on membership of their age group).

data geographies   The charting of the spatial patterns and mobilities of data. How data are produced, organised, governed, shared, and used is ordered across space, varying across jurisdictions and scales from the local to the global. Data are produced at particular sites, with local customs, culture, politics, and governance inflecting data practices. The *data assemblages* of companies and states are composed of a complex topology of ICT infrastructures, *data centres*, and places of work interconnected across locations, with *data services* and products circulating between them. These topologies are inflected by the global space economy (how trade is organised and operates across space and scales) and geopolitics (how places and activities are governed and managed). Data about places can vary in their production, volume, and *granularity*; for example, the substantial differences in coverage in OpenStreetMap, or entries about locations in Wikipedia, with the Global North having significantly richer data than the Global South. *Administrative data* and commercial data are often georeferenced and organised with respect to a *statistical geography* enabling the data to reveal geographical patterns through mapping and spatial analysis. These data can be used to spatially sort individuals and places, reproducing and deepening inequalities (see *geodemographics*; *redlining*). Data-driven systems are being used to manage and govern locales and to mediate spatial behaviour, as for example with the development of smart city technologies and mobility-focused platforms. Data geographies examine these topologies and mobilities and chart other related geographies.

Further reading

Graham, M. and Dittus, M. (2022) *Geographies of Digital Exclusion: Data and Inequality*. Pluto Press, London.

Pickren, G. (2018) 'The global assemblage of digital flow: Critical data studies and the infrastructure of computing', *Progress in Human Geography*, 42(2): 225–43.

data governance   The framework and procedures through which data-driven systems are managed and regulated, and strategic ambitions realised. Data governance ensures that data systems operate as intended and that the *data practices* and uses comply with legal, regulatory, and ethical requirements. Data governance concerns principles, policies, and procedures with respect to organisational issues relating to roles and responsibilities, personnel issues and the actions of those managing data, operational aspects such as how data are processed, managed, shared, stored, secured, and utilised (documented in *data management plans*), and compliance issues relating to *transparency*, oversight, *accountability*, and redress. There are a number of different data governance models that vary in ethos, strategic aims, and operation, and which might be specific to particular domains (e.g., health, national statistics). Having weak data governance can be a costly business; risks include the reputational damage and costs of a *data security* breach, or being fined for not meeting *data protection* regulations, or a system underperforming due to *data fragmentation* and poor *data quality*. See also *data controllers and processors*, *data management*, *data maturity frameworks*.

Further reading

Ladley, J. (2020) *Data Governance: How to Design, Deploy, and Sustain an Effective Data Governance Program*. Second edition. Academic Press, London.

data habitus   The normalised, unconscious ways of producing and using data, shaped by prevalent social dispositions such as attitudes, beliefs, practices, and skills. A habitus is the habitual, routine, usual state of affairs that shapes everyday life and reproduces the status quo with respect to social order without conscious thought or effort. Walter and Andersen (2013) extended the concept to data, arguing that the generation of state data and national statistics is the product of a habitus, with the need for such data and the way they are created largely uncontested and an accepted process; it is just the way things are. From an Indigenous community perspective, the habitus of state data is rooted in settler colonialism, with the normalised means of producing data about Indigenous people failing to recognise that the methods of *national statistics organisations* see Indigenous communities through settler dispositions, and that these communities have a different understanding of themselves and about data and possess different knowledges. The power of the habitus is that Indigenous policy actors become invested in the state's means of producing data about Indigenous communities, which become further naturalised through their use. The habitus then works to produce a *data doxa* that maintains the status quo. Beyond Indigenous matters, the normalisation of *surveillance capitalism* has created a data habitus in which people are predisposed to mass *datafication*; it is just an expected part of living in a digital society. This normalisation of data practices makes it more difficult to envision and propose alternatives. See also *CARE principles*, *decolonising data*, *Indigenous data*.

Further reading
Walter, M. and Andersen, C. (2013) *Indigenous Statistics: A Quantitative Research Methodology*. Left Coast Press, Walnut Creek, CA.

data history   The historical analysis of datasets, data institutions, or the uses of data. The conceptualisation of data changes over time (see *data*), as do the processes through which data are generated (see *big data*), shared, and analysed (see *data analytics*), and how data are utilised to produce knowledge and manage society and economy. The data landscape is constantly in flux as new ways of producing data are invented, new methods of processing and analysing data become available, and new data products and means of extracting value are developed, replacing older ideas, practices, and products. Even longitudinal datasets that seem relatively stable, such as national *censuses*, alter over time as questions are tweaked, added, and removed, and the means of enumerating and processing the survey change with new procedures and technologies. Historical analyses of data examine these changes, focusing on key actors and institutions, their actions, motivations, and relationship to others, key events and initiatives, the creation and implementation of policy and legislation, the iterative development of data products and services, and how data has impacted individuals, places, and knowledge, and shaped society and economy over time. Tracing these histories is not always straightforward (see *archives*, *oral history*); on the one hand in terms of sourcing necessary evidence, and on the other because this evidence can be contested and incomplete. Careful *genealogical* analysis is therefore needed to make sense of how a particular historical story unfolded. The history of individual datasets should be recorded in their data *lineage*.

Further reading

Poovey, M. (1998) *A History of the Modern Fact: Problems of Knowledge in the Sciences of Wealth and Society.* University Chicago Press, Chicago.

Koopman, C. (2019) *How We Became Our Data: A Genealogy of the Informational Person.* University of Chicago Press, Chicago.

data holding   The storage of data without a long-term *preservation* strategy or formalised *data governance*. A data holding lacks the policies, procedures, and governance of an *archive* or *trusted digital repository*. The data might meet *data standards* and be organised within a database, and files may be structured within ordered directories and possibly include some *metadata*; but there might also be a degree of ad hoc management and maintenance, a lack of *documentation*, and no long-term plan with regards to future storage or *re-use*. For example, the data of most researchers is stored on local and external hard drives, or in the *cloud*, using the *data formats* and file structures decided by them. There is usually no documentation about the files, with knowledge of what data are stored in what file, or how the data are structured in databases, known only by the researcher (and their team if they are shared resources). Metadata are often partial or missing. In the absence of archiving the data in a repository, over time files might be deleted or lost, especially when the researcher retires or dies. Data holdings can often become *stranded data* since they lack standardisation of format and structures that would enable *interoperability* and *data fusion*.

data hugging   A colloquial term that describes the refusal of data owners to share *primary data* or *derived data* with others. Data are a valuable resource and provide their owners with competitive advantage. Data owners then can be reluctant to share their data, instead holding them tight. In addition, there are a number of disincentives that hinder data sharing, including a lack of rewards for doing so, limited resources to prepare data for sharing, and concerns over how the data might be used. Loosening the grip of data owners on their data is the primary aim of the *open data movement*. See also *data philanthropy, data sharing, re-use*.

Further reading

Borgman, C.L. (2012) 'The conundrum of sharing research data', *Journal of the American Society for Information Science and Technology*, 63(6): 1059–78.

data humanitarianism   The rapid generation or sharing of data and the use of data-driven systems to tackle disasters and conflicts and support their relief operations. Given that disasters can severely disrupt existing ICT infrastructure and associated systems, as well as change the local landscape (e.g., an earthquake, hurricane or tsunami destroying buildings, transport/ utility infrastructure, and land cover), or can take place in locations where official data have poor *coverage* or weak *granularity*, data humanitarianism seeks to rapidly provide an evidence base to direct emergency response operations. In general, the aim is to be able to manage a situation in real-time, coordinate activities, perform needs assessments, monitor post-emergency social response (e.g., health and disease, crime and violence), and evaluate the effectiveness of the ongoing response. Data practices might involve generating new data via aerial surveys and deploying sensors, gathering together, fusing, and sharing existing data sources, collating data from across social media and other platforms that might reveal local conditions in isolated places, and volunteers based elsewhere studying aerial imagery and making maps of the new landscape. Part of this process might involve *data philanthropy*, with corporations gifting datasets to aid the relief effort. Data humanitarianism has been critiqued for driving technocratic responses to emergencies, failing to produce sufficient actionable and high quality data, ignoring ethical data practices, undermining local cultures and governance and deepening state power, and over-promising on its capabilities, particularly with respect to fusing disparate data, real-time monitoring, and inter-linking systems. See also *data ethics, data fusion, interoperability, real-time data.*

Further reading

Read, R., Taithe, B., and MacGinty, R. (2016) 'Data hubris? Humanitarian information systems and the mirage of technology', *Third World Quarterly*, 37(8): 1314–31.

data imaginaries   The ways in which data are imagined and envisioned, which shapes how they are understood and mobilised within narratives and discourses, and how they are used in practice. Data and the ways they are used can be imagined in diverse ways, some rooted in established modes of knowing and doing and existing ideas and concepts, others more speculative, innovative, and fictive. People can construct varying data imaginaries relating to the nature of data, the data lifecycle, and how data are used and for what purpose, with these imaginaries contributing to *data valences*. Data imaginaries are important as they shape how people approach, think through, and engage with data, and allow new *data affordances* to be conceived that open up fresh possibilities in designing and building data-driven processes and systems.

Further reading

Benabdallah, G., Kaneko, M.A., and Desjardins, A. (2023) 'A notebook of data imaginaries', in Byrne, D. et al. (eds), *Proceedings of the 2023 ACM Designing Interactive Systems Conference (DIS '23)*. Association for Computing Machinery, New York, pp. 431–45.

data infrastructure   The digital means of storing, processing, and analysing *data holdings* and *archives* and sharing them across the internet. An open *data repository* or *trusted digital repository* are data infrastructures. A data infrastructure provides the supporting data and infrastructural resources for apps and other digital services to be built on top of its foundations. For example, a travel app might utilise the *API* and *open data* of a transit company. A data infrastructure can be understood as a crucial constituent of a *data assemblage*; a socio-technical arrangement composed of a number of technologies (e.g., servers, computers, software, files, databases) whose *data architecture* and ongoing operation is shaped by a range of *contextual* and *contingent* factors, such as institutional politics, interpersonal relations, resources, governance arrangements, standards, policies, and laws. Moreover, the data held within a data infrastructure usually forms part of a wider *data ecosystem*; for example, housing data stored within the data infrastructure of a government department forms part of a wider housing data ecosystem, wherein housing datasets that are stored on many organisations' data infrastructures might be combined to conduct housing analysis. Making sense of a data infrastructure requires unpacking the nature of its assemblage, charting how it works contingently and relationally in practice, mapping its relations to other data infrastructures, and situating the analysis in its local and wider framing. See also *spatial data infrastructure*.

Further reading

Bates, J., Goodale, P., Lin, Y., and Andrews, P. (2019) 'Assembling an infrastructure for historic climate data recovery: Data friction in practice', *Journal of Documentation* 75(4): 791–806.

Williamson, B. (2018) 'The hidden architecture of higher education: Building a big data infrastructure for the "smarter university"', *International Journal of Educational Technology in Higher Education*, 15: article 12.

data ingestion   The importing of existing data into a new system, retaining their data format and structure. For example, data records held within a *data holding* might be ingested into an *archive*, or *metadata* within an *archive* ingested into a federated *data repository*. Usually the data are imported from several sources, resulting in a much larger collection of data in a single *data infrastructure*. Typically, ingestion uses a process of *automation* unless there are *data quality* and *data format* issues with the records to be imported. A particular form of data ingestion is *ETL (extract, transform, load)*, which, rather than ingesting the data as-is, processes and transforms the data into the form required by the new host system. See also *data fusion*.

data integration, see *data fusion*

data integrity   The robustness, stability, and quality of a dataset. Data integrity helps engender and maintain trust in a dataset. A dataset with integrity is one that has comprehensive *metadata*, including full *methodological transparency*, is not tampered with or altered over time, and has assured *data quality* with minimal *error*, gaps or *bias*. Integrity might be assured through transparent *data governance*, including *data audits*, external *validation*, certification, and *accountability* and redress procedures. See also *blockchain*, *data security*, *veracity*.

data intermediaries Organisations that mediate between data actors and provide services that add value to *data infrastructures* and *data ecosystems*. A data intermediary usually contributes specialist data knowledge and skills to other data actors and acts as a middle agent in some data processes. For example, a data intermediary might take public *administration data*, apply *data cleaning*, *data wrangling*, *data fusion*, and *data enrichment*, and then sell on an enhanced data product and services to clients. In general, they unlock and add value to datasets, create data tools and perform *data analytics*, provide training and consultancy services (e.g., preparing data strategies for other organisations), and act as *data policy* advocates. They are vital actors in a data ecosystem as they act as interlocutors who interlink organisations, drive progress, and ensure key activities happen. See also *data services*.

Further reading
van Schalkwyk, F., Willmers, M., and McNaughton, M. (2016) 'Viscous open data: The roles of intermediaries in an open data ecosystem', *Information Technology for Development*, 22(S1): 68–83.

data journalism The use of data and *data analytics* to investigate and report on an issue and to tell news stories. Mass *datafication* and the advent of *big data* have led to massive stores of data that can provide a source for investigative journalism and for *data stories* about a particular phenomenon. A prominent example of the former was the 'Panama Papers' in which 11.5 million documents were leaked and analysed to reveal the shady or illegal offshore financial transactions of over two hundred thousand entities. Data analytics can be applied to these data sources to reveal relationships and associations that might not be spotted otherwise. These analytics are used as part of the reporting, being shared with readers. Journalists have long used *facts* and *statistics* to construct *data narratives* that aid their news storytelling.

With the move to online reporting, journalists can provide more detailed evidence in the form of interactive *data visualisations* and maps which can be embedded into webpages and explored by readers. In addition, data and analytics can be used to produce anticipatory stories, such as using political polling data to predict election outcomes. What the latter has highlighted, given that predictions often do not transpire, is that data journalism is reliant on good *data quality* and data analytics is prone to *ecological fallacies*.

Further reading

Bounegru, L. and Gray, J. (eds) (2021) *The Data Journalism Handbook: Towards a Critical Data Practice*. Amsterdam University Press.

Mutsvairo, B., Bebawi, S., and Borges-Rey, E. (eds) (2020) *Data Journalism in the Global South*. Palgrave Macmillan, Cham, Switzerland.

data journeys   The movement of data along a path from their place of generation, through sites of downstream processing, and on to users. The path might involve passing through *data repositories* or *data intermediaries*, who might transform and add value to the data. The term is used as an alternative to data flow to signify that, like a journey, the movement has breaks and pauses, can involve different modes of travel (e.g., via passed pen drives, posted CDs, electronic transfer of different kinds of files), and can take different routes and detours. A journey also denotes that there can be change along the way as data are transformed through *data cleaning, data wrangling, data fusion*, and other processing. Moreover, the movement might involve other 'passengers', such as *metadata* and *documentation*, as well as other datasets and artefacts, and the journey can serve different purposes. And just as journeys are *contingent*, unfolding with circumstances and *context*, the same is the case for the movement of data. See also *data circulation, data mobilities, data threads*.

Further reading

Bates, J., Lin, Y.-W., and Goodale, P. (2016) 'Data journeys: Capturing the socio-material constitution of data objects and flows', *Big Data & Society*, 4(2): 1–12.

Leonelli, S. and Tempini, N. (eds) (2020) *Data Journeys in the Sciences*. Springer Open, Cham, Switzerland.

data justice   Fairness and equity with respect to how people are treated by the operations of data-driven systems. Data justice applies the ideas and ideals of social justice theories to *data power* and the (re)production of data-related inequalities and harms. Those seeking data justice identify the ways in which data and *data regimes* are implicated in processes of discrimination, oppression, exclusion, and inequity, the *data practices* through which they are enacted, and the structural conditions that enable them, and consider how these might be addressed through a redistribution of data power, a reconfiguring of *data infrastructures*, and the creation of *data rights* to ensure fair treatment.

   There are five types of data justice that advocates aim to achieve. Instrumental data justice focuses on purposes and impact and seeks the fair use of data and the creation of just outcomes. Procedural data justice focuses on data practices and processes and seeks the fair handling, *data management*, and extraction of value from data. Distributional data justice focuses on 'who gets what' and aims to ensure a fair distribution of data resources and data-driven outcomes. Recognition seeks equal respect, rights, and treatment across all *data subjects*. Representation aims for equal voice and ability to shape data regimes across all data subjects. How these are conceptualised varies depending on the underlying moral philosophy adopted, with most conceptions of data justice rooted in feminist (see *data feminism*), postcolonial (see *postcolonialism and data*), Marxist (see *data capitalism, political economy of data*) or Indigenous (see *Indigenous data*) values.

   Much of the work on data justice and the development of its core ideas has been undertaken with respect to the Global South and Indigenous populations. Structural inequalities tend to be more pronounced in these contexts, political regimes can be more authoritarian, and there are weaker frameworks in place for seeking and claiming rights, meaning data injustices can be pronounced. In the Global North, data justice is often focused on the injustices faced by specific groups defined by *race, ethnicity*, class, *gender*, sexuality (see *queer data*), *disability*, and others. Achieving data justice is not straightforward since those who experience injustices often have less access to the tools and resources needed to counter data power, are more politically disenfranchised, having weaker political representation and political capital to influence how systems and policies are enacted, and have poorer levels of *data literacy*, providing a more limited understanding of issues and potential solutions. In addition, attempts to enact data justice through *counter-data actions* are resisted by those with data power seeking to maintain the status quo.

Further reading

Dencik, L., Hintz. A., Redden, J., and Trere, E. (2022) *Data Justice*. Sage, London.

Heeks, R. and Renken, J. (2018) 'Data justice for development: What would it mean?', *Information Development* 34(1): 90–102.

data labour   The work performed to ensure that the full life-cycle of data takes place, and that data circulate and are used to produce value. There are a number of forms of data labour, such as *data entry, data curation, data cleaning, data maintenance and repair,* and *data analytics*. These are generally undertaken by specialist workers, such as archivists, data engineers, and data scientists, and are coordinated by managers, such as *chief data officers*. Data labour often consists of *articulation* work; that is, aligning and performing a set of tasks to produce coordinated action that enables a *data infrastructure* to function. A focus on data labour reveals the many *data practices* employed to ensure data infrastructures function and the variations in how they are performed (see *embodiment*), as well as how they are experienced (see *affect*) and produce *datafied agency*. Data labour reveals the *liveliness* of data and the *contingency* of *data assemblages*. Beyond working with data infrastructures, people in jobs using digital technologies or monitored with *metrics* find themselves 'working for data'; that is, their work is directed by data (e.g., a driver following a calculated route) or they are trying to satisfy expected productivity targets. See also *data sweat*.

Further reading

Evans, L. and Kitchin, R. (2018) 'A smart place to work? Big data systems, labour, control, and modern retail stores', *New Technology, Work and Employment*, 33(1): 44–57.

Nadim, T. (2016) 'Data labours: How the sequence databases GenBank and EMBL-Bank make data', *Science as Culture*, 25(4): 496–519.

data lifecycle   The full lifecycle through which data pass from their generation through to their deletion. This lifecycle consists of a number of phases, including data generation, *data cleaning* and *data wrangling*, *documentation*, *data storage*, *data sharing*, analysis, interpretation, and *deletion*. In some cases, this lifecycle occurs very quickly; for example, *exhaust data* might be produced, have their value extracted immediately (if at all), and then be deleted. In other cases, data might persist for generations if it is preserved in an *archive*. In some cases, the full length of a data lifecycle might be legally mandated. For example, *data minimisation* rules of the GDPR in the European Union mandate that data should be kept only for the duration required to achieve their original purpose. In some cases, the minimum or maximum duration of storage is set; for example, telecom companies in the European Union have to retain call and internet records of customers for at least six months but no more than two years. All *data controllers and processors* then have to put in place a data lifecycle management plan to ensure that data are processed as required at every stage of the lifecycle and that they are deleted at the appropriate time.

data lineage, see *lineage*

data literacy   The skills and knowledge to generate, process, analyse, and interpret data. Weak data literacy results in a poor ability to create, handle, and make sense of data, whereas strong data literacy is reflected in an ability to think creatively and reflectively about all aspects of the *data lifecycle*, be competent at *data management*, possess good analytical skills, and be able to use data to competently solve questions and problems. Data literacy is not an innate set of skills and competencies, but requires education, training, mentoring, and practice. *Critical Data Studies* scholars have extended this traditional notion of data literacy to also include an understanding of the politics of knowledge production and the operations of *data power* and *data politics*. Critical data literacy involves developing a critical consciousness towards the politics and praxes of the data lifecycle and the ways in which data-driven systems shape society and economy, as well self-*reflexivity* with respect to one's own *data practices* and *positionality*. Possessing traditional and critical data literacy is important because they enable an individual to undertake their own data work, make sense of and critique the work of others, seek *data justice*, enact *counter-data actions*, and claim *data sovereignty*.

Further reading

Klidas, A. and Hanegan, K. (2022) *Data Literacy in Practice*. Packt Publishing, Birmingham.

Pangrazio, L. and Selwyn, N. (2023) *Critical Data Literacies: Rethinking Data and Everyday Life*. MIT Press, Cambridge, MA.

data loss   The *deletion*, corruption, or stranding of data on inaccessible media. Data can be deleted for good reason (e.g., to comply with *data protection* legislation), but they can also be erased thoughtlessly or accidentally. Digital records are easily overwritten or deleted and *data storage* media have a short life-span. For example, it is estimated that 50 per cent of webpages have different content or are deleted within a year. A pen drive typically lasts a handful of years before the storage media starts to decay. Moreover, storage hardware, software, and data formats evolve rapidly and quickly become obsolescent, meaning data can become inaccessible. Unless data are regularly transferred to new media and formats they can become lost and forgotten. *Archives* and *data repositories* have technology transfer policies for this reason. See also *stranded data*.

Further reading

Kitchin, R. (2021) *Data Lives: How Data Are Made and Shape Our World*. Chapter 13. Bristol University Press, Bristol.

data maintenance and repair   The upkeep of the *data architecture* of *data infrastructures* and systems. This upkeep differs from *data cleaning* and *data wrangling*, in that these relate to preparing datasets for downstream processing, analysis, and use, whereas data maintenance and repair refer to the architectures that support the operational systems and infrastructure that perform data work. IT systems, *archives, data repositories, databases*, network infrastructure, and all other related technologies that support the production, handling, analysis, storing, and sharing of data are fragile entities. They suffer from *glitches*, breakdowns, and cyberattacks (see *data security*), and they are in a constant state of upgrading as new software versions are released and new technical innovations are introduced. To continue to function they need constant monitoring and maintenance, including firmware patching and software updates, as well as repairs and replacement of physical components. Without this maintenance and repair a system will atrophy and eventually stop working altogether. With respect to the storage of data, without *curation* and transferring data across *data formats* and storage media (e.g., from floppy disk to CD to cloud) it is vulnerable to bit rot and *data loss*.

Further reading

Graham, S. and Thrift, N. (2007) 'Out of order: Understanding repair and maintenance', *Theory, Culture & Society*, 24(3), 1–25.

Mattern, S. (2018) 'Maintenance and care', *Places Journal*, https://doi .org/10.22269/181120

data management   The practices of administering all aspects of the *data lifecycle* to ensure that the data can be used as intended. Data management involves a suite of data handling practices including data generation, *data ingestion*, *data cleaning*, *data wrangling*, *data maintenance and repair*, *data enrichment*, *data fusion*, *curation*, *data storage*, *data sharing*, and *deletion*. Data management should align with an organisation's or project's *data policy* and *data strategy* and comply with a *data management plan* and *data governance* expectations. Poor data management will lead to issues of *data integrity* and reduce the value that can be extracted from the data.

Further reading

Corti, L., Van den Eynden, V., Bishop, L., and Wollard, M. (2019) *Managing and Sharing Research Data: A Guide to Good Practice*. Second edition. Sage, London.

data management plan   A formalised plan as to how data will be managed within a project. A data management plan details the policies and procedures as to how data will be generated, handled, and stored, who owns the data, who the data can be shared with, what the data will be used for, how *data practices* will comply with *research ethics*, *data regulations*, and the *law*, and how the data will be *preserved* and *archived* for future *re-use*. It will also detail the resourcing required and the roles and responsibilities for implementing the plan. A data management plan is a live document, meaning that it continues to be updated as a project unfolds. At the end of a project a revised plan is published that details the data management performed over the lifetime of the project and any archiving or disposal arrangements, including stating why some data cannot be shared.

Further reading

Donnelly, M. (2012) 'Data management plans and planning', in Pryor, G. (ed.), *Managing Research Data*. Facet Publishing, London, pp. 83–104.

data markets   The trading of data, *data analytics*, and *data services* as a commodity. There is a wide variety of data markets in operation globally. These include: the rent or sale of specific forms of data as provided by *data brokers*; *cloud* storage services; data analytics as a service; and consultancy services relating to *data management, data maintenance and repair, data policy* and *data strategies* provided by *data intermediaries*. Transactions do not always have to be monetary based, but could be in-kind trades (swapping one dataset for another, or for a service). The operations of data markets are somewhat opaque; there are open questions concerning their regulation since they often span jurisdictions, and concerns relating to anti-trust violations and data mis-use regarding *Fair Information Practice Principles*. See also *data capitalism, data colonialism, data regulation, surveillance capitalism*.

Further reading

Taylor, L., Mukiri-Smith, H., Petročnik, T., Savolainen, L., and Martin, A. (2022) '(Re)making data markets: An exploration of the regulatory challenges', *Law, Innovation and Technology* 14(2): 355–94.

data materiality   The material constitution of data and data work. Data are most often conceived as being representational, symbolic, and semiotic in nature, rather than understood in material terms. However, data do possess a materiality in three main senses. First, data can be autographic in nature, inscribed into the materiality of the phenomenon being examined (see *autographic data*). Second, data are stored on and made mobile by physical entities; for example, a table of numbers on a sheet of paper, magnetic atoms storing bits on a hard drive, packets of bits that

are transmitted across internet infrastructure (see *analogue data,
digital data*). Data possess material properties that affect how
data can be stored and circulated (see *data centre*) and what they
represent and how they can be used. Third, data are the product
of the material conditions of their generation, processing, storage,
and sharing, which are imprinted on the structure and form of the
data, their *data formats, data access,* and *data management*. Data is
a discursive-material entity and what can be achieved with data is
not simply related to what they represent.

Further reading

Dourish, P. (2017) *The Stuff of Bits: An Essay on the Materialities of
Information.* MIT Press, Cambridge, MA.

data maturity framework   A means of assessing the current
state of play in an organisation with regards to data, *data management, data governance,* and *data literacy,* and devising a *data strategy* to improve the quality of procedures and processes to reach
defined targets. A data maturity assessment involves *benchmarking* data integrity and data-related activities (e.g., *data security,*
data management, data governance, *data analytics, data storage*)
against pre-defined levels within a prescribed framework. There
are several data maturity assessment frameworks available, each
designed to work for different types of organisation and sectors.
These vary in their scope, the specific aspects of data management assessed, and how they are applied. Once an assessment is
completed, the findings are used to draw up a strategy designed
to increase data maturity across the assessed criteria, usually over
a period of three to five years. During this period, the criteria are
monitored to make sure progress is being made. The benefits of
implementing a data maturity framework are: the organisation
and its staff has a better awareness of data-related activities and
data management expectations; a unified approach to data management and governance is adopted; the risks arising from low
data maturity can be mitigated; the value extracted from data is
increased; and new opportunities can be identified.

Further reading

Henderson, D. and Earley, S. (eds) (2017) *DAMA-DMBOK:
Data Management Body of Knowledge.* Second edition. Technics
Publications, Basking Ridge, NJ.

data minimisation principle   *Personal data* should only be produced when needed, used solely for the purpose for which they were generated, be retained only until this task is complete, and should not be made available to others without the *consent* of the *data subject.* The data minimisation principle is also termed the 'use limitation principle' and it is core to *Fair Information Practice Principles, data protection,* and *privacy* legislation. Such a principle is antithetical to the rationale of *big data* and *data markets,* both of which desire to extract as much value as possible from datasets. As a consequence, actors such as *data brokers* have devised strategies to circumvent the principle, such as *deidentification,* using *pseudonyms,* classifying data subjects into defined 'measurement types' (profiles that share the same characteristics as the data subject), or creating *derived data* and deleting the original data. These transformed data can then be used as desired without the need to inform the data subject or gain their consent as data minimisation only applies to original captured data. See also *privacy by design, surveillance capitalism.*

Further reading

Tene, O. and Polonetsky, J. (2012) 'Big data for all: Privacy and user control in the age of analytics', *Northwestern Journal of Technology and Intellectual Property,* 11(5): 240–73.

data mining   A set of analytical techniques to find and extract data, patterns, and relationships in very large datasets. Data mining uses supervised or unsupervised *machine learning* to detect, classify, and segment meaningful patterns in datasets. A variety of different statistical and algorithmic techniques are used to perform different types of data mining tasks, each selected depending on the purpose of analysis and data type (*structured data, semi-structured data* or *unstructured data*). For example, cluster analysis might be used to segment data; Bayesian statistics, decision-trees or neural networks for *classification*; social network analysis or regression techniques to discover associations; outlier detection or evolution analysis to detect deviations; or natural language processing to uncover patterns in text. The power of data mining is that it has enabled the analysis of enormous amounts of data that would have been all but impossible by hand or by using traditional methods of *quantitative analysis* and *qualitative* *analysis,* particularly for unstructured data. Data mining is not without criticism, however. It has been critiqued for encouraging *data dredging* and for increasing *ecological fallacies* in analysis; for example, through apophenia (detecting patterns in random or meaningless data) or confusing *noise* for pattern.

Further reading

Han, J., Pei, J., and Tong, H. (2022) *Data Mining: Concepts and Techniques.* Fourth edition. Morgan Kaufmann, Waltham, MA.

data mobilities An approach to data that recognises that a fundamental aspect of their lifecycle and use is their fluid and mobile nature. Rather than understanding the world as largely fixed, with some movement between locales, the mobilities turn in the social sciences posits that it is more productive to recognise that everyday life consists of mobile practices. People, objects, data, knowledge, and other entities that make up the world (e.g., animals, the elements, etc.) are constantly on the move. Data mobilities seeks to understand, holistically and relationally, the movement and circulation of data, as well as their supporting technologies and *data infrastructures,* management and governance practices, economy and *data capitalism,* and environmental effects. It examines *data journeys* and *data threads,* wider patterns of *data circulation,* the seams that facilitate movement, and the *data frictions* that limit it. See also *seamfulness and seamlessness.*

Further reading

Kitchin, R., Davret, J., Kayanan, C., and Mutter, S. (2024) 'Data mobilities: Rethinking the movement and circulation of data', *Data Stories Working Paper 3,* https://mural.maynoothuniversity.ie/18716

data model A conceptual mapping of how all the data within a system relate to one another and to specific processes within a system. It is often displayed as a graphical chart that details the collections of data held, how these data logically relate and connect to one another, and how these relations are structured within a *database* design (a data model is sometimes referred to as data structure, and data modelling referred to as database design). A well-structured data model enables all desired operations and analysis to be performed by allowing datasets to be linked together to answer specific queries. It also aids *data standardisation*, *data fusion*, and *data management* by applying a consistent data model across a system. See also *modelling*.

data monopolies   Companies who hold a disproportionate share of a *data market*. As a valuable asset, data have become a major business enterprise to the extent that highly data-centric companies lead the list of the top ten most valuable companies globally (e.g., Amazon, Apple, Facebook, Google, Microsoft). These companies hold massive amounts of *personal data* and commercial data, and through their platforms and *data services* dominate positions in their respective markets. They form data monopolies making it difficult for other actors to enter the market and to grow. Indeed, the wealth of data monopolies allows them to buy and merge with smaller rivals, acquiring their *intellectual property rights*, patents, and data reserves, with their data assets providing them with strategic market intelligence that enables them to maintain and further extend their position. Data monopolies have been criticised for stifling competition and evading anti-trust actions, and there are concerns that the concentration of *data power* has implications for *data protection*, *privacy*, consumer choice, non-discrimination rights, freedom of speech, democracy (through controlling information channels), and how traditional economic markets work (e.g., Airbnb reshaping local real-estate markets). There is a sense that present laws and regulations focus inadequately on the symptoms of data monopolies, and do little to limit their formation, dismantle them or curtail their data power. See also *data capitalism*, *data colonialism*, *surveillance capitalism*.

Further reading

McIntosh, D. (2019) 'We need to talk about data: How digital monopolies arise and why they have power and influence', *Journal of Technology Law & Policy* 23(2): 185–213.

data narratives   The construction of meaning-making and argument using data. Data do not speak for themselves but must be narrated, embedded into narratives that present, contextualise, and interpret them for different purposes and for varying audiences. Different ways of presenting and animating data aid in this process, such as tables, *data visualisations*, maps, and text, structuring and parsing the data to enable *data stories* to be told and meaning-making to take place. Through their mobilisation in narratives data gain *data affordances* and are translated into *situated knowledge*. All academic papers, evidence-informed policy documents, *data journalism*, and any other media using data to support an argument will have constructed a data narrative to make their case and persuade their audience. With mass *datafication* and the increasing use of data in public discourse, marketing, advertising, strategic plans, and other discursive materials, data narratives are becoming more common and are reshaping narrative practice more generally. See also *data literacy*, *data imaginaries*, *discursive regime*.

Further reading

Dourish, P. and Gomez Cruz, E. (2018) 'Datafication and data fiction: Narrating data and narrating with data', *Big Data & Society*, 6(2): 1–10.

data ontology   How data are defined and formally organised. In philosophy, *ontology* concerns the nature of being and reality and what exists and can be known. A data ontology concerns how aspects of the world are defined, classified, and organised into an intelligible form that is suitable for making sense of a phenomenon and undertaking analysis. An ontology might be an informal set of categories or a formalised *taxonomy*. *Archives* and libraries have long used formal, standardised data ontologies to enhance searching for material. With mass *datafication*, *big data*, the huge growth in *unstructured data* or *semi-structured data*, and the need to improve *interoperability* between systems and datasets and to extract value from data (including the use of *artificial intelligence* and semantic media), there has been significant investment in creating standardised data ontologies. See also *categorisation and classification*, *semantic web*.

Further reading

Iliadis, A. (2019) 'The Tower of Babel problem: Making data make sense with Basic Formal Ontology', *Online Information Review*, 43(6): 1021–45.

data ownership, see *ownership*

data performativity   Data do not simply represent aspects of the world, they also incite work in the world. Or to put it another way, rather than being mirrors of phenomena, data act as engines, making things happen. Data are performative in the sense that their affordances mediate viewpoints, inflect subjectivities, shape behaviours, and prompt action (see *data affordances*). Data and their analysis produce knowledge, inform policy, and enable commercial systems to function. How we come to know and act in relation to a phenomenon or process is not just reflected in data, it is shaped by those data. In this sense, data produce what they represent. Data incite people to adopt certain roles or behave in particular ways. The data within a CV or citation ranking, or a dating app or *surveillance* system, modulate subjectivity (how people perceive themselves and others) and compel individuals to act in response to those data and also to try to change them (they work for and to the data) (see *datafied agency*). Such performativity is contextually framed with respect to *data valences* and circumstances.

Further reading

Matzner, T. (2016) 'Beyond data as representation: The performativity of Big Data in surveillance', *Surveillance & Society*, 14(2): 197–210.

data philanthropy   Private datasets are made available for public good initiatives. In the big data era, private enterprise generate massive amounts of granular and timely data about every aspect of society. These data are potentially of enormous benefit for understanding an issue or reacting to a situation (such as a humanitarian crisis), but since they are a private resource they are not accessible to researchers, policy makers, civil society actors or responding agencies. Data philanthropy involves a donor company making a selection of data available to particular organisations or as *open data*. What data are shared is controlled by the donor and access to and use of the data might involve terms and conditions. While data philanthropy can be highly valuable, it is also relatively uncommon. In the case of emergencies, it has been argued that companies should be compelled to make key data available. See also *data access, data humanitarianism*.

Further reading

Taddeo, M. (2016) 'Data philanthropy and the design of the infraethics for information societies', *Philosophical Transactions of the Royal Society* A, 374(2083): 37420160113.

data phronesis   The situated and context-dependent practical wisdom enacted by different actors in order to care with or for data. The concept was introduced by Ślosarski (2024) to explain how various stakeholders draw on their experience and knowledge to define good care, and use *sensor data* to practise care with respect to air quality, but also practice *data management* and *data maintenance and repair* to perform data care. This care is collectively manufactured through the collaborations and contestations between actors who may have different values, aims, and purposes. Data phronesis in this sense is the contextual, practical, embodied, and negotiated enactment of an *ethics of data care*.

Further reading

Ślosarski, B. (2024) 'Data phronesis and the duality of care in the air quality data politics', *Information, Communication & Society*, doi: 10.1080/1369118X.2023.2296926

data physicalisation   The conversion of data into a physical form whose measurements and material properties encode the data values. Typically, a data physicalisation is both tactile and visual, produced by encoding data into 3D model shapes or using crafts such as sculptures, knitting, and quilting. For example, encoding annual global temperature change in a knitted scarf, where each row of stitches is coloured to reflect the temperature in an individual year, or a tactile map that encodes *spatial data*. Data can also be encoded with respect to other senses such as smell and taste (e.g., data encoded as shapes and flavours of chocolates). In addition, data can be map-projected onto other entities such as buildings or 3D models, using their physical form as means to encode or simply communicate the data. Data physicalisation often produces *visceral data*.

Further reading

Huron, S., Nagel, T., Oehlberg, L., and Willett, W. (eds) (2022) *Making with Data: Physical Design and Craft in a Data-Driven World*. CRC Press, London.

Offenhuber, D. (2020) 'What we talk about when we talk about data physicality', *IEEE Computer Graphics and Applications*, 40(6): 25–37.

data pipeline The ordered sequence through which data are generated and made ready for use. The production of data involves a number of stages, including a pre-generation phase of preparation (e.g., setting up and readying equipment, designing a survey), the generation of data, processes of *data cleaning, data wrangling* and *data transformation, data fusion,* and *data storage* and *data sharing.* Once the data pipeline sequence has been completed the data are ready for use and analysis. This sequence of phases is not simply technical, consisting of the rote implementation of a set of defined techniques and practices, but is *socio-technical,* mediated by people, cultural norms, learned behaviours, scientific conventions, regulations and laws, amongst other factors. This is even the case in fully automated systems as these possess secondary agency, performing the work as designed by their programmers.

data policy Policy that is designed to address data-related issues and promote data-led work. Governments formulate policies in order to drive an agenda and achieve certain outcomes with respect to an issue or phenomenon. For example, an *open data* policy promotes the publication of open data, providing guidance and targets for public bodies to adequately achieve this task. A *data standards* policy sets out the rationale for improving standards and stipulates how this will be achieved by reaching defined milestones at particular points in time. The formulation of data policies involves significant *data politics* as different vested interests seek to influence the orientation, goals, and specific actions. Organisations who are responsible for executing data policy often produce *data strategies* and implementation plans to guide how they will achieve the policy ambitions. Policy relating to any issue where the argument is supported or driven by data is termed evidence-based or evidence-informed policy.

data politics The political ambitions, negotiations, and debates related to data. The data lifecycle and the uses of data do not take place in a political vacuum. The ways in which data are produced, for what purposes, and in whose interests is full of politics relating to points of view, agendas, ideologies, choices and decisions, and the reproduction and contestation of *data power*. Data are reflective of the values and politics of those that produce and use them. *Data policies* arise out of political debate and serve political interests. Data are used to undertake political work in terms of shaping debates about social and economic phenomena, transforming public values, and driving institutional response. The use of data and the practices of data politics produce political subjects, marked by the political work of data or acting as advocates or opponents of political positions. Data politics is practised through all forms of political organising and activity: formal politics and the debates between political parties; the lobbying of corporate interests and other stakeholders; the expression of identity politics relating to *race, ethnicity, gender,* sexuality (see *queer data*), and other social markers; the organising of *data activism* and grassroots resistance to data power; and in the micro-politics of inter- and intra-organisational machinations and interpersonal relations.

Further reading

Bigo, D., Isin, E., and Ruppert, E. (eds) (2019) *Data Politics: Worlds, Subjects, Rights.* London: Routledge.

Koopman, C. (2021) 'The political theory of data: Institutions, algorithms and formats in racial redlining', *Political Theory*, 50(2), 337–61.

data power   The ability to shape and control processes, extract value, and to assert claims through the production and use of data. Power is the ability or right to control and claim entities (e.g., people, objects, territory) and processes, and to act as desired at the expense of others. Digital technologies and *data infrastructures* are designed to serve the interests of those that fund and create them, with power invested into, mobilised, and enacted through the constitution and operations of data-driven systems in order to influence, manage, and govern people, to profile, sort, and differently treat groups, to exploit labour, to leverage profit, and to maintain and extend dominant relations. There are pronounced asymmetries in data power, with the state and corporations holding more authority and control than subjects and customers, owners and managers wielding more influence than workers, and other asymmetric divisions along the lines of social identities such as *gender*, *race*, class, *disability*, *ethnicity*, and sexuality (see *queer data*). Data power is also expressed in geopolitical terms, contributing to the relations between nation states with respect to *data regulations*, transnational *data markets*, border controls, *data security* and cyberwar, amongst a range of data-related and mediated issues. Asymmetrical and hierarchical relations of power underpin the organisation and functioning of a *data regime*, with this regime reproduced as a *data doxa* through the maintenance of dominant, hegemonic structural relations and the operations of *data politics*. Differential data power raises concerns with respect to civil liberties, *data sovereignty*, *data protection* and *privacy*, unfair and discriminatory treatment, *accountability* and redress. To address concerns and counter data power, states have mandated *data regulations*, legislation, and *data rights*. In addition, civil liberty organisations have promoted *data ethics* and revised *data citizenship*, while community groups have mobilised *data activism* designed to produce *data justice*, enable citizens to claim data sovereignty, and *decolonise data* regimes. A great deal of *Critical Data Studies* research focuses on exposing the constitution and operations of data power and considering how this power can be resisted and countered, and what alternative, more just data regimes might be created. See also *discursive regime*, *power/knowledge*, *social sorting*.

Further reading

D'Ignazio, C. and Klein, L.F. (2020) *Data Feminism*. MIT Press, Cambridge, MA.

Söderström, O. and Datta, A. (eds) (2023) *Data Power in Action: Urban Data Politics in Times of Crisis*. Bristol University Press, Bristol.

Thatcher, J. and Dalton, C. (2022) *Data Power: Radical Geographies of Control and Resistance*. Pluto Press, London.

data practices   Forms of embodied behaviour and action that contribute to the *data lifecycle* or produce data-involved outcomes in the world. With respect to the data lifecycle, data practices are the ways in which work is undertaken in relation to *data management* in all its forms; for example all the tasks employed in *data cleaning* and *data wrangling*. In relation to data-involved outcomes, data practices are the actions employed to translate data into knowledge production, decision-making, and the services and products being delivered; for example, all the tasks involved in creating *data narratives* and the *data stories* of policy-making or *data journalism*. Data practices are embodied, performed through bodily actions, but also affective, inflected by mood, feelings, and pre-cognitive thoughts (see *affect, embodiment*). The kinds of practices utilised and how they are enacted can be prescribed by *data regulations* and law, and framed within social norms. Over time they can become routine and habitual, helping to reproduce the workings of a *data regime*. They are, though, never static and stable, but always situated and unfolding in *contingent*, relational and citational ways, imperfectly repeating previous performances and varying with *context*, circumstances, and subjectivities (even if this variance is almost imperceptible). Over time then, practices can slowly change, with new routines and habits forming. This change might be more radical if a new regime of best practices is introduced; for example, in response to a *data maturity* assessment.

Further reading

Ruppert, E. and Scheel, S. (2021) 'Data practices', in Ruppert, E. and Scheel, S. (eds), *Data Practices: Making Up a European People*. Goldsmiths Press, London, pp. 29–48.

data protection The set of laws and regulatory tools for safeguarding *personal data* and protecting against *privacy* harms. Outside of the European Union, data protection is often framed as privacy legislation. Both data protection and privacy regulations draw on *Fair Information Practice Principles* (FIPPs) and are concerned with individual rights with respect to the production of personal data, how these are processed and used, and their disclosure to third parties. Data protection, as defined by the EU through GDPR (General Data Protection Regulations), differs from privacy regulations in that it relates to all datasets holding personal data and the responsibility for compliance lies with organisations (see *data controllers and processors*), whereas privacy legislation can vary by domain (e.g., in the United States, health data can have different privacy regulations to transportation data) and responsibility lies with individuals. In addition, which principles from the FIPPs are adopted can vary, with just four of the eight principles (*notice, consent,* access, and *data security*) adopted by the Federal Trade Commission in the US, and privacy regulations only being applied to some practices (such as credit rating, employment, and insurance) but not others. Neither data protection nor privacy regulations tackle *group privacy* harms arising from the use of *demographically identifiable information*. Great strain is being placed on data protection through mass *datafication, dataveillance,* the creation of *data markets, data capitalism* and *surveillance capitalism*. In these cases, data controllers and processors often find workarounds to bypass the regulatory requirements, using, for example, *pseudonyms, aggregation* or *inferred data,* since data protection rules apply to *personally identifiable information* rather than anonymised and derived data, the use of which does not need *data subject* consent. See also *privacy by design, law and data*.

Further reading

Krzysztofek. M. (2021) *GDPR: Personal Data Protection in the European Union*. Kluwer Law International, Netherlands.

data provenance, see *provenance*

data publics   Citizens who are interested in data, *data politics,* and *data governance,* undertake data work either personally or through group initiatives, and who discuss the uses and effects of data in their lives and society more generally. The term was introduced by Ruppert (2015) to refer to people who are data-minded. That is, they have an active interest in data, either with respect to a particular issue or in a broader, more general sense, and they think about and seek to influence data practices and narratives. Data publics might relate to those working in data-related employment, or those who take part in *citizen science, civic hacking* or *crowdsourcing* initiatives, or undertake *data activism*. See also *communities of practice*.

Further reading

Ruppert, E. (2015) 'Doing the transparent state: Open government data as performance indicators', in Rottenburg, R., Merry, S.E., Park, S.-J., and Mugler, J. (eds), *A World of Indicators: The Making of Governmental Knowledge Through Quantification*. Cambridge University Press, Cambridge, pp. 127–50.

data pyramid The concepts of *data power* and *data capitalism* mapped onto population demographics, with the small percentage of the world's richest people residing at the top of the pyramid and the large percentage of the world's poorest people at the base. Introduced by Arora (2016), her analysis focused on the 'bottom of the data pyramid' – the roughly four billion poorest members of the Global South. This group are positioned by companies and states as beneficiaries of *datafication*, gaining empowerment and upward mobility through being new data consumers and becoming new *data subjects* of the state. In contrast, others caution that those at the bottom of the data pyramid are being mobilised as a new *data market* and being enrolled into *bureaucracy* and *surveillance* structures as knowable and calculable subjects, which may further marginalise vulnerable populations. While digital technologies may create empowered consumers or citizens through access to digital services, they also enrol them into capitalist and neoliberal *data regimes* without protecting them from data extraction as *data rights*, *data protection*, and *data literacy* are limited. Arora argues that the last three issues need redress, and that new models of digital inclusivity are needed. See also *data colonialism*.

Further reading

Arora, P. (2016) 'The bottom of the data pyramid: Big data and the Global South', *International Journal of Communication* 10: 1681–99.

data quality How clean, untainted, and consistent a set of data is. The higher the quality of the data, the stronger the *data integrity* and the level of *veracity* and trust in data analysis and interpretation. High quality data are *error* free, possess no *bias*, have *completeness*, *consistency*, strong *veracity*, and appropriate *coverage*. Poor quality data are the opposite and might also consist of *gamed data*, *fake data* or weak *proxy data* or *inferred data*. The consequences of using poor quality data are manifold and all negative; as the adage goes 'garbage in leads to garbage out'. In other words, even if all other aspects of analysis arc impeccable, if the data are poor the integrity of the process is compromised to varying degrees. Very few datasets are perfect and it might be the case that despite data quality issues the data used are considered *good enough data.* In addition, it is possible to improve data quality through *data management* processes such as *data cleaning, data wrangling,* and *data transformation.*

Further reading

Hawker, R. (2023) *Practical Data Quality.* Packt Publishing, Birmingham.

data ratcheting   The process by which an organisation undergoes gradual data-driven change management as new digital technologies and processes are introduced that reshape services, products, and labour and shift organisational goals and governance. The term was introduced by Heaphy (2019) in his study of how a public transport provider gradually became more data-driven over time, using *real-time data* to monitor infrastructure and vehicle movements, plan timetabling and routing, and share data with the public through real-time passenger information signs and apps. New innovations were ratcheted iteratively on top of previous changes and were informed by developments in other places (i.e., examples of international best practice) and the need to meet emerging industry standards. Data ratcheting has three primary phases: data expansionism (the development of new datasets through the deployment of new technologies, especially through the production of *big data*); data experimentalism (development of new functions, products, and services); and operational consolidation (the embedding of new innovations in the everyday work of an organisation).

Further reading

Heaphy, L. (2019) 'Data ratcheting and data-driven organisational change in transport', *Big Data & Society* 6(2): 1–12.

data refuge   A site where data rescued from potential deletion is stored and protected. The concept was first imagined and introduced in the United States in 2016. After the election of Donald Trump, and in the context of the growing voice and influence of climate change deniers, there was a well-founded concern that federal environmental and climate science data would be removed from *open data* sites and *deleted.* Concerned citizens started to systematically create backup copies of datasets to *preserve* them for future use, initiating the Data Refuge project and running a number of data rescue events (see datarefugestories.org; see *citizen science*). There are concerns about the need to place other open datasets and declassified data in data refuges, with some instances of the latter being reclassified and thus removed from the public record.

Further reading

Chapman, R.E.T. (2022) 'When the goalposts move: Government information, classification, and censorship', *Legal Reference Services Quarterly*, 41(3–4): 117–55.

Currie M.E. and Paris B.S. (2018) 'Back-ups for the future: Archival practices for data activism', *Archives & Manuscripts*, 46(2): 124–42.

data regime   A dominant, interlocking set of ideas, norms, practices, and technologies that shape how data are understood and produced, and how they are legitimately used within society and domains. A strong data regime operates as a *data doxa*; that is, as a commonsensical, normalised, and accepted approach to data (its production, management, governance, regulation), the role and *data labour* of different actors, and the use of data and expected and acceptable outcomes. The nature and operation of a data regime is shaped by the wider *political economy, data capitalism, data citizenship, governmentality,* and *data politics*, as well as the situated and contextual factors and norms within specific domains, and its rationalities and logics are justified through a supporting *discursive regime*. While a general data regime operates at a societal level, there can be particular data regimes in place within domains and sectors; for example, the data regime within the health sector will have norms and expectations that partially match but also differ from that of the retail sector. Data regimes also differ across jurisdictions, relating to cultural and governance norms, and regulatory and legislative contexts. Data regimes can change over time as new technologies, practices, laws, and strategies are introduced and as social expectations shift; for example, the introduction of *big data, open data,* and the *cloud* has reconfigured the data regimes of many domains. *Data activism*, and calls for *data ethics* and *data justice*, actively seek to challenge, disrupt, and change data regimes. A *calculative regime* is a particular form of data regime, relating to how data are used in managing and governing populations and systems. See also *data habitus*.

Further reading
Ricaurte, P. (2019) 'Data epistemologies, the coloniality of power, and resistance', *Television & New Media*, 20(4): 350–65.

data regulation   The control and management of data practices and uses. Given the value of data, its many applications, the unevenness and inequalities in its impact and benefits, and the operations of *data power*, *data politics*, and *data capitalism*, the need for data regulation is well understood. As a consequence, there is a long history of different forms of data regulation – conventions, *data standards*, regulations, directives, laws – designed to ensure that best practice procedures are put in place and are enforced with respect to *data practices*, *data governance*, *data labour*, *data rights*, *data ethics*, *intellectual property rights*, *data markets*, and the use of data that is prejudicial, discriminatory, and harmful. This might include the introduction of formal roles, such as *chief data officers*, *data protection* or *privacy* officers and *information commissioners*, or approval and oversight bodies such as audit and governance boards and *institutional review boards*, as well as market self-regulation. Data regulation varies across jurisdictions and sectors. See also *accountability*, *research ethics*.

data repository   A shared *data infrastructure* for the storing, archiving, and sharing of data. In effect, a data repository is a multistakeholder *archive*, in which several organisations deposit their data in the same data infrastructure, though their various data collections might not share *data formats* or *data standards*. A single-site repository hosts all the data collections in a single data infrastructure accessible through a single website address. A federated repository might host some of the data collections on a central data infrastructure, along with the metadata of other data collections stored in an organisation's own digital archive. In other words, the data are stored across multiple sites, but are accessible through a single portal. While data formats and standards might vary within a repository, there will be shared *data governance*, *data policies*, and *data strategy*, and agreed *data regulations* regarding *data quality*, *metadata*, and *data integrity*. Data repositories might also provide some *data services* beyond search and retrieval, such as basic *data analytics* and *data visualisation*. Building and maintaining a data repository is not simply a technical exercise, but involves a lot of personal and institutional politics and negotiations regarding all aspects of its development, maintenance, and operation. See also *trusted digital repository*.

Further reading

Rice, R. and Southall, J. (2016) *The Data Librarian's Handbook*. Facet Publishing, London.

Schöpfel, J. and Rebouillat, V. (eds) (2022) *Research Data Sharing and Valorization: Developments, Tendencies, Models*. ISTE/Wiley, London.

data rights   The rights that are conferred to individuals, groups, and owners with respect to data. Rights are morally and normatively framed, concerning what entitlements and treatment different actors can expect in particular circumstances. These are enshrined in regulations and legislation, and in the social norms of society. With respect to individuals, *data subjects* have the right to *data protection* and *privacy* in relation to their *personal data*. They also have rights conferred through *data citizenship* and their membership of a polity (including, depending on the jurisdiction, the right to *freedom of information* and the *right to be forgotten*). Groups can have rights with respect to their social identity, defined in legislation or equality, diversity, and inclusion policies and regulations, that protect their community knowledge and heritage (as in the case of *Indigenous data*) or seek to limit discrimination (in relation to *race*, *ethnicity*, and *gender*, amongst others). Data owners have rights with respect to data they generate, such as *intellectual property rights* and the right to extract value from these data as long as they do not infringe the rights of data subjects. There is an inherent tension between data subjects and data owners when the latter seek to skirt the rights of the former in order to leverage value and profit (see *data controllers and processors*, *data capitalism*, *data colonialism*, *ownership*, *surveillance capitalism*).

Data   Science   An   interdisciplinary   field   that   uses computationally-driven *statistics*, informatics, *modelling*, applied mathematics, and bespoke programming to produce *knowledge* from data. The core approach is to develop and use *data analytics* (including *data mining*, *statistics*, *simulation*, and *visual analytics*) to draw insight from datasets (typically *big data* or large sets of *administrative data*) about a domain (e.g., transport, health, climate). A relatively young field, Data Science has been able to grow rapidly due to a surge in computational power that has allowed massive volumes of calculations to be performed quickly. While Data Science is now well established internationally as a vibrant field, it has also been the subject of critique. Some applications of its approach have been criticised for practising empiricism (letting the data speak for themselves) rather than *data-driven science*. Applications adopting the more traditional *scientific method* have been critiqued for their *positivist*-rooted analyses of social phenomena (see *computational social sciences*). In addition, there are concerns that Data Science performs analysis on domains in which it has little expertise, producing ill-informed insights; practises a form of data solutionism in which data analytics (as opposed to other forms of analysis) are seen as providing the best answer to any issue; and often does not properly engage with *research ethics* regarding *personal data* (incorrectly assuming that if one is using secondary data and examining issues or systems rather than people, then research ethics does not apply). In response to these critiques, some have sought to develop critical data science, in particular drawing on feminist philosophy to create a post-positivist approach that recognises *positionality*, practices ethics, and produces *situated knowledges*. See also *data feminism, critical GIS, feminist data science, radical statistics*.

Further reading

Kelleher, J.D. and Tierney, B. (2018) *Data Science*. MIT Press, Cambridge, MA.

Neff, G., Tanweer, A., Fiore-Gartland, B., and Osburn, L. (2017) 'Critique and contribute: A practice-based framework for improving critical data studies and data science', *Big Data*, 5(2): 85–97.

data scraping Automatically downloading and processing web content, or using an undocumented *API* to capture data displayed on publicly available websites. Given that sharing data with the public is an essential feature of many platforms (e.g., displaying product details and prices), these data are amenable to being scraped in an automated fashion by a bespoke scraping program. For example, Inside Airbnb has constructed a longitudinal database of Airbnb rental data for cities worldwide by scraping Airbnb's website (see insideairbnb.com). Data scraping raises ethical and legal questions. While data might be viewable on a website, that does not necessarily mean it is *open data* that can be re-used as one wishes, even if it has public interest value. There are ongoing debates with regards to consent, *ownership*, *intellectual property rights*, control of data use, and how the law should treat data scraping (e.g., as trespass or theft).

Further reading

Scassa, T. (2019) 'Ownership and control over publicly accessible platform data', *Online Information Review*, 43(6): 986–1002.

data security   Protecting data from being hacked and stolen. Data security is a core principle of the *Fair Information Practice Principles* and *data protection*, committing *data controllers and processors* to ensuring that *personal data* remains inaccessible to those without access rights. Given the value of data to organisations, data security extends beyond personal data to include all the data that they hold. Networked digital systems are vulnerable to various forms of cyberattack, such as hacking, malware, and phishing, which can result in a *data breach* that can be very costly for the organisations and the *data subjects* to whom the data refer. Cybersecurity measures – technical interventions (e.g., firewalls, access controls, encryption, virus scanners, patching) and training and education – are designed to prevent such breaches. However, these measures constantly need to keep up with new vulnerabilities and forms of attack.

Further reading

Lenhard, T.H. (2021) *Data Security: Technical and Organizational Protection Measures Against Data Loss and Computer Crime*. Springer, Wiesbaden, Germany.

data services   The provision of services centred on data-related work. A number of *data intermediary* companies specialise in providing a range of data services. These include operational services, such as undertaking *data management*, conducting *data audits*, and performing *data security* work, and consultancy services, such as undertaking *data analytics* and interpretation, performing *data maturity* assessments, writing *data policy* or *data strategies*, and delivering training and education. Given the value of data to organisations and the increasing *datafication* and digitalisation of services and operations within public and private organisations, data services have become a significant global industry. See also *data brokers*, *data capitalism*, *data markets*, *surveillance capitalism*.

data shadows, see *data footprints and shadows*

data sharing   The sharing of datasets with other parties for *re-use*. Traditionally, data sharing was relatively limited given the cost and resources needed to copy and transfer *analogue data* (see *data access*). In addition, organisations practised *data hugging* to protect valuable assets and maintain their competitive advantage. In the age of *digital data*, the cost and resource barriers to sharing data have been eroded. Digital data are non-rivalrous (more than one entity can possess the same data), non-excludable (they are easily copied and it takes effort to block sharing), and their reproduction has a zero marginal cost (copying is effectively free). If the data are accessible via the internet, then they can be easily transferred, avoiding the time and effort it takes to visit an *archive* in person. Moreover, the *open data movement* has made a compelling case for the sharing of state-held data as *open data*, and many jurisdictions now have open data policies and repositories. There are still good reasons to not share data, such as commercial interest or sensitivity and to comply with *data protection* and *privacy* regulations, but it is much easier to share and access data. This is particularly the case for the informal sharing of data, such as emailing a file, or transferring data onto a pen drive, or placing a *small data* holding online. However, the large-scale *preservation, curation*, storage, and sharing of data through the *data infrastructures* of archives, *data repositories*, and *trusted digital repositories* entails significant overheads in terms of material and staffing costs. This investment and the ongoing operational costs are viewed as being worthwhile due to the spillover and intangible benefits of many people being able to extract value from the shared data. See also *community archives*.

Further reading

Borgman, C.L. (2015) *Big Data, Little Data, No Data: Scholarship in the Networked World*. MIT Press, Cambridge, MA.

OECD (2019) *Enhancing Access to and Sharing of Data: Reconciling Risks and Benefits for Data Re-Use Across Societies*. OECD Publishing, Paris.

data silo Data are isolated for use in a single system and are not made available to other systems or for other uses. A common argument of those advocating for data-driven governance is the need for *data fusion*, breaking down the walls between data silos so that additional value can be extracted from the data. For example, smart city advocates contend that city administrations have too many data silos and that by creating integrated *control rooms*, wherein several services can be monitored and managed from a single site and the data fused to enable further insights, more effective urban governance will be facilitated. While this might be the case, from a *data security* perspective, data and system silos prevent the contagion created when a cybersecurity breach into one data-driven system provides access to others. Data silos can often produce *stranded data*.

data sovereignty The principle that individuals should have control over the data relating to them – both with respect to if and how data are extracted and in relation to how they are used – and others recognise and respect that sovereignty as legitimate. At present, individuals often have little control with respect to their data, with *data power* wielded largely by state bodies and companies. They are, however, afforded some *data rights* and protections through legislation (such as *data protection* and *privacy* regulations and *laws*; see *Fair Information Practice Principles*) enforced through third parties (*data controllers and processors, information commissioners, institutional review boards*). Data sovereignty seeks to enhance the role of individuals and communities in data governance and extend their personal control over *data practices* and use. The idea has its roots in the claims of Indigenous people to be able to control and protect their traditional knowledge, cultural heritage and territory, and the data relating to them (see *Indigenous data*). This claim to sovereignty is a response to centuries of exploitative data extraction, where those data have been used to marginalise and dispossess Indigenous people. See also *data commons, FAIR principles*.

Further reading

Kukutai, T. and Taylor, J. (eds) (2016) *Indigenous Data Sovereignty: Towards an Agenda*. Australian National University Press, Canberra.

data spectacle The visual presentation of data that provides aesthetic pleasure and visual allure. Introduced by Gregg (2015), the data spectacle refers to the scopic power of witnessing *data visualisations* (particularly of *big data*, the extent and complexity of which are difficult to comprehend) created to induce wonder, intrigue, and to promote the uses of data, but also to provide insight. Walls of screens in *control rooms*, infographics on advertising screens, immersive 3D *digital twin* models, *dashboards*, spatialisations, and various forms of *visual analytics* all display 'beautiful data' which have performative effects, shaping how we see and think about the world through their allure and visual spectacle.

Further reading

Gregg, M. (2015) 'Inside the data spectacle', *Television & New Media* 16(1): 37–51.

Halpern, O. (2014) *Beautiful Data: A History of Vision and Reason since 1945*. Duke University Press, Durham, NC.

data standards The technical specifications that detail the consistent production, handling, and storing of data. The aim of data standards is to produce standardised data – data that are uniform in definition, type, *data format* and schema, and fit within a standard *data model* – through the implementation of standardised processes. Data standards help improve *data quality* and allow *interoperability* and *data fusion*. Typically a data standards framework is applied at an organisation or domain level. Within this framework, data standards packages are applied to particular tasks such as *data cleaning* or *data storage*, with a package consisting of an assembled set of discrete component standards relating to the specific qualities of the data, processes, and work flow. In some cases, such as with *national statistics organisations*, data standards are enforced to ensure *data integrity*, whereas in others they are somewhat aspirational and haphazardly applied. The development of data standards is a contested and negotiated process, and which sets of data standards are adopted can have a marked impact on the *data infrastructures* and data work of an organisation.

Further reading

Gal, M. and Rubinfeld, D.L. (2019) 'Data standardization', *NYU Law Review*, 94(4): 737–70.

Star, S.L. and Lampland, M. (eds) (2009) *Standards and Their Stories: How Quantifying, Classifying and Formalizing Practices Shape Everyday Life*. Cornell University Press, Ithaca, NY.

data stewardship   Custodial responsibility and *accountability* with respect to an organisation's data and *data management* and *data governance*. Data stewardship refers to any activity by members of an organisation that seeks to cultivate good practice, protect data assets, and leverage value from these assets. Data stewards might have formal, defined roles or simply practice stewardship through their daily practice. Formal data stewards perform roles centrally concerned with data management and data governance. These roles include responsibility for meeting *data standards* and *data regulations*, complying with *data controller and processor* expectations, producing *documentation*, creating and managing *metadata* and *data dictionaries*, maintaining *data quality*, fulfilling a *data strategy*, providing education and training, and executing data governance. Data stewards oversee the work of those in an organisation who deal with data but are not data specialists. See also *chief data officer*.

data storage   The storing of data on media from which they can be accessed and re-used. *Analogue data* has traditionally been stored on paper, and in the twentieth century also on vinyl, film, magnetic tapes, and microfilm. Digital data are stored on a variety of optical disks, semiconductor chips, and hard disks. The bulk of long-term data storage uses hard disks, an electro-mechanical device that stores and retrieves digital data using magnetic disks. A hard disk is the secondary memory in a digital device (the primary being the central processing unit and random access memory), but it can also be external to the device in the form of a portable pen drive or hard drive, or in the *cloud* on servers in *data centres*. Given mass *datafication* and the growth in *big data*, data storage has had to expand enormously. Digital storage media do not have a long lifespan and are vulnerable to *data loss*, meaning that data need to be transferred to new media periodically to ensure their long-term *preservation*.

data stories   Stories in which the narrative is driven by data. A data story can be about a phenomenon, using data to support the meaning-making, interpretation or case being made, or be a story about some aspect of the *data lifecycle* or how data shape some aspect of society or economy. In the former case, data are used to produce 'evidential stories', where data in the form of facts, statements, *data visualisations* or other representational forms are used to form data narratives that scaffold and justify the argument being made. The use of a story form aids *data literacy* by helping the reader make sense of the data. In the latter case, fiction, audio, visual media (e.g., film, animation), or creative non-fiction, documentaries, and podcasts, including the use of *data imaginaries* and speculation, are used to explore and critique data and its consequences. Using a story form provides a different lens through which to think through data and helps translate ideas, concepts, and critiques for a wider audience. See also *arts-based methods, data journalism, research-creation*.

Further reading

Feigenbaum, A. and Alamalhodaei, A. (2020) *The Data Storytelling Workbook*. Routledge, London.

Kitchin, R. (2021) *Data Lives: How Data Are Made and Shape Our World*. Bristol University Press, Bristol.

data strategy   A strategy for how an organisation is going to improve its approach to data over a set period. As organisations employ digital systems to mediate their work, handle ever more data, and become more data-driven in their decision-making, they are having to change their approach to data. No longer the remit of a small number of IT and data specialists, data are moving to be a core aspect of all employees' work. To guide the transition to being a data-driven organisation, it is becoming common to devise and implement a data strategy. A strategy typically runs for a period of three to five years and sets out the aims and ambitions with regards to core data competencies such as *data infrastructures, data management, data governance, data literacy*, and training and education. A data strategy might be linked to a *data maturity framework* and assessment, with the strategy aiming to address specific weaknesses identified. The strategy is usually accompanied by an implementation plan that sets out roles and responsibilities, required resources, timelines and milestones, and *key performance indicators* for monitoring progress.

Further reading
Wallis, I. (2021) *Data Strategy: From Definition to Execution*. BCS, Swindon, UK.

data structure, see *data model*

data subject   The individual to whom *personal data* and associated *attribute data* relate. The data subject is a key figure in *data protection* and *privacy* legislation since most data-related laws provide rights specifically to individuals. *Fair Information Practice Principles*, for example, relate to individual *data rights* with respect to *data practices* performed on personal data. Within academic research, a data subject is each participant in a study or to whom data specifically refers.

data sweat   A bodily metaphor for *exhaust data* that represents the *data labour* invested in the production of those data. Introduced by Gregg (2015), data sweat signifies that the investment of labour in contributing and curating data across systems and platforms is a form of sweat equity for the digital economy. The term also captures the work that those systems and platforms do in terms of sweating the data; that is, extracting as much value for as minimal investment as possible. See also *data colonialism*.

Further reading
Gregg, M. (2015) 'Inside the data spectacle', *Television & New Media* 16(1): 37–51.

data threads   The entanglement of data as they move, get transformed, and encounter other data. First proposed by White (2017), the idea of data threads is an alternative conceptualisation of *data mobilities* that counters the notion of *data journeys*. The latter concept, in White's view, gives the impression that data movement is a linear, sequential process along a path from origin to destination. Instead, the path is more complex, with data taking circuitous routes, encountering dead-ends, and looping back on themselves, and the movement can occur with no clear sense of the destination. Moreover, the paths of different data can be threaded together to form knots, or fray and split apart. *Data materiality* and the discursive are also bound together, with data travelling simultaneously as socio-cultural and material entities passing through discursively inscribed material processes, such as inscription and translation. See also *data circulation*.

Further reading

White, J.M. (2017) 'Following data threads', in Kitchin, R., Lauriault, T.P., and McArdle, G. (eds), *Data and the City*. Routledge, London, pp. 85–97.

data transformation   1. The process of converting a dataset from one *data format*, type, schema or structure to another in order to aid *data management, interoperability, data fusion*, and *data storage*. 2. The application of a mathematical function to each data point in a dataset in order to convert it into a new value suitable for *statistical* analysis or *data visualisation*. In the first case, datasets might be saved into a new format, or be transformed from *qualitative data* to *quantitative data* or from *interval data* to *ordinal data*, or be re-categorised or reclassified, or be converted into a new structure through *data wrangling*. In the second case, the data are transformed to address a limitation that hinders statistical analysis, such as applying a function to transform a skewed distribution to a normal distribution. It might also consist of data augmentation, such as rotating or flipping images to create variation for training computer vision. If and how the data should be transformed is informed by the statistical analysis to be undertaken.

data trusts   Organisations that provide data stewardship on behalf of their members. A data trust consists of a confederation of members who form a partnership for pooling and *data sharing* with each other and with other trusted individuals and organisations, which might include the general public for some or all of the data held. A trust has an agreed set of objectives and a model of *data governance*, and might be constituted as a legal entity. There are a number of different forms of data trusts. Public data trusts seek to pool data for the public good, with stakeholders including state agencies, research bodies, private enterprise, and civil society groups. The data might not be published as *open data*, but rather only made available to trusted actors; for example, commercial data might be made selectively available for academic or policy research. Data sharing pools are industry-led data trusts wherein commercial data are exchanged on an open trust basis (rather than financial exchange) between business partners in order to produce innovations and services. Data cooperatives are collectively owned by individuals with a shared business interest (such as farmers) or by civic organisations. The cooperative is a communal resource designed to claim *data sovereignty* on behalf of its members, to leverage value from the data, and to oppose and resist *data monopolies* (such as large agribusiness conglomerates).

Further reading

Micheli, M., Ponti, M., Craglia, M., and Suman, A.B. (2020) 'Emerging models of data governance in the age of datafication', *Big Data & Society*, 7(2): 1–15.

data universalism   The notion that the nature of data, our understanding of them, and how they are used is universal in conception and practice. In other words, the definition of data, how they are constituted, the practices applied to them, and the forms of analysis undertaken are understood in the same way across people, places, and contexts. Moreover, according to this view, the operations of *data power* and *data capitalism* work in all places and at all times in the same way. This is the logic of the *scientific method* and capitalism – they are universal in their conception and operation. It is also evident in many of the entries in this book, in which concepts are expressed and explained in a way that is universal in its scope and assertion. This data universalism has been challenged by a number of scholars who make a set of related arguments. They note that there is *contingency* and relationality in how data are understood (see *data valences*) and produced, shaped by local *contexts*, cultures, and economies, jurisdiction-specific regulations and laws, and other factors (see *data assemblages*). As Loukissas (2019) contends, 'all data are local', not universal. Similarly, Global South and Indigenous scholars have made the case that *datafication, data imaginaries, data citizenship, data power,* and *data sovereignty* are understood and operate differently across space and communities, with this variance not adequately captured in Western conceptions of data-related phenomena. They argue instead for a more nuanced, contextual understanding of data, including a de-Westernisation and decolonisation of *Critical Data Studies* (see *decolonising data*).

Further reading

Loukissas, Y. (2019) *All Data Are Local: Thinking Critically in a Data-Driven Society*. MIT Press, Cambridge, MA.

Milan, S. and Treré, E. (2019) 'Big data from the South(s): Beyond data universalism', *Television & New Media*, 20(4): 319–35.

data valences   How data are perceived and valued by different people, which mediates expectations about how data should be utilised. Valences refer to relative values with respect to a phenomenon; in relation to data they concern the social values placed on data and how those mediate the work that data performs in a particular domain. A focus on data valences reveals orientations and expectations towards data and how these are rhetorically evoked in *data narratives* and *data practices*. The concept was introduced by Fiore-Gartland and Neff (2015) who used it to examine how patients and different health care professionals held different values and expectations with regards to the same data, rather than sharing a common understanding. How these groups made sense of and utilised data, and their expectations of outcomes arising from analysis of the data, were informed by quite different data valences, creating tensions between groups as they tried to prioritise their views and values. The interplay of these different valences shapes the unfolding of a *data assemblage*. Data valences are not stable over time and are not consistently evoked; they vary with circumstances or context, and are subject to change as peoples' viewpoints evolve through learning and rhetorical debate. See also *discursive regime*.

Further reading

Fiore-Gartland, B. and Neff, G. (2015) 'Communication, mediation, and the expectations of data: Data valences across health and wellness communities', *International Journal of Communication*, 9: 1466–84.

data visualisation   The practice of turning data into graphical representations. There are a wide variety of data visualisation methods, including various forms of graphics, spatialisations, *mapping*, 3D datascapes, and infographics, that vary in their visual form and the degree of generalisation and abstraction employed. The use of digital devices (computers, graphics cards, touchscreens, heads-up displays, and immersive headsets) has increased the ability to visualise very large datasets and to produce more dynamic, interactive displays, leading to the development of *visual analytics*. Visualisations are used analytically to perform *exploratory data analysis*, to communicate complex information, and to construct and support *data narratives* and the creation of *data stories* in specialist and popular media (see *data journalism*). The visualisation method employed depends on the data type (e.g., *qualitative data* and *quantitative data*) and the purpose of the visualisation. Data visualisation has itself become the object of critical analysis, with research examining the *data politics* and *data practices* of creating visualisations, as well as their circulation and the ways in which they are used. See also *dashboards*.

Further reading

Engebretsen, M., and Kennedy, H. (eds) (2020) *Data Visualization in Society*. Amsterdam University Press, Amsterdam.

Halpern, O. (2015) *Beautiful Data: A History of Vision and Reason Since 1945*. Duke University Press, Durham, NC.

data walks   A set of methods that use walking as a means to investigate or produce data. A data walking tour involves an exploration of a place in order to observe and reflect on the *data infrastructures* in that environment, the data they produce and process, and the data-driven work they perform. A data walkshop is a participatory, collective form of data walking tour that uses exercises, such as 'locate data-calm or data-rich places', to prompt critical reflection on *datafication*, *data politics*, and *data power*, and how these might be countered. A walking interview consists of walking around an environment with a participant asking them questions relating to data issues. Data walking involves collecting *sensor data* by walking along a prescribed route; repeating the walk at subsequent dates enables the monitoring of change over time. See also *data dérive*.

Further reading

Powell, A. (2018) 'The data walkshop and radical bottom-up data knowledge', in Knox, H. and Nafus, D. (eds), *Ethnography for a Data-Saturated World*. Manchester University Press, Manchester, pp. 212–32.

van Es, K. and de Lange, M. (2020) 'Data with its boots on the ground: Datawalking as research method', *European Journal of Communication*, 35(3): 278–89.

data walkthrough A method that follows the sequence of steps used in performing data work. It is adapted from the app-walkthrough method to specifically focus on data and has two main forms. First, the researcher interacts with a digital system in a systematic way in order to identify how data are being generated and processed; for example by following a sequence of *data entry* screens and inputting the required data. Second, an interview is conducted with a data worker as they are undertaking their usual *data labour*, with the interviewer noting the various actions and asking questions about what is occurring. This might involve video recording the *data practices* being performed. The aim is to identify and understand the *socio-technical* nature of *data assemblages* and the ways in which data production and *data management* are undertaken in practice (rather than in theory). One outcome of a data walkthrough might be a set of data flow diagrams detailing the *data journeys* within a system or the workflow sequence, or the construction of a *data dictionary*. See also *data audits, data dérive, follow the data*.

Further reading

Arantes, J. (2023) 'Educational data brokers: Using the walkthrough method to identify data brokering by edtech platforms', *Learning, Media and Technology*, doi: 10.1080/17439884.2022.2160986

data witnessing The use of data and data practices for documenting and responding to human rights abuses. Data witnessing is a complement to human witnessing at a scene and personal testimony, enabling the production of evidence of injustices at a distance and across time. With mass *datafication*, including *digitisation* of historical records, high definition satellite imagery, and networked, mobile digital devices capable of capturing and transmitting photographic, video, and audio data, it is possible to analyse such data for evidence of abuses and to practise *data activism* in pursuit of *data justice*. Organisations such as Amnesty International have actively sought to employ data witnessing.

Further reading

Gray, J. (2019) 'Data witnessing: Attending to injustice with data in Amnesty International's Decoders project', *Information, Communication & Society*, 22(7): 971–91.

Richardson, M. (2024) *Nonhuman Witnessing: War, Data, and Ecology after the End of the World*. Duke University Press, Durham, NC.

data wrangling A set of practices for preparing data to improve *data quality* and make data more useful for analysis and sharing. These practices include *data cleaning*, data *standardisation*, adding *metadata*, reformatting data values, data *validation*, restructuring datasets, *anonymisation*, *data enrichment*, *data fusion*, *data transformations*, and saving data into alternative *data formats* for use in other systems. Since datasets are very rarely produced analysis-ready, data analysts can spend a significant amount of time and effort performing data wrangling. Many of these practices are now being subject to *automation*. See also *derived data*, *ETL (extract, transform, load)*.

database An organised collection of data that are structured into a form that enables *data storage* and efficient search, queries, retrieval, and modification of data via software. Databases also enable a straightforward means of *data sharing*. The first digital databases, which used a flat or hierarchical structure, were produced in the 1950s. Relational database design, which organised data into a set of interlinked tables, was invented in 1970 and quickly became popular due to the development of relational database management systems and the ability to perform sophisticated querying of *structured data* using SQLs (structured query languages). In the 2000s, NoSQL database designs were introduced for handling *big data*, particularly those that consisted of *unstructured data* or *semi-structured data*. NoSQL databases have a simpler structure and more limited *data model*, but are more flexible in organisation and are rapidly extensible due to being distributed across many machines (see *cloud*), making them better able to deal with *volume* and *velocity*. *Metadata* and *indexical data* are essential for databases, enabling users to understand the data they contain and to link sets of data together. As with *data*, databases are not simply technical and neutral in nature. Rather they are *socio-technical*, created by actors who make choices and decisions in their design and maintenance, framed within conditions set by *data regulations*. Database design is not then predetermined, but emerges through *contingent* and *contextual* practices. The design and choices concerning what data are stored, and which are not, and how data are organised, make a difference to what queries can be asked and thus what databases can reveal.

Further reading

Driscoll, K. (2012) 'From punched cards to "big data": A social history of database populism', *communication +1*, 1(1): 1–33.

Ruppert, E. (2012) 'The governmental topologies of database devices', *Theory, Culture & Society*, 29: 116–36.

data-driven science   A version of the *scientific method* in which hypotheses and insights are 'born from the data' rather than 'born from theory'. Data-driven science incorporates an initial stage of *induction*, using *exploratory data analysis* and *data mining* to spot patterns or relationships that might be worthy of further examination, before then swapping to a traditional *deductive* approach. The process of induction is not random in application, but uses guided knowledge-discovery techniques that are informed by established knowledge. The utility of the inductive stage is that it potentially identifies new questions to explore that knowledge-driven science would fail to spot. Its advocates argue that data-driven science is much more suited to the *big data* age as it is better able to extract insights from large, interconnected datasets.

Further reading

Kitchin, R. (2014) 'Big data, new epistemologies and paradigm shifts', *Big Data & Society* 1(1): 1–12.

datafication   The capture of ever more aspects of social life and economic activity as data. As all aspects of society and economy become mediated by digital technologies they become captured as data. Many of these technologies are designed to produce an excess of data, capturing data that are not required to perform a task or function; for example, websites and apps hosting third party trackers, or smartphone apps requesting access to unrelated storage media or device sensors (see *data minimisation principle*). The data produced have high *granularity*, *exhaustivity*, and *velocity*, creating a highly detailed view of a domain. Datafication is seen as a vital process for creating data-driven systems that will improve state services and enable companies to increase productivity and efficiency, create new products, and identify and target markets. It also enables mass *surveillance* and *dataveillance* and raises concerns about the strengthening of state and corporate *data power*. See also *data doubles*, *data footprints and shadows*.

Further reading

van Dijck, J. (2014) 'Datafication, dataism and dataveillance: Big Data between scientific paradigm and ideology', *Surveillance & Society*, 12(2): 197–208.

datafied agency A condition in which human agency is inflected through an engagement with data. The term was introduced by Kennedy (2018) to consider the ways in which *datafication* is lived, felt, and experienced in everyday life. What it means to be human and our capacities to act are being shaped by data, either through how data-related processes impinge on our life choices or how we mobilise and use data to do work for us. Kennedy suggests examining this datafied agency through a phenomenological approach that explores human agency in datafied conditions, or examining people's data-related capabilities and their abilities to mobilise datafied agency and to uncover its associated emotional aspects (see *affect*). See also *data anxieties*, *embodiment*.

Further reading

Kennedy, H. (2018) 'Living with data: Aligning data studies and data activism through a focus on everyday experiences of datafication', *Krisis: Journal for Contemporary Philosophy*, 38(1): 18–30.

dataism The ideological belief and faith in widespread *datafication* and the logics of a data-driven society and economy. Data-driven systems and their work, whether practised by states or companies, are viewed as essential for supporting and progressing human activity, managing populations, and growing business. Big *data analytics* are necessary for advancing science. Dataism has a normalised view of present hegemonic formations of *data power*, *data citizenship*, and *data capitalism* as rational, commonsensical, legitimate, and trustworthy. *Critical Data Studies* strongly critiques this position, contending that dataism is an ideological position that seeks to create a *data doxa* that maintains the status quo.

Further reading

van Dijck, J. (2014) 'Datafication, dataism and dataveillance: Big Data between scientific paradigm and ideology', *Surveillance & Society*, 12(2): 197–208.

datascape   An amalgam of *data infrastructures* that enable *data journeys* to occur. Introduced by Tarantino (2019), a datascape is the interlinking of several data infrastructures into a wider system, whereby data flows between these infrastructures undergo *data cleaning* and *data transformations*, *data enrichment* and *data fusion* at each site before being transferred to the next. For example, a planning system has a datascape that might consist of several IT systems used at different scales by different actors (local government, national government, other public bodies) through which planning application data might be passed as it is processed and decisions made and appealed. Charting a datascape involves mapping out the relationships, data journeys, *data frictions*, and *socio-technical* relations between systems, thus recognising that each data infrastructure constitutes a *data assemblage*. See also *data ecosystem*.

Further reading

Tarantino, M. (2019) 'Navigating a datascape: Challenges in automating environmental data disclosure in China', *Journal of Environmental Planning and Management* 61(3): 67–86.

dataveillance   *Surveillance* conducted by processing and analysing data records. Given the extensive generation of *data footprints and shadows*, a wealth of information exists in relation to individuals and organisations. These data and their associated *metadata* can be monitored and analysed to track, regulate, and predict activity. Mass dataveillance is possible because the means of sifting and sorting data to identify individuals or activities that fit certain parameters has been largely *automated*. Moreover, it is easier to interlink datasets to identify relationships and patterns that might otherwise go unnoticed. Dataveillance routinely transgresses the principle of *data minimisation* by *repurposing* data that was never intended to be used for surveillance. Dataveillance, alongside associated practices of *social sorting* and predictive *profiling*, has raised a number of concerns relating to *privacy*, civil liberties, *data protection*, and *data justice*.

Further reading

Degli Esposti, S. (2014) 'When big data meets dataveillance: The hidden side of analytics', *Surveillance & Society* 12(2): 209–25.

decolonising data   A process of addressing unequal and discriminatory effects of *data power* by challenging the prevalent *data doxa* and divesting from dominant *epistemologies* and *data governance* frameworks. Decolonising data means shifting the control and framing of data to those whom the data represents. The drive for data decolonisation has it roots in the demands of Indigenous communities for *data sovereignty*, in which they own and control data relating to their communities (see *Indigenous data*), and to replace colonial settler epistemologies and data norms with Indigenous ways of knowing and doing. Likewise, in postcolonial states (see *postcolonialism and data*) there have been calls to challenge the *data universalism* of colonial metropoles and to replace their data legacy with *data regimes* that reflect local values and cultures, including those of Indigenous and other marginalised populations. Strategies to decolonise data include the use of *data activism* and *data politics* to challenge dominant *discursive regimes*, promote Indigenous epistemologies and *methodologies*, and enact Indigenous *data governance*.

Further reading

Carroll, S.R., Rodriguez-Lonebear, D., and Martinez, A. (2019) 'Indigenous data governance: Strategies from United States Native Nations', *Data Science Journal* 18(4): article 31.

Ricaurte, P. (2019) 'Data epistemologies, the coloniality of power, and resistance', *Television & New Media*, 20(4): 350–65.

deduction   A mode of logical reasoning that seeks to make a definitive claim about causes and effects based on empirical evidence. Deduction is the primary logic underpinning the application of the traditional *scientific method*, in which *hypotheses* are empirically tested to establish their *veracity*. The hypothetico-deductive method involves deducing whether a hypothesis is true, and what consequences follow, then testing whether that deduction holds true in practice through empirical analysis. If the prediction proves to be false, then the deduction has been fallacious and a new hypothesis needs to be formulated. See also *abduction, induction*.

deidentification   The process of ensuring that the identity of a *data subject* cannot be revealed via the data held within a system. Deidentification aims to ensure that the *privacy* of a data subject is not infringed. There are several means of implementing deidentification including *anonymisation* techniques and the use of *pseudonyms*. There are concerns, however, that many of these techniques do not sufficiently deidentify datasets and that by combining datasets and using *data mining* and other techniques it is possible to reidentify individuals. There have been several high-profile cases where this has occurred. Care then is needed to ensure any deidentification undertaken conforms to expected *data protection* and *privacy* expectations.

Further reading

Garfinkel, S.L. (2015) *De-Identification of Personal Information*. NIST Report 8053, National Institute of Standards and Technology, Gaithersburg, MD. 20899-8930

deletion   The erasure of data from a dataset or the removal of a data file from a computer/server. Deletion is an integral part of the *data lifecycle*. *Data protection* legislation and many *data ethics* policies stipulate that personal and other captured data need to be deleted after a certain period of time and cannot be indefinitely retained. This can be circumvented by deleting the original sourced data, but retaining *derived data* or *inferred data*. Deletion usually involves using the 'delete' or 'cut' function in software or file deletion commands within an operating system. In the latter case, the data might be recoverable unless a data erasure method is used, such as reformatting the storage device which overwrites all previously stored data. See also *data refuge, transient data*.

demographically identifiable information Data that enables an individual or group of individuals to be profiled based on a demographic group identity such as *race, ethnicity,* class, *gender,* sexuality (see *queer data*), age, *disability,* location, occupation or other markers. By assigning individuals to demographic classifications, decisions can be taken in relation to them without knowing *personal identifiable information.* Instead, inferences are made that members of the same classification will share other characteristics; for example, that people in this group are 'more likely to buy' or 'more likely to default' (see *inferred data*). How a group is characterised has consequences for individuals, but since no personal identifiable information is being used it is not subject to *privacy* regulations or *data protection* as these give rights to individuals not groups (see *group privacy*). Hence, the use of demographically identifiable information is an approach often used by data brokers for *social sorting* and targeting people. This has the effect of reproducing discrimination by indiscriminately targeting group members through a practice that generates *ecology fallacy* issues, such as assuming all members of the group have the same profile. See also *geodemographics, redlining.*

Further reading

Raymond, N.A. (2017) 'Beyond "do no harm" and individual consent: Reckoning with the emerging ethical challenges of civil society's use of data', in Taylor, L., Floridi, L., and van der Sloot, B. (eds), *Group Privacy: New Challenges of Data Technologies.* Springer, Cham, Switzerland, pp. 67–82.

derived data Data that are created from other data, rather than being captured directly from a source. For example, the percentage change in population between two time periods is derived via a calculation using population counts from those periods. *Aggregated* data are derived through the combination of source data. Derived data are generated for a number of reasons, including to produce more meaningful data (e.g., through *standardisation*) and to reduce the volume of data for processing and analysis.

descriptive statistics The provision of summary descriptions of a set of data. Descriptive statistics detail the characteristics of a dataset, usually in a numerical or visual form. It includes basic summary statistics such as mean, median and mode, standard deviation, levels of *error* and *uncertainty*. These can also be presented visually, along with other *data visualisations* such as graphs and charts (e.g., scatterplots, histograms). Several variables can also be compared to one another, including change over time. More sophisticated descriptive statistics include the use of graph theory to identify the properties of networks and descriptive *spatial statistics* that describe geometry or clustering. Descriptive statistics might provide necessary insights, but they can also be used as *exploratory data analysis* (e.g., to assess whether a dataset has a normal distribution) before analysing the data using *inferential statistics*.

Further reading

Scott Jones, J. and Goldring, J. (2022) *Exploratory and Descriptive Statistics*. Sage, London.

determinism, see *data determinism*

digital data   Data that are recorded and stored in a digital form. At their base level, data are recorded in sequences of digital bits (0s and 1s), and stored in digital databases in various digital file types (e.g., image or sound files). As digital data they can be efficiently processed using computational techniques and analysed using a range of sophisticated software programs capable of performing calculations that would be all but impossible by hand (see *data analytics*). *Analogue data* can be converted to digital data using *digitisation* techniques.

digital humanities   An interdisciplinary approach that applies digital *data management, descriptive statistics, mapping, data mining,* and *data analytics* to the forms of *qualitative data* that are traditionally used in humanities research. Such data include manuscripts, photographs, artworks, audio recordings, video, social media content, and other cultural media. The field brings together scholars from across the humanities (e.g., historians, linguists, literary and media scholars) with librarians, archivists, and computer, data and information scientists. These researchers often work with other stakeholders such as archives, museums, galleries, and media companies. Digital humanities research undertakes the *digitisation* of historical *analogue data*, builds *data infrastructures* to preserve, store, and curate these new data, and creates and applies digital tools and analytics to extract insights from these data. Rather than performing a close reading of a small sample of data sources, such as a handful of novels or a selection of images, a distant reading of thousands, or even millions, of books and images is undertaken, which was previously impossible to perform. For example, it is now relatively straightforward to search for terms across millions of documents and examine the relationships between terms, or to identify reoccurring patterns across tens of thousands of images. For some, digital humanities research brings methodological rigour to scholarship that has been reliant on the subjective interpretation of the observer. For its detractors, a careful, contextual reading of documents that are full of meaning is sacrificed for a mechanistic, flat, surface reading that provides at best shallow insights: *algorithms* are good at spotting patterns, but are poor at deciphering meaning and placing it in social and political context. Many in the field tread a middle line, arguing that a distant reading provides an *exploratory data analysis* that suggests promising lines of inquiry for a close reading.

Further reading

Gardiner, E., and Musto, R.G. (2015) *The Digital Humanities: A Primer for Students and Scholars*. Cambridge University Press, Cambridge.

digital rights management (DRM)   The legal protection of access to *digital data*. DRM was introduced to try to protect the *intellectual property rights* of those holding *copyright* or patents rights since the non-rivalrous nature of digital data makes it easy to copy and share (see *data sharing*). DRM employs a set of technical tools, such as access control (e.g., *licensing*) and *encryption*, to try to limit illegal copying or pirating of digital works, such as music or software. Advocates argue that DRM protects the intellectual property of creators and ensures that they can be paid for their work. Detractors argue that it restricts legal usage of a digital product, can lock a user into a *proprietary data* format (which might become obsolete if a company goes out of business), and can shift a once-only purchase into a subscription model, unfairly extracting payment for continued use.

Further reading

Lemmer, C.A. and Wale, C.P. (eds) (2016) *Digital Rights Management: A Librarian's Guide.* Rowan & Littlefield, Lanham, MA.

digital twin   The synonymous twinning of physical systems and environments with a virtual counterpart that represents their structure, registers changes over time, and provides for reciprocal feedback for monitoring and control. For example, an aircraft engine being paired with a virtual 3D, interactive model of the engine, which can be used for optimising the design, manufacturing the engine in the factory, monitoring its performance using sensors, and potentially controlling aspects of its behaviour in operation. *Real-time data* flows link the physical and virtual models, so that any change in the engine updates the model, and any amendments to the model alter the engine's performance. A traffic *control room* is a form of digital twin, utilising a digital representation of the system to mediate traffic flow, with real-time data relating to traffic movement modulating the traffic model, which then alters the traffic light phasing and how cars move on streets. The virtual twin can be used for testing, monitoring, *simulation*, guiding maintenance, and managing its physical twin over its lifecycle.

Further reading

Grieves, M. and Vickers, J. (2017) 'Digital twin: Mitigating unpredictable, undesirable emergent behavior in complex systems', in Kahlen, J., Flumerfelt, S., and Alves, A. (eds), *Transdisciplinary Perspectives on Complex Systems.* Springer, Cham, Switzerland, pp. 85–113.

digitisation   The process of capturing and transforming *analogue data* as *digital data*. For example, scanning a book page and storing the scanned text in a digital format. Digitisation is undertaken to make the new digital data available for *data sharing* and wider *re-use* and *repurposing*, or to make the data amenable to linking to other datasets, processing and analysis by *software*, and to the application of *data analytics*. The digital copy also acts as a *preservation* precaution if the original analogue data are vulnerable to *data loss*. See also *archive, data respository*.

disability data   Data about disabled people or the issues that disable people. Data about disability have long been generated in the medical and health sciences related to the physical and mental conditions of individuals. These data have been used in relation to medical treatments, to research ways to cure or alleviate conditions, and in the provision of health and social services, with *classification* and *social sorting* shaping the lives of individuals. These data have generally been used within what is referred to as the medical model of disability, in which the daily issues disabled people face are rooted in their impairment. As many disability scholars and activists note, this framing and its *data practices* have perpetuated a negative orientation to disability and discriminatory practices. In contrast, the social model of disability contends that society disables people by failing to accept them for who they are and to provide facilities and infrastructure accessible for all. Data with respect to the latter might include maps that detail how accessible an urban environment is with respect to different conditions. Data themselves might also be inaccessible; for example, many *open data* sites do not comply with internet standards that enable web content to be accessed by visually impaired people.

Further reading

Bannon, O. (2018) 'Disability studies, big data and algorithmic culture', in Ellis, K., Garland-Thomson, R., Kent, M., and Robertson, R. (eds), *Interdisciplinary Approaches to Disability, Volume 2*. Routledge, Abingdon, pp. 45–58.

Deitz, S., Lobben, A., and Alferez, A. (2021) 'Squeaky wheels: Missing data, disability, and power in the smart city', *Big Data & Society*, 8(2): 1–16.

disclosure data   Data that are generated on a legal basis in order to monitor compliance with regulations and laws. For example, companies handling hazardous waste needing to produce a toxic release register that details any emissions of toxic materials during a reporting period. In many cases, these disclosure data are self-produced and reported, meaning that it is the company that undertakes data generation and the managing of the dataset. Depending on the consequence of a negative disclosure – such as a poor performance review, a fine or another penalty – perverse incentives can be created that encourage employees to *juke the stats* or to produce no data at all, thus undermining the *veracity* and *data integrity* of the datasets. Consequently there have been calls for greater independence and transparency regarding the full *data lifecycle* of disclosure data and how they are used in order to ensure *accountability* and trust.

Further reading

Poirier, L. (2022) 'Accountable data: The politics and pragmatics of disclosure datasets', *FAccT '22: Proceedings of the 2022 ACM Conference on Fairness, Accountability, and Transparency*. ACM, New York, pp. 1446–56.

discourse analysis   A method for analysing how meaning is constructed and conveyed through language and narrative. It is usually applied to written texts, such as media stories, policy documents, marketing material, and fiction, as well as audio and visual media, such as speeches, hearings, television and radio debates. Discourse analysis aims to understand meaning within context and in so doing reveal something of the writer or speaker, rather than just the linguistic structure of language. For example, a discourse analysis of a *data strategy* document will examine how the strategy and its specific goals are framed and expressed, taking account of the wider context of the prevalent *data regime*, and what this reveals about the organisation and its intentions. It is a commonly used method within *Critical Data Studies* for understanding the *discursive regime* relating to data work.

discursive regime   An interlocking set of arguments that justify, legitimate, and sustain a *data regime* and maintain a *data doxa* through the production of *power/knowledge*. These arguments work to persuade people that a particular way of thinking about data and performing data work is commonsensical and logical. A discursive regime with respect to the use of data-driven technologies in smart city initiatives draws on discourses of efficiency, productivity, safety, security, competitiveness, and sustainability to justify their implementation. These discourses reinforce each other, close down alternative counter-arguments, and can be difficult to argue against (who wants to live in an inefficient, unproductive, unsafe, insecure, laggard, non-sustainable city?). Nonetheless, discursive regimes are open to challenge and being reconfigured through *data activism* and *counter-data actions*. For example, limited *data access* and *proprietary data* were a standard feature of state data regimes until the late 2000s when the *open data movement* constructed an alternative discursive regime which – using discourses of *transparency, accountability, data sharing, re-use,* open government, and social entrepreneurship – persuaded the public and state and private actors that publishing their data as *open data* was more commonsensical than the data remaining closed. See also *data imaginaries, data valences.*

documentation   Descriptive and instructional material relating to the operation, maintenance, and use of a *data infrastructure.* Documentation describes and explains how a data infrastructure, or one of its component processes, works and instructs readers on how to perform particular tasks. Documentation might take the form of a user guidebook, online help, or a short instructional video, and will refer to technical, legal or governance processes and practices. Like *metadata,* documentation is important because it helps users understand a system and how to undertake their work. It is particularly useful in a handover process to new staff.

doxa, see *data doxa*

E

ecological fallacies   False conclusions about a phenomenon caused by *data quality* issues with a dataset or with the *methodology* and techniques of analysis used. Ecological fallacies are a serious issue as they misrepresent the real situation with regards to a phenomenon and its relationship with other factors and negatively impact any related interpretation and decision-making. There are several different forms of ecological fallacy, which arise from poor or deliberate practice. These include *sampling* bias (extending the findings from a specific sample to an entire population); false causality (wrongly assuming that a statistically significant result confirms a relationship between variables rather than being a random effect); *data dredging* (analysing a dataset in different ways to find a statistically significant result rather than testing a specific *hypothesis*); cherry-picking (carefully selecting data or results that lead to a desired finding); and *aggregation* effects (the removal of variance in a dataset hiding the real underlying pattern). *Big data* and *data analytics* suffer in particular from ecological fallacies. The size of the datasets means that traditional statistical techniques detect multiple *false positives and false negatives* in which the relationship is actually random. *Data mining* techniques can produce apophenia (detecting patterns in random or meaningless data) or mistaking *noise* for information, and changing the weights within models or using different *modelling* techniques can yield profoundly different answers. See also *bias, composite indices, juking the stats, lying with statistics, statistical geography, veracity.*

embodiment   How data are produced and managed by people, and the effects they have on individuals, is mediated by and mediates human action. Individuals perform data work in embodied ways – fingers tap on keyboards and swipe screens, skin and body motion interacts with wearable devices, eyes stare at interfaces, and voices talk to microphones. They react in embodied ways to the commands of data-driven systems – following routes, operating machines, and entering information. These embodied encounters can be mundane and habitual or more visceral and occasional (e.g., passing through a body scanner at an airport). Interactions with data and *data labour* consist of performative encounters that produce *datafied agency* and generate *affect*. Phenomenological accounts of data seek to chart the embodied, sensory, and affective human-data entanglements that shape how encounters with data are experienced.

Further reading
Lupton, D. (2020) *Data Selves*. Polity Press, Cambridge.
Smith, G.J.D. (2016) 'Surveillance, data and embodiment: On the work of being watched', *Body & Society*, 22(2): 108–39.

encryption   A process of encoding data so that it cannot be accessed without a password key. Encryption does not stop data being copied or shared, but it does limit the ability to access the encrypted material. Encryption is used for *data protection* to ensure that sensitive data cannot be accessed by others, and also to perform *digital rights management* to protect *intellectual property rights*.

end-user licence agreement (EULA) A legal contract between the user of software or a digital service and its provider. The contract sets out in detail the legal rights and restrictions for the user, and the rights, role, and warranties of the provider. This can include how the data produced through using an app or a web-delivered service can be used and shared. EULAs are designed to protect the *intellectual property rights*, including *copyright*, of developers, but also work to maximise their opportunities with regards to *data colonialism*, and to minimise their liabilities. In most cases, EULAs are non-negotiable; one either accepts the terms and conditions or forgoes using the app or service. A major problem with EULAs is that they can be very long documents full of legal jargon, meaning that most people do not read them, or if they do they cannot understand them, so accept the terms with limited knowledge of the potential consequences. See also *digital rights management*.

enrichment, see *data enrichment*

environmental sustainability, see *political ecology of data*

epistemic community A network of knowledge, policy, and industry experts with recognised competencies who share a world-view and a common set of normative beliefs, values, and practices with respect to an issue and help decision-makers identify and deploy solutions to solve problems. With respect to data, there are several large epistemic communities operating across scales (locally, nationally, and internationally); for example, in relation to *open data*, and *big data* across different domains (e.g., big data and health or smart cities). These epistemic communities work together to forward a vision, create a policy response that will enable this vision, use their influence to lobby for policy adoption, and provide advice, support, and social learning to aid its rollout. They differ from interest groups through their claim to authoritative knowledge. Data-related epistemic communities have been highly influential in promoting *datafication* and the adoption of data-driven technologies and industries, reinforcing *discursive regimes* and new *data doxas*. See also *community of practice*.

Further reading

Kitchin, R., Coletta, C., Evans, L., Heaphy, L., and MacDonncha, D. (2017) 'Smart cities, urban technocrats, epistemic communities, advocacy coalitions and the "last mile" problem', *it – Information Technology*, 59(6): 275–84.

epistemology A theory of how we come to know and make legitimate claims about the world. In essence, epistemology is a theory of knowledge production that asserts how knowledge is and should be created. It is one of the foundational components of philosophy, alongside *ontology*, *methodology*, and ideology/*ethics*. Different philosophical schools hold varying epistemological views as to how the world can be legitimately known. For example, *positivism*, which uses the *scientific method*, adopts an epistemology that favours direct observation of measurable phenomena and rejects an analysis of metaphysics (questions about the nature of being, beliefs, and opinions) as these cannot be directly observed and measured. In contrast, phenomenology holds that metaphysics can be observed through behaviour and teased out through the use of *qualitative methods* (e.g., *interviews*, *participant observation*) and legitimate conclusions drawn. The epistemology underpinning a study can have a profound effect on the methodology adopted, the data produced, how these data are analysed, and the claims that can be made based on them. See also *feminist data science*.

Further reading

Pernecky, T. (2016) *Epistemology and Metaphysics for Qualitative Research*. Sage, London.

Pietsch, W. (2022) *On the Epistemology of Data Science*. Springer, Cham, Switzerland.

error In statistical terms, error is the difference between a measured and a real value. In more general terms, error encompasses a number of issues that affect the *accuracy and precision* of a dataset, generate *uncertainty*, and weaken trust and *validity* in analysis. These include absences (e.g., missing data), mistakes (e.g., duplicate records, miscoding or misclassification), false data (e.g., noise in sensor recordings), poor data management or analytical techniques (e.g., misapplied *transformations* or weak *inferencing*), and the inclusion of *gamed data* (e.g., workers seeking to *juke the stats*) or *fake data* (e.g., bot-produced social media data). In some cases, a certain amount of error in datasets is tolerated as an acceptable degree of variance. In others, *data cleaning* is undertaken, along with *modelling* and *calibration*, to reduce the degree of error in a dataset. A number of statistical procedures seek to identify the degree of error in the analysis undertaken so that it can be taken into account in interpretation (e.g., identifying residuals).

ethics, see *data ethics*

ethics of data care   An approach to data harms that is rooted in the notion of an ethics of care; that is, caring and protecting people based on their needs, rather than in relation to a universal set of rights. Social justice, which underpins *data justice*, is concerned with rights, entitlements, and responsibilities and the generalisable standards, rules, and principles that enforce them. An ethics of data care recognises that people have different circumstances and universal rules will provide some, but not all, the data care they require. Instead, it advocates for an approach rooted in reciprocity and practical action wherein people care for each other, treating others with dignity and fairness and as they themselves expect to be treated. *Slow computing* advocates for an ethics of data care in which people seek to claim *data sovereignty* and to reduce data harms (e.g., *data breaches*, *data protection* and *privacy* infringements, *profiling* and *social sorting*) by practising collective care – aiding those with weaker *data literacy*, undertaking political campaigning and lobbying, creating *data commons*, undertaking *counter-data actions* and *data activism* – and self-data care, in which they try to minimise their *data footprints and shadows* by curating what data they share and using open source software.

Further reading

Kitchin, R. and Fraser, A. (2020) *Slow Computing: Why We Need Balanced Digital Lives*. Bristol University Press, Bristol.

Leurs, K. (2017) 'Feminist data studies: Using digital methods for ethical, reflexive and situated socio-cultural research', *Feminist Review*, 115: 130–54.

ethics washing Using ethics initiatives to give the impression that ethics are being taken seriously and meaningful action is occurring with respect to *data power*, when the real ambition is to maintain the status quo and avoid regulation and legislation. Ethics washing is a form of performative ethics and virtue signalling, providing superficial support for an ethical position and prioritising appearance over action. The hope is to reassure the public, policy-makers, and government with respect to any concerns they might have, while at the same time using the initiative to promote their aims and interest. With respect to business, a number of companies have founded ethics advisory boards to counsel on how they handle and profit from data. These boards have generally had little effect on the policies and practices of the companies, despite the good intentions of those recruited to serve on them, but they allow the company to state that they are taking *data ethics*, *data regulations*, and calls for *data justice* seriously.

Further reading

Wagner, B. (2018) 'Ethics as an escape from regulation: From ethics-washing to ethics shopping?', in Hildebrandt, M. (ed.), *Being Profiled: Cogitas Ergo Sum*. Amsterdam University Press, Amsterdam, pp. 84–9.

ethnic data Data that relate to a person's cultural heritage and shared identity. An ethnic group is a set of people who share a common culture, language, religion, *race*, and history and identify with each other based on these traits. Ethnic data consists of people classified into ethnic groups (see *categorisation and classification*). Such data are generated through social *surveys*, such as a *census*, and also through *bureaucracy*, recorded in *administrative data*. In some cases, it might include *biometric data*. The data can be used to understand the ethnic make-up of populations, and their geography and sociology. It can also be used to *socially sort* individuals and to perpetuate discrimination, with ethnic groups singled out for particular attention and differential treatment. Ethnic data are a key marker, for example, in border controls. In a worst-case scenario, the data can be used to direct war and genocide by identifying people belonging to a particular ethnic group and their location. See also *demographically identifiable information*, *Indigenous data*.

Further reading

Amoore, L. (2024) 'The deep border', *Political Geography*, 109: 102547.

Vogt, M., Bormann, N.-C., Rüegger, S., Cederman, L.-E., Hunziker, P., and Girardin, L. (2015) 'Integrating data on ethnicity, geography, and conflict: The Ethnic Power Relations data set family', *Journal of Conflict Resolution*, 59(7): 1327–42.

ethnography, see *data ethnography*

ETL (extract, transform, load) A three-phase process wherein data are extracted from a system, transformed, and then loaded into a new destination. The transformation phase can consist of a number of related processes, such as *data cleaning*, *data wrangling*, *data enrichment*, *data fusion*, and *data transformations* that improve *data quality* and conformity with *data standards* and the *data format* and structuring requirements of downstream systems. ETL is often automated, enabling routine *data journeys* and data processes to occur across systems. See also *data ingestion*.

exhaust data Data that are inherently produced by a device or system as part of their use. Browsing the internet or using a smartphone app generates a trail of *big data* relating to the interactions and transactions performed. Some of these data are *transient data* and are deleted immediately after generation and use. Others are stored for potential future *re-use*. For example, a fitness wearable device might display *real-time data*, but only retain key sampled or descriptive statistical data for later viewing. Exhaust data can be *repurposed* to extract additional value from them. For example, social media platforms produce a massive amount of exhaust data through all the posts and comments users make; these data have been repurposed for all kinds of academic studies to investigate social issues. Social media companies extract value from these data through targeted advertising and also sell them to *data brokers* who use them to undertake profiling. See also *data market*, *privacy*, *surveillance capitalism*.

exhaustivity The exhaustive capture of all data within a domain; that is, in *sampling* terms, n=all. Exhaustivity is a key attribute, along with velocity, of *big data*. For example, the cameras of an automatic licence plate recognition system capture all vehicles passing the cameras, not a sample of them. Likewise, a store loyalty card system captures every transaction of its members, and a social media platform captures every post and comment of its users. *Small data*, in contrast, is not exhaustive but is sampled, capturing data about a selected sample of a population (e.g., one person in every ten). That said, while big data systems are exhaustive to a system, they are nonetheless still a sample since not every vehicle passes a camera, not every shopper is a member of a loyalty card scheme, and not all members of society are users of a social media platform. Exhaustive data capture has significantly extended the scope and extent of *datafication* and mass *surveillance*.

exploratory data analysis (EDA) An initial investigation into the characteristics of a dataset, undertaken without assumptions, prior to the main phase of analysis. The aim is to gain an understanding of the underlying structure and features of the data that might inform further analysis (e.g., whether it has a normal distribution or large residual values or anomalies) and of any issues that need attention (e.g., missing values). EDA typically uses *descriptive statistics* and *data visualisation* to examine datasets. See also *data cleaning*.

extensionality The flexibility and adaptability of the *data model* in a digital system. Many digital systems have strong extensionality, regularly changing the data they capture, with fields added and deleted as the system is developed and iterated through new designs and functionality. Extensionality is considered by some to be a core attribute of *big data*; however, many big data systems have little extensionality due to the need for a fixed data model to maintain stability, robustness, and comparability of data records over time (e.g., financial systems).

F

fact   An incontrovertible piece of data that reveals a *truth* about the world. A fact is a knowledge claim that is generally accepted as valid and possessing integrity and *veracity* by a community. Facts seek to be *immutable mobiles*; that is, independent, legible, and understandable beyond their site of production as their generation and framing share common, universal principles (e.g., GDP is calculated in the same way across jurisdictions and is easily interpreted without local knowledge). Given their claim to be autonomous, stable, reliable knowledge, facts form important pieces of evidence in social, legal, and scientific debates – truths that are seemingly indisputable and self-evident. Facts thus have an elevated status in relation to data, evidence, and inference. However, as with data more generally, facts are produced, being the outcome of decisions made during the generation, processing, and analysis of data. Facts then are not incontrovertible truths, but rather give this impression through the *fixation of evidence*.

Further reading

Poovey, M. (1998) *A History of the Modern Fact: Problems of Knowledge in the Sciences of Wealth and Society*. University Chicago Press, Chicago.

Shepard, M. (2022) *There Are No Facts: Attentive Algorithms, Extractive Data Practices, and the Quantification of Everyday Life*. MIT Press, Cambridge, MA.

FAIR data principles   A set of fourteen principles relating to *open data* organised into four main principles that state that data need to be findable, accessible, interoperable, and re-usable. They were introduced in 2016 by a consortium of scientists who wished to improve the *data sharing* and *re-use* of research by providing a guiding set of principles for best practice. In particular, the FAIR data principles emphasise the production of *machine-readable data*, accompanied by good quality *metadata*, that would facilitate automated search and *ETL (extract, transform, load)* processes. They have been complemented by the *CARE principles* (collective benefit, authority to control, responsibility, and ethics) that aim to ensure *data sovereignty*.

Further reading

Wilkinson, M., et al. (2016) 'The FAIR guiding principles for scientific data management and stewardship', *Scientific Data* 3: 160018.

Fair Information Practice Principles (FIPPs)   A set of eight principles that are designed to protect the privacy of individuals. Introduced in 1980 by the OECD, FIPPs define the obligations of *data controllers and processers* and how personal data can be generated, used, and shared. The eight principles are: *notice, consent, choice, data security, data integrity, data access, data minimisation* (use limitation), and *accountability*. These principles have been codified in *data protection* and *privacy* legislation within OECD countries and transnationally within the European Union. Not all principles are included in this legislation or given the same priority, and the principles have been under sustained pressure through mass *datafication* and *big data* and the lobbying of *data brokers* and other stakeholders.

Further reading

Woodrow, H. (2016) 'The inadequate, invaluable Fair Information Practices', *Maryland Law Review*, 76(4): 952–83.

fake data   Data that have been invented or data derived from fake entities, such as social media bots. Not all data are produced through a process that is seeking to create data with strong *data quality* and *data integrity*. In some cases, data are falsified, usually for the purpose of duplicity, such as inventing data in a scientific study to gain the desired result (the website redactionwatch .com regularly details papers redacted for using fake data). Either specific fields can be falsified or an entire dataset. Datasets can inadvertently contain fake data through including data generated by entities designed to disrupt a platform or process. For example, capturing a sample of Twitter/X data that includes data produced by bot accounts as well as those of real people. The inclusion of the fake data in the analysis will create *bias* and *ecological fallacies* unless *data cleaning* is undertaken to identify and remove the fake data.

false positive and false negative   A false positive is an incorrect assumption or test result being recorded as true (e.g., a pregnancy test indicating that a woman is pregnant when she is not). A false negative is the opposite – when a condition or relationship is true but is recorded as false (e.g., a pregnancy test indicating that woman is not pregnant when she is). In statistical testing, false positives lead to type I errors in which a significance test result (see *statistical significance*) leads to the null hypothesis being incorrectly rejected, and false negatives produce type II errors in which the null hypothesis is incorrectly accepted. If not identified and corrected, false positives and negatives produce *ecological fallacies*. In big data, as the number of variables and volume of records increases, the rate of false positives and false negatives multiplies.

Further reading

Ferguson, C.J. (2018) 'The problem of false positives and false negatives in violent video game experiments', *International Journal of Law and Psychiatry*, 56(1): 35–43.

feminism, see *data feminism, feminist data science, gender and gendered data*

feminist data science   An approach to *Data Science* that 1. challenges and seeks to replace the predominant scientific *epistemology*; 2. advocates for a progressive framing of Data Science that contests *data power* in Data Science itself and within society. Feminist data science draws on the epistemology and politics of intersectional feminism to consider the ways in which Data Science makes sense of the world and reproduces inequalities and injustices, and to reconstitute both to produce a new approach. Feminism has long critiqued the *scientific method* for its mechanistic, reductionist, and determinist view from nowhere, and its claim to *objectivity* and political neutrality. Instead, feminist data science advocates for acknowledging a researcher's *positionality*, producing *situated knowledges*, and for Data Science to reconfigure its data power to contribute to progressive politics. With respect to the latter, feminism has always sought to change not simply study the world. Feminist data science uses *data analytics* to tackle inequalities and produce *data justice*, often adopting a *participatory methods* approach and working with local communities.

Importantly, while patriarchy, sexism, and the inequalities relating to women are a focus, feminism is centrally concerned with the operations of different forms of power across society. Feminist data science then is concerned with contesting data power in all its guises in relation to any group or issue within the practices of Data Science and in society. This is evident in a feminist data 'Manifest-No' published in 2019 that compels its adoptees to refuse to support harmful *data regimes*, to not commit data injustices through research, and to pledge to create better *data futures*. See also *ethics of care, data feminism*.

Further reading

Cifor, M., Garcia, P., Cowan, T.L., Rault, J., Sutherland, T., Chan, A., Rode, J., Hoffmann, A.L., Salehi, N., and Nakamura, L. (2019) *Feminist Data Manifest-No*, www.manifestno.com

D'Ignazio, C. and Klein, L.F. (2020) *Data Feminism*. MIT Press, Cambridge, MA.

fit for purpose   Whether the data being used are of sufficient *data quality* and *veracity* to be able to perform the task being asked of them. Fit for purpose can consist of different dimensions, such as data quality, *timeliness*, suitability, and *reliability*. For example, the data might be highly suitable and be of good quality and veracity, but if they are twenty years old and a lot has changed during those two decades then they are unlikely to be fit for purpose. A related notion is *good enough data*; that is, the data are not perfect but they are good enough to serve a purpose. See also *proxy data*.

fixation of evidence   The production of a generalisable truth wherein data and their interpretation become accepted as valid and true. The process of producing a *fact* and then persuading others that this fact and the theory used to interpret it have *validity* consists of fixing the evidence in place so that people believe it is a *truth* and form a consensus in that view. The persuasion is performed by various mechanisms and processes of translating evidence into a form that conveys its validity (e.g., a visual representation), by providing supporting argument that explains why the findings and interpretation have *veracity* and why alternative views can be discounted, and by being used and reaffirmed by others so it seems indisputable and stable. The fixation of evidence enables *hypotheses* and theories to be accepted by a community. See also *data bounds, immutable mobiles*.

Further reading

Walford, A. (2019) 'Raw data: Making relations matter', in Jensen, C.B. and Morita, A. (eds), *Multiple Nature-Cultures, Diverse Anthropologies*. Berghahn Books, Oxford, pp. 65–80.

focus group   A collective *interview* in which several people participate in a facilitated group discussion about an issue. A focus group is facilitated by the researcher who asks questions, prompts responses, and moderates discussion between group members. The format is semi- or unstructured in nature and aimed at allowing a relatively free-flowing, evolving conversation amongst participants. A focus group can take place in person or online, with the latter enabling asynchronous interactions (spread over time) and *anonymous* participation. Focus groups can be used to explore the views of participants in relation to any aspect of data.

follow the data   A method for tracing *data journeys* and *data circulation* in which the production, consumption, and movement of data as a commodity is tracked. It is adapted from the 'follow the things' method used to trace the movement of commodities in the global economy from sites of production to sites of consumption. The method involves a multi-sited *data ethnography* at different points along the data commodity chain to understand local roles, processes, and systems and how onward movement is facilitated.

Further reading

Akbari, A. (2020) 'Follow the thing: Data. Contestations over data from the Global South', *Antipode* 52(2): 408–29.

forgetting   In the context of data, the practice of strategically using *data loss* and *deletion* in order to halt the persistent storage of data. With mass *surveillance, dataveillance,* and *sousveillance,* more and more data about people are being generated and stored. These records form a long-term memory of activities, including text, photos, video, movement logs, weblogs, transactions, communications, and interactions with others. In the case of large *platforms,* the data are generally persistent (e.g., Facebook does not delete any posts, comments, photos, etc.). In contrast, human memory suffers loss such as transience (loss of memory over time), absentmindedness, blocking, misattribution, and misremembering. This forgetting is useful as it allows people to move past their mistakes and practise reconciliation and forgiveness. Digital *memory*, however, is persistent, though it might turn into *zombie data* or *stranded data*. An ethics of forgetting argues that the state of persistent memory of *personal data* needs to be complemented by forgetting so that people can escape their pasts if desired. See also *ethics of data care, right to be forgotten*.

Further reading

Dodge, M. and Kitchin, R. (2007) '"Outlines of a world coming in existence": Pervasive computing and the ethics of forgetting', *Environment and Planning B*, 34(3): 431–45.

Eichhorn, K. (2019) *The End of Forgetting: Growing Up with Social Media*. Harvard University Press, Cambridge, MA.

format, see *data format*

fragmentation, see *data fragmentation*

freedom of information   The freedom for individuals to be able to share and consume information, including being able to access information held by public bodies. Freedom of information is seen as a prerequisite for a democratic society in which citizens can voice their opinions, share data openly, and freely source information, with limited forms of censorship (e.g., prohibiting hate speech). Many states have introduced freedom of information laws (also termed *right to information* laws) designed to ensure the *transparency* and *accountability* of government by enabling access to state-held information. However, in some jurisdictions it can be expensive and difficult to perform freedom of information requests.

friction, see *data friction*

fusion, see *data fusion*

futures, see *data futures*

G

gamed data Data that have been massaged to create a particular impression. Unlike *fake data*, where the data are entirely invented, gamed data are generated or presented in a manner that bends the rules but does not entirely break them, or works inside the rules while breaking the spirit or morals of the exercise. For example, an individual may selectively record data about their performance in a way that shows their work in a good light and meets the expectations of managers (see *juking the stats*). Gamed data usually arise where there is self-reporting in a system of rewards and punishments (e.g., performance management).
Further reading
Deschamps, C. (2022) 'Performance management in public service organizations: Can data be useful to managers even when it is flawed or gamed?', *International Public Management Journal*, 25(5): 704–21.

gaps and exclusions Data that have not been generated, or are withheld, and are thus absent from a dataset. Gaps refer to entire sets of absent data, rather than missing data fields in a data sequence (i.e., an entire variable being absent, rather than some values in a variable sequence, which are referred to as missing data). In some cases, gaps might be deliberate exclusions, the data not generated because of what it might show; in other cases, it may be an oversight. In both cases, there is a *data politics* at work. Deliberate omission is the work of *data power* seeking to hide an inconvenient truth. Oversight is often because of the lack of a *data strategy* and a formal process of working out what data are needed to provide necessary insights or outputs. In some cases, gaps are the result of the data being too resource intensive to produce. Gaps in data produce gaps in information and knowledge, and limit the utility and value of datasets. See also *completeness, data pyramid, uncounted*.

gatekeeping The process of controlling access to a resource. A gatekeeper with respect to data acts to decide who can access a dataset, or acts to filter a dataset so that only some elements are available to selected individuals (see *data access*). For example, an archivist for a *data repository* acts as a gatekeeper to decide who has permission to access a dataset; the *open data* manager in a public body decides which data will be made openly available to the public and in what form, and what will remain closed from view. Gatekeeping is an exercise in *data power* and is informed by *data politics*, especially when exclusions are at the discretion of the gate-keeper as opposed to being dictated by legal and regulatory obligations. Prevention of access can have a number of consequences in terms of limiting the ability to know what has occurred and to seek redress (see *right to information*).

GDPR (General Data Protection Regulations), see *data protection*

gender and gendered data   Data related to gender, gender biases in data, and *data practices* and processes that reproduce sexist, misogynist, and patriarchal relations. As feminist analysis has extensively documented, there are significant, long-standing inequalities and inequities between men and women in society. These differences in status and roles are reflected in a range of *administrative data* and *official statistics*. They are also reflected in the absences and gender biases in datasets. Historical records in *archives* are much more likely to relate to men and their lives and achievements than to women. Administrative household records that refer to the 'head of household' are more likely to be tied to men. Data relating to the public domain and to work are more likely to concern men. The sexist and misogynist attitudes that have pervaded society are built into *bureaucracy* and data-driven systems, both mostly designed and implemented by men and imbued with their values. This can be particularly harmful for those who do not exist within the gender binary, with many data systems offering only two options, effectively erasing nonbinary and transgender people (see *queer data*). The *scientific method* has similarly been critiqued for its detached, masculinist *epistemology*. The logics and operations of patriarchy are evident in datasets and reproduced through their use. *Data feminism* has sought to expose the gendered nature of data and *data politics*, challenge and recon-figure patriarchal data relations and *data power*, and create new approaches to thinking about and conducting data work (e.g., *feminist data science, ethics of data care*).

Further reading

D'Ignazio, C. and Klein, L.F. (2020) *Data Feminism*. MIT Press, Cambridge, MA.

Perez, C.C. (2018) *Invisible Women: Data Bias in a World Designed for Men*. Vintage, London.

genealogy   A methodological approach that seeks to trace out the emergence of ideas, practices, technologies, and other phenomena over time and space. Rather than producing a teleological historiography, in which a linear story of how a way of thinking or acting developed over time is set out, a genealogy acknowledges that how a phenomenon comes into being is rarely straightforward or determined by simple cause-effect relations. Instead, phenomena emerge from several sources, interactions, conflicts and resolutions and unfold in *context* in *contingent* and relational ways. A new mode of *surveillance*, for example, might have several origin points, develop through competition, be stimulated by particular events, and be accepted or resisted by societies in different places. Genealogy seeks to untangle, contextualise, and chart these various intersecting strands in order to understand the multiple, complex ways in which forms of *data, data infrastructures, data policies, data regimes,* and other data-related phenomena emerge, develop, are debated, taken up and discarded, and the roles of various actors (e.g., individuals, organisations) and actants (e.g., media, technology, policy, legislation) in these processes. In so doing, it identifies how *data assemblages* form and develop contingently over time and space.

Further reading

Browne, S. (2015) *Dark Matters: On the Surveillance of Blackness*. Duke University Press, Durham, NC.

Koopman, C. (2019) *How We Became Our Data: A Genealogy of the Informational Person*. University of Chicago Press, Chicago.

generalisation, see *data generalisation*

geodemographics   The profiling of people living within a geographic area in order to target them with marketing and services.

Geodemographics works on the principle that the same kinds of people, with the same kinds of outlook and tastes, generally live in the same places. By determining the socio-economic characteristics of people living in an area, they can be spatially sorted by matching them up against possible interests, previous patterns of purchases, and disposable income (see *social sorting*). This means that a company does not waste resources by sending marketing materials for a luxury car to a working-class neighbourhood where people are unlikely to be able to afford one, or a political party can match its electoral message to the interests of local residents. Businesses can also use the information to decide where best to locate a new store, or a local government to identify locations in need of targeted policy interventions. A typical means of creating a geodemographic profile is to use socio-economic variables in a *census* to classify census districts into household profiles. A company then might add to this by factoring in the purchase history of loyalty card holders living in an area. With the advent of *big data*, geodemographic profiling has become more sophisticated, *granular*, and dynamic. Much more data linked to places can be used in *profiling*, the spatial scale has become more granular (street-level rather than districts), and the profiles can be constantly updated in relation to unfolding contexts. This is facilitating dynamic pricing, wherein people living in different places are offered varying prices for the same goods and services, and these can change in real-time in response to circumstances. Geodemographics inherently places a value on places and the people who live there and has led to discriminatory practices such as *redlining*. See also *demographically identifiable information*.

Further reading

Dalton, C.M. and Thatcher, J. (2015) 'Inflated granularity: Spatial "big data" and geodemographics', *Big Data & Society*, 2(2), https://doi.org/10.1177/2053951715601144

Webber, R. and Burrows, R. (2018) *The Predictive Postcode: The Geodemographic Classification of British Society*. Sage, London.

geography, see *data geographies*

glitches   Accidental, dysfunctional events wherein digital technologies and systems work incorrectly or not at all. Glitches may arise due to software errors, packet loss in data flows, and data *errors* (e.g., *noise*, missing fields, misclassification, duplication). Glitches lead devices and systems to perform sub-optimally or not as anticipated, or to fail entirely, and can seriously disrupt data-driven work (see *unanticipated consequences*). They are tackled through workarounds, quick fixes, and software and firmware patching. Glitches, as some feminist scholars note, also reveal how data-driven systems are grounded in the messiness of everyday life and are open to rupture, and thus intervention and reconfiguration. They have advocated for a focus on the glitch, both to highlight the contingent and contextual nature of data-driven systems, but also as a strategy of disruption and refusal in practising *data politics* and *data activism*. See also *maintenance and repair*.

Further reading

Russell, L. (2020) *Glitch Feminism*. Verso, London.

Leszczynski, A. (2020). 'Glitchy vignettes of platform urbanism', *Environment and Planning D: Society and Space*, 38(2), 189–208.

good enough data   Data that enable a task to be performed as required despite *data quality* or alignment issues. Very few datasets are perfect in terms of their quality or their fit with a task; that is why *data cleaning*, *data wrangling*, and *data transformation* are very common *data management* tasks, and *proxy data* and *exhaust data* are often used. Instead, a key consideration for a data analyst or system designer is whether the data are 'good enough' to provide an answer that is *fit for purpose*. What is considered good enough data varies with task and context. For example, the data in a planning IT system might be good enough to make a decision on whether to grant planning permission, but not of sufficient *accuracy and precision* to satisfy a legal dispute over a property boundary. In most cases, it is good enough data that are being used and a common concern is whether good enough data are actually good enough, or whether issues with a dataset sufficiently compromise the process as to raise serious doubts about the *veracity* and *validity* of the data analysis.

Further reading

Gabrys, J., Pritchard, H., and Barratt, B. (2016) 'Just good enough data: Figuring data citizenships through air pollution sensing and data stories', *Big Data & Society*, 3(2): 1–14.

governance, see *data governance*

governmentality   The logics, rationalities, and techniques that inform and underpin how governance is enacted. Since the Enlightenment and the rise of *bureaucracy*, data-based ways of monitoring society have been a component of governmentality. Bureaucracy and *surveillance* became central elements in an interlocking set of institutions, procedures, laws, technologies, and social norms that produced *power/knowledge* and instilled self-disciplining, wherein people act in expected ways for fear of being monitored, disciplined, and punished. The rise of digital technologies, mass *datafication*, and *automation* has widened and deepened the data gaze and the scope of disciplinary governmentality, but also produced a new mode of control governmentality, and new forms of technocratic, algorithmic, and anticipatory governance. Control is where the means of performing a task is the only way it can be undertaken and is also the means of monitoring performance. This form of governmentality is enacted when tasks are digitally mediated, with people compelled to act in the way the system wants. With respect to work, data-driven systems are changing the nature of labour and how staff are managed, overseen, and regulated, with behaviour steered and nudged as well as disciplined. Data and *dataveillance* are at the heart of this process, used to monitor action and to make decisions. This shift in governmentality raises political and ethical questions about the effects of *big data* and digital technologies on how society is governed. See also *calculative regime, data labour, data regime, data power*.

Further reading

Evans, L. and Kitchin, R. (2018) 'A smart place to work? Big data systems, labour, control, and modern retail stores', *New Technology, Work and Employment*, 33(1): 44–57.

granularity   The resolution of data within a dataset. With respect to populations, individual-level data are highly resolute, with granularity dissipating at the levels of household and demographically classified data. Similarly, spatial granularity is a reflection of the spatial *scale* at which spatial data are produced and published (e.g., individual address points, streets, neighbourhoods, districts, counties, regions, nations). Ideally, to increase the precision and veracity of a study's findings, analysis is undertaken on data with a high degree of granularity. The coarser a dataset is in its granularity, the more likely *ecological fallacies* will occur in analysis. See also *accuracy and precision, aggregation.*

ground-truthing, see *validation*

group privacy   A privacy right that is extended to groups or communities. Legal approaches to *data protection* and *privacy* are presently centred on individual rights and *personal data.* Such an approach fails to recognise that many privacy harms are applied to groups of people indiscriminately. That is, all members of a group are targeted through group *profiling.* This is particularly the case with mass *datafication* and the rise of *surveillance capitalism. Pattern recognition* enables individuals to be assigned to multiple groups depending on context (e.g., *gender, race, ethnicity,* purchasing, voting), with members of these groups treated in the same way without being personally profiled and targeted. Group profiling can extend discrimination with respect to groups who are already marginalised, by deepening the levels and consequences of targeting. Since there is no *personally identifiable information* in a group profile, it is not subject to privacy protections. This has led to calls for legislative reform that will protect groups from collective privacy harms. See also *demographically identifiable information.*
  Further reading
  Taylor, L., Floridi, L., and van der Sloot, B. (eds) (2017) *Group Privacy: New Challenges of Data Technologies.* Springer, Cham, Switzerland.

H

habitus, see *data habitus*

hackathon   An event in which teams of participants use data and digital technologies to design and build prototype solutions to an issue. Hackathons are a form of *civic hacking* that usually takes place over a weekend, with participants competing as teams. The aim is to leverage the technical and domain knowledge of participants to address a local problem by developing multiple potential solutions, some of which might be viable. Teams are provided with key data-sets and guidance, and if needed access to specialist software and hardware. The winning team often receives seed funding to further develop the prototype into a possible product. Hackathons have been used extensively to promote the use of *open data*, with teams asked to consider how value might be extracted from these data. Some have sought to enact *data justice* and to produce *counter-data actions* (e.g., Data for Black Lives). Hackathons have been critiqued for promoting technological solutionism (every issue can be fixed with a technical solution), their top-down organisation (usually run by state bodies or companies that choose their theme), and the lack of diversity and domain knowledge of participants (usually young men working in the tech sector who are tech-savvy but know little about the issue being tackled).

Further reading

Irani, L. (2015) 'Hackathons and the making of entrepreneurial citizenship', *Science, Technology and Human Values*, 40(5): 799–824.

heterogeneity, see *variety*

historical analysis, see *data history, genealogy, oral history*

history, see *data history*

humanitarianism, see *data humanitarianism*

hypotheses Formal statements about assumed truths that require testing to be verified. A hypothesis is usually expressed as a deductive statement: if A and B then C (see *deduction*). For example, if patient A has symptoms B, then patient A has disease C. This statement is empirically tested to establish its veracity, seeking to establish if all patients with symptoms B do in fact have disease C, or whether they have a different condition. If, after testing, a hypothesis is disproved then its underlying reasoning can be dismissed or reformulated for re-testing. Hypotheses are a core component of the *scientific method*, providing formal statements of the research questions under investigation.

I

imaginaries, see *data imaginaries*

immutable mobiles   Information that can be circulated across places and contexts without significant alterations to its inherent characteristics and meaning. *Facts*, statistical findings, *data visualisations*, and maps (see *mapping*) are all considered to be immutable mobiles, a concept introduced by Latour (1986). These forms of data can all be transported independently of the means of their production and remain interpretable to non-proximate populations. For example, the form, structure, and symbology of maps has become standardised internationally, meaning that maps are stable, legible forms of knowledge, portable and interpretable across space and time without local knowledge. Immutable mobiles only give the impression of being immutable by reinforcing a dominant mode of knowledge that seeks to be universal by silencing other ways of knowing (e.g., *Indigenous data*/knowledge; see *data universalism*). Moreover, as some have noted, in the digital age information can be simultaneously mutable and immutable; that is, (im)mutable. For example, a digital map of Dublin is immutable in its base form, but also mutable through being overlain with placemarks, annotations, images, videos, and user-generated content, with maps containing varying combinations of these.

Further reading

Graham, M., De Sabbata, S., and Zook, M.A. (2015) 'Towards a study of information geographies: (Im)mutable augmentations and a mapping of the geographies of information', *Geo: Geography and Environment* 2(1): 88–105.

Latour, B. (1986) 'Visualization and cognition: Thinking with eyes and hands', *Knowledge and Society: Studies in the Sociology of Culture Past and Present* 6: 1–40.

indexical data   Datapoints that uniquely identify the source of *attribute data*. Indexical data related to a building might be its latitude and longitude or electricity meter ID, and for a person their social security and passport numbers, *biometric data*, bank account and credit card numbers. Other indexical data include digital object identifiers, and order and shipping numbers. Indexical data are vital components of datasets as they connect attribute data to their source and enable data held across different *databases* to be linked and combined together and to be *machine-readable*. See also *personally identifiable information*.

Further reading

Dodge, M. and Kitchin, R. (2005) 'Codes of life: Identification codes and the machine-readable world', *Environment and Planning D: Society and Space*, 23(6): 851–81.

Whittington, J., Calo, R., Simon, M., Woo, J., Young, M., and Schmiedeskamp, P. (2016) 'Push, pull, and spill: A transdisciplinary case study in municipal open government', *Berkeley Technology Law Journal*, 30(3): 1899–966.

indicator data   Quantified, time-series measurements that enable the monitoring of a phenomenon. For example, an economic indicator might be the monthly unemployment rate. Indicators are often displayed as a graph to visually depict how the measured rate is changing over time. Single indicators consist of a single measure of a phenomenon. Ideally, the indicator measure should be well defined, unambiguous, and have strong *veracity* (see also *proxy data*). *Composite indicators* consist of several single measures combined together to produce a new single derived measure and are designed to track multidimensional phenomena such as social deprivation. Descriptive indicators are designed to provide trend information. Target indicators aim to assess performance against a desired outcome (see *key performance indicators*). Predictive indicators provide measurements that reveal present conditions and can also be used to predict and simulate future outcomes (e.g., meteorological indicators for making weather forecasts). *Metrics* consist of a suite of indicators being used together to monitor a phenomenon or issue.

Further reading

Morse, S. (2019) *The Rise and Rise of Indicators: Their History and Geography*. Routledge, London.

Indigenous data   Data that relate to Indigenous communities. These data are primarily generated by state agencies, whose approach to population data and statistics is rooted in the ideologies and practices of settler colonialism, and by Indigenous communities themselves, who have their own traditions of knowledge creation. *Administrative data* regimes and *official statistics* are grounded in a *governmentality* and *bureaucracy* designed to monitor and administer populations. While some individuals have a degree of liberal autonomy in the conduct of their lives, other subjects – designated along lines of *race*, *ethnicity*, class, *gender*, sexuality (see *queer data*), and *disability* – are liable for closer monitoring and governance that aims to discipline and civilise them to meet the social expectations of the ruling class. In colonial states, Indigenous communities were, and continue to be, subject to a *data regime* that marks them out, or deliberately excludes them (see *uncounted*), depending on circumstance, and that is used in their governance. At the same time, data related to their cultural heritage, knowledge, and territories is either dismissed as parochial and invalid, or appropriated for value extraction. Indigenous communities have enacted *data activism* to claim *data sovereignty* with respect to state data relating to them, as well as their own self-generated data, demanding the right to determine and govern how data related to them are generated, analysed, documented, owned, stored, shared, and used in accordance with Indigenous values and collective interests. This claim to data sovereignty relates to all organisations that hold Indigenous data, including companies, and is enshrined in the *CARE principles* developed by the Global Indigenous Data Alliance. Indigenous data sovereignty is recognised by a number of national states, such as Australia, Canada, and New Zealand, and is also enshrined in the United Nations Declaration on the Rights of Indigenous Peoples. Nonetheless, there is still significant *decolonisation* work to be undertaken globally with respect to state data regimes. See also *data universalism*.

Further reading

Kukutai, T. and Taylor, J. (eds) (2016) *Indigenous Data Sovereignty: Towards An Agenda*. Australian National University Press, Canberra.

Walter, M. and Andersen, C. (2013) *Indigenous Statistics: A Quantitative Research Methodology*. Left Coast Press, Walnut Creek, CA.

induction A mode of logical reasoning that seeks to infer general principles and conclusions from a body of evidence rather than make definitive claims (see *deduction*). While deduction formalises a theoretical statement, which it then seeks to verify or falsify through testing, induction seeks to construct a theory from generated evidence. In so doing, induction works from the level of the particular (e.g., the experiences of individual app users) to make inferences at the general level (e.g., the effects of app use), while recognising that these inferences are probable but not guaranteed.

inferencing, see *inferred data*, *inferential statistics*

inferential statistics   A set of statistical techniques for making inferences or predictions relating to a population based on a *sample* of data. In contrast to *descriptive statistics*, inferential statistics test whether there are patterns and relationships within a dataset as set out in a *hypothesis*, and aim to establish the strength and significance of any association (see *statistical significance*). Inferential statistics include *non-parametric statistics*, *parametric statistics*, and probability statistics. They are used widely in *data analytics*.
Further reading
MacInnes, J. (2022) *Statistical Inference and Probability*. Sage, London.

inferred data   Data that has been estimated or predicted based on other data. For example, one might use data that records purchasing or internet browsing history to infer what other products a person might be interested in; or one might use a socioeconomic profile and social media data to infer which political party someone might vote for. Inferred data are usually produced without consultation with the *data subject*. Inferred data are often used to fill missing gaps within datasets (see *data cleaning*). In general, inferred data contain more *false positives and false negatives* than declared data (i.e., data that is directly captured) given that they are estimated or predicted values based on a set of assumptions. See also *data derivatives*, *profiling*.
Further reading
Custers, B. (2018) 'Profiling as inferred data: Amplifier effects and positive feedback loops', in Bayamlioğlu, E., Baraluic, I., Janssens, L., and Hildebrandt, M. (eds), *Being Profiled: Cogitas Ergo Sum*. Amsterdam University Press, Amsterdam, pp. 112–15.

information   The organised accumulation of data into a mean-ingful form. Information is variously understood across disciplines and schools of thought, though they all position information as sitting between *data* and *knowledge*. Data are converted into information through processing, organisation, and analysis; infor-mation into knowledge through collation and interpretation. For some, information is the accumulation of associated data, or the signal (pattern) that can be identified in the data. For others, information must possess an inherent sense of meaning that can be extracted. For example, records (data) can be turned into a graph (information) where the visualisation conveys the relationship between datapoints. Others identify different forms of information that have varying relationships to data. As well as being composed of data, information may also be instructional (e.g., commands, recipes) or convey useful facts (e.g., timetables, product lists and prices, maps). *Critical Data Studies* is interested in uncovering the praxis and politics involved in translating data into information (see *data narratives*, *data stories*, *data visualisation*).

information commissioners   A government regulator and ombudsman with respect to *privacy* and *data protection*, and for *freedom of information*. The role and functions can vary across jurisdictions (usually nation state and federal state level), but they are principally concerned with protecting *personal data*, censor-ship, the *right to information*, the *right to be forgotten*, compliance with *open data* directives, and fair data trading and *data monopolies*.

infrastructure, see *data infrastructure*

ingestion, see *data ingestion*

institutional review board (IRB)   A panel of *research ethics* experts who assess whether a proposed *research design* meets acceptable standards of ethical conduct. An IRB ensures that every research project that involves people or animals actively considers potential ethical issues ahead of initiating the study, and while underway, complies with moral expectations, regula-tions, and legislation, and avoids malpractice and litigation. Any university-led study that generates or uses *personal data* should receive IRB scrutiny to ensure it complies with *Fair Information Practice Principles*, *data protection*, and *privacy* regulations.

integrity, see *data integrity*

intellectual property rights (IPR)   The legal protection of intellectual ideas and work from unauthorised re-use. IPR include *copyright*, patents, trademarks, *digital rights management*, and *end-user licence agreements* that seek to provide the creator of a new idea or a creative work with property rights, usually for a set period of time, so that they can derive value from their mental and innovation labour. These rights, their advocates argue, create incentives to innovate and to drive social and economic progress. The digital technologies that have driven the present data revolution are wrapped up in IPR that controls their use and many company buyouts and mergers occur to acquire and consolidate valuable patents. The *open access*, open source software, open licensing, and *open data movements* aim to provide an alternative IPR landscape in which ideas are freely shared for the public good rather than private gain. See also *data access*, *data monopolies*, *data rights*, *data scraping*, *law*, *licensing*.

Further reading

Harms, L.T.C. (2012) *The Enforcement of Intellectual Property Rights: Case Book*. Third edition. World Intellectual Property Organization.

intermediaries, see *data intermediaries*

interoperability   The ability of different digital systems and technologies to interconnect and work cooperatively together in a coordinated manner. This includes the ability to conduct *data sharing*, *data fusion*, and *data enrichment* through straightforward, *automated* processes (see *ETL (extract, transform, load)*). Interoperability is aided by shared *data standards* and *data formats*, and shared or overlapping *data models* and *data dictionaries*. It might also include aligned *data governance*, *data strategies*, and *data policies*, which enable *data sharing* agreements, coordinated work flows, and the building of trust between partners. Interoperability is seen as essential for creating coherent *digital markets* at scale. For example, the European Interoperability Framework (EIF) provides forty-seven recommendations to improve interoperability across public sector digital services within and across jurisdictions to help create a Digital Single Market in Europe. See also *data silos, seamlessness and seamfulness, stranded data.*

Further reading

European Union (2017) *New European Interoperability Framework: Promoting Seamless Services and Data Flows for European Public Administrations.* Publications Office of the European Union, Luxembourg, ec.europa.eu/isa2/sites/default/files/eif_brochure_final.pdf

interval data   *Quantitative data* that are ordered along a scale that has fixed intervals and an arbitrary origin and end point, but where ratios are not meaningful. For example, the Celsius temperature scale has 100 equal sized intervals (centigrade) between the freezing point and boiling point of water, with the scale extending below 0°C and above 100°C. Addition or multiplication by a constant will not alter the interval nature of the observations. However, zero is not absolute and ratios do not apply as 30°C is not twice as hot as 15°C (unlike temperature on a Kelvin scale, which are *ratio data*). Time when measured from an arbitrary point such as AD, location using latitude/longitude, or direction from north are also interval data. Interval data can be analysed using *descriptive statistics* and *visualisations,* and using *parametric statistics.* See also *nominal data, ordinal data.*

interviews   A form of conversational exchange in which an interviewer asks an interviewee questions about their experiences, opinions, beliefs, aspirations, thoughts, and feelings in relation to an issue or phenomenon. Interviews take three main forms. Structured interviews ask a set sequence of questions to all interviewees, with little room for deviation, providing directly comparable responses. Semi-structured interviews take a guided form in which the interviewer has a list of questions they want to cover, but these do not need to follow a sequence and there is more scope to ask follow-up questions and to explore answers further. A semi-structured interview is thus more conversational, but all the key questions are asked. An unstructured interview is an open conversation, where an initial prompt focuses attention on a particular issue or phenomenon and the discussion follows interesting lines of exchange, directed as much by the interviewee as the interviewer. Interviews can be undertaken face-to-face or via online video, or be asynchronous in nature, conducted via email or messaging. They might involve prompts such as photos or quotes to stimulate conversation. Interviews are used extensively in *Critical Data Studies*. For example, interviewing people who perform data roles such as *chief data officers*, data scientists, archivists, *data controllers and data processors*, or members of *data governance* teams, or interviewing members of the public about their opinions on and experiences of *datafication* and data-driven systems or their efforts to conduct *data activism* and *counter-data actions*. See also *data ethnographies*, *data walks*, *focus groups*, *oral histories*.

Further reading

Ash, J., Kitchin, R., and Leszczynski, A. (2024) *Researching Digital Life: Orientations, Methods and Practice*. Chapter 5. Sage, London.

J

journalism, see *data journalism*

juking the stats   A colloquial term describing the deliberate alteration of data to produce a particular outcome (see *gamed data*). For example, workers altering how their performance is measured by omitting, inflating or miscoding aspects of their work to meet expected targets. Juking the stats reveals explicitly the ways in which data are 'cooked' (see *cooked data*).

justice, see *data justice*

K

key performance indicators (KPIs)   A form of *indicator* that measures activity and outcomes against an expected target to monitor and evaluate performance. In workplaces, KPIs (e.g., the volume of sales per month or rate of production) are used to monitor individual, unit, organisational, process or system performance. A range of indicators might be used to monitor performance. KPIs often have rewards and punishments linked to specific targets that are designed to ensure those targets are met or exceeded. The KPIs of individuals and organisations are often ranked to *benchmark* relative performance (e.g., school league tables or global university rankings) to encourage competition that improves performance. KPIs are designed to inform strategic and operational planning and decision-making. They have been critiqued for: reducing the diverse tasks that individuals and organisations do to overly simple measures; fostering behaviour that seeks to game the KPI, which in turn changes the processes it is monitoring (see *gamed data*, *juking the stats*); and encouraging excessive work behaviour (e.g., working hours beyond those that are waged) which is exploitative and can cause stress and ill health. For KPIs to be meaningful, they also need to be standardised; for example, averaging factory output against numbers of workers rather than simply benchmarking total output regardless of factory size. There are related critiques with respect to benchmarking. See also *metrics*.

Further reading

Kitchin, R. (2021) *Data Lives: How Data Are Made and Shape Our World*. Chapter 18. Bristol University Press, Bristol.

knowledge   An understanding of, and know-how relating to, the world. *Information* is translated into knowledge through analysis and interpretation that create insight and the basis for action and decision-making. Knowledge is not necessarily rooted in captured *data*, but can also build from practical experience, developing know-how, and through teaching and conversational exchange. There are a number of ways of conceptualising knowledge that are rooted in different epistemological positions, with *epistemology* being the study of the nature of knowledge, how it is produced, and how it is used and contested.

Further reading

Lemos, N. (2020) *An Introduction to the Theory of Knowledge*. Second edition. Cambridge University Press, Cambridge.

L

labour, see *data labour*

law and data　A formalised set of rules and principles used to govern data and data-related activities, established by a political authority and enforced by a policing and legal system. Laws relating to *intellectual property rights* are long-standing: patents can be traced back to fifteenth-century Italy; copyright to sixteenth-century Britain. Laws concerning *bureaucracy* and its conduct and record-keeping are also long-standing, as are trade competition laws. The right to *privacy* can be traced to the late nineteenth century. The law has thus had an enduring impact on the generation, sharing, and trading of data and on its uses, both within jurisdictions and internationally. In the digital era, *datafication* and *data capitalism*, and new governance and business practices and processes, have placed pressure on old-standing laws and led to legal and political debate and revised and new legislation. These include laws relating to *data protection*, privacy, *digital rights management, licensing, data access,* the *right to be forgotten,* the *right to information,* and *data security*. Given the rate of technological innovation, the law often struggles to keep pace with new developments. See also *data rights, data scraping, Fair Information Practice Principles*.

legacy systems　An old technology or system that is still in use. Legacy systems may still be actively maintained and updated, but are no longer considered the optimal means of undertaking the work they perform. In some cases, they are locked into an old configuration. They do, however, work, which is why they have not been abandoned. The reason a legacy system stays in place varies, including vendor lock-in, the cost of a replacement system, the embeddedness of associated work practices, the need for staff retraining, and the disruption of transferring between systems that make change management difficult. Legacy systems maintain a *path dependency* and can stifle innovation. They can limit *interoperability* with newer systems and also create *data security* vulnerabilities such as *data breaches* due to poorer cybersecurity measures. Many *data infrastructures, data formats,* and *data standards* are legacy systems, and understanding contemporary *data assemblages* means charting their historical development and identifying the points at which technological and organisational innovation and new investment falter and its downstream consequences.

Further reading

Bellotti, M. (2021) *Kill It With Fire: Manage Aging Computer Systems (and Future Proof Modern Ones)*. No Starch Press, San Francisco, CA.

licensing Providing permissions to a user granting them the right to use goods or services under certain conditions. Licensing is designed to provide *intellectual property rights* to creators, protecting their ability to leverage value from their intellectual labour and innovations, including data and software (see *copyright*). Data licensing usually places limits on *re-use* and what can be done with a dataset and data derived from it, commercial resale and derived services, the publishing of insights drawn from the data, the sharing of the data, and the timeframe in which the data can be used. Licensing often involves paying a fee to the licence holder. Creative commons licences allow dataset creators to permit free re-use with conditions relating to attribution, commercial use, modification and adaptation, and how a licence is applied to derived work. Copyleft licensing allows the right to freely distribute the data, but only on the condition that derived work is shared using a copyleft licence. See also *data access, digital rights management, end-user licence agreement.*

lifecycle, see *data lifecycle*

lineage The history of a dataset, including details of the source material, methods used, data flows, and any transformations or processes applied. Ideally lineage information should enable a step-wise audit from data generation through to publication. *Methodological transparency* is a central component of lineage, along with information on *data management.* Lineage is important as it allows an understanding of how a dataset was produced and the ability to trace back through the processes undertaken to identify the causes of any issues.

linked data *Structured data* and *semi-structured data* that is interlinked with other data across the internet. Linked data are associated with the idea of the *semantic web* in which the internet is transformed from a web of documents to a web of data through the tagging of content into a *taxonomy* and which can be queried (see *XML*). Linked data are *machine-readable data* enabling automated processing and linking, and efficient data mining and semantic querying; that is, being able to identify associations and relationships between data. There have been calls for all *open data* repositories to become linked data sites to enhance the value that can be leveraged from the data, but to date most only publish a limited set of linked data, if at all.

Further reading
Sakr, S., Wylot, M., Mutharaju, R., Le Phuoc, D., and Fundulaki, I. (2018) *Linked Data*. Springer, Cham, Switzerland.

literacy, see *data literacy*

liveliness A condition of *contingency*, meaning that things do not always unfold in neat, predictable ways but are open to difference, rupture, and unanticipated events. The liveliness of data is evident in its contingent, relational, and contextual unfolding and the ways in which they are diversly experienced. Data production does not always unfold as planned, with people deviating from the planned procedures in unconscious and conscious ways, so that what is produced has *errors*, *gaps*, and *biases* (see *cooked data*). *Automated* technologies are lively in their work as well, as demonstrated by *glitches*. Liveliness demonstrates the *socio-technical* nature of data. See also *affect, embodiment, unanticipated consequences*.

Further reading
Lupton, D. (2017) 'Feeling your data: Touch and making sense of personal digital data', *New Media and Society*, 19(10): 1599–614.

location data, see *spatial data*

longitudinal data/analysis   Data that is consistently produced over time, which can be analysed to show long-term trends and patterns. Longitudinal data and analysis can be quantitative and qualitative in nature. Longitudinal *quantitative data* and analysis are often used in *metrics*, forming the basis for *key performance indicators* and temporal *benchmarking*, and are displayed in *dashboards* using *data visualisation* such as time-series graphs. *Administrative data* and *official statistics* are examples of publicly produced longitudinal data, with some sets of data, such as those generated within *censuses*, being comparable back to the nineteenth century in many countries. While *consistency* in data production might last a number of years, longitudinal data are vulnerable to breaks in continuity caused by instability in what is being measured and the *methodology* or *data standards* employed, or data generation might be halted altogether. Discontinuities in the data produced potentially create *ecological fallacies* as an exact like-to-like comparison over time is not being undertaken. Longitudinal *qualitative data* might involve tracking individuals and communities over time, undertaking a temporal sequence of *interviews* or *participant observation* over a sustained period of time, and undertaking *oral histories*.

Further reading

Gayle, V. and Lambert, P. (2020) *Quantitative Longitudinal Data Analysis*. Bloomsbury, London.

Neale, B. (2021) *The Craft of Qualitative Longitudinal Research*. Sage, London.

lying with statistics   Presenting statistical findings in a way that is misleading. A commonly associated phrase is 'lies, damn lies, and statistics', attributed to Benjamin Disraeli and popularised by Mark Twain. In relation to statistical analysis, lying with statistics can be achieved in a number of ways. Examples include the use of carefully selected data, or *gamed data* or *fake data*, or how *categorisation* or *aggregation* are applied to data, or by amplifying the importance of a statistically significant finding which might well be a spurious outcome, or generalising a statistically significant finding from a limited sample to a wider population. In relation to *data visualisation*, the statistical properties of the data can be misrepresented through how the graphs and charts are constructed,

such as using non-continuous scales on a graph, or only showing a portion of the graph and exaggerating the scale. See also *data wrangling*, *data dredging*, *ecological fallacies*, *juking the stats*, *tortured data*.
Further reading
Barker, H. (2020) *Lying Numbers: How Maths and Statistics are Twisted and Abused*. Robinson, London.

M

machine learning   A set of automated algorithmic processes for generating and training models to fit a dataset's features and relationships. The model can then be used to perform further analysis, inference or prediction on new examples of similarly structured data. Machine learning is a form of *artificial intelligence* and its development has enabled insights to be extracted from *big data* through the automation of *data analytics*, which would be difficult to undertake manually. Machine learning techniques seek to acquire the ability to recognise patterns, build an associated model, and to perform certain calculations based on this model, iteratively improving its outcomes. There are two broad types of machine learning: supervised and unsupervised. In supervised learning, the model is trained to match inputs to known outputs using *training data* (e.g., to spot objects in a set of images by matching to a set of reference images of objects). In unsupervised learning, the model seeks to teach itself to identify patterns and structures in a dataset without using training data by spotting clusters and associations (e.g., to classify customers by spotting common patterns in purchases). In both case, the model evolves through a learning process that is determined by a set of rules and parameters, with the model determining how to adjust these to improve performance. While the process is automated, the analyst remains important for judging and guiding the process and assessing intermediate results.
Further reading
Alpaydin, E. (2020) *Introduction to Machine Learning*. Fourth edition. MIT Press, Cambridge, MA.
Barocas, S., Hardt, M., and Narayanan, A. (2023) *Fairness and Machine Learning*. MIT Press, Cambridge, MA.

machine-readable data   Structured data that can be read, processed, and analysed automatically by digital systems without human aid. Machine-readable data can be digital data that use a common *data standard*, or be in an analogue form that can be read by a sensor; for example, a printed barcode can be automatically scanned, the item identified, and a related process executed. Ideally, *open data* repositories publish their collections as machine-readable data and in some countries this is a legal requirement for some organisations (e.g., federal agencies in the US). See also *ETL (extract, transform, load)*, *linked data*, *semantic web*.

maintenance, see *data maintenance and repair*

management, see *data management*

mapping   The relative positional plotting of *location data* and *spatial data*. Mapping provides a powerful form of *data visualisation*. Conventionally, maps adopt a Cartesian rationality, placing spatial data onto a linear plane to show the relative location of sites. Cartography as a discipline and practice has a highly evolved set of techniques and standards for producing maps and a wide variety of mapping techniques exist, including a number which are designed to display statistical data (e.g., choropleth maps, proportional symbol maps, cartograms). The digital era has had a major impact on mapping. There has been an explosion in spatial base data (e.g., satellite imagery, photogrammetry, GPS, laser ranging tools) and spatial attribute data (data that are geographically referenced), leading to increased generation and use of maps. In addition, there has been a change in the technical constitution of maps, which are no longer static paper products but interactive and dynamic digital displays. Geographic information systems (GISs) enable the storage, mapping, and analysis of multiple spatial datasets in a single system, while online maps can display *real-time data* and can be queried. More recently, spatial data has been displayed in 3D interactive models and other spatial media.

Further reading
Crampton, J.W. (2011) *Mapping: A Critical Introduction to Cartography and GIS*. Wiley-Blackwell, Chichester.

Kitchin, R., Lauriault, T.P., and Wilson, M. (eds) (2017) *Understanding Spatial Media*. Sage, London.

markets, see *data markets*

materiality, see *data materiality*

memory   1. The recollection of, and engagement with, a remembered past. 2. Data stored on digital media for future *re-use* (see *data storage*). Memories are the means by which the past (such as events, moments, thoughts, and emotions) is remembered and experienced in the present. Memories might be surfaced through encountering people, visiting places, engaging with objects, or performing practices. For example, a photograph of old friends might prompt memories of a specific event. Photo albums, scrapbooks, diaries, memorials, rituals, and *archives* are designed to preserve and surface personal and collective memories, as are memory prompts on social media that display old posts. As these examples make clear, memories are stored in the human mind, but also as prosthetic memory recorded on various media. *Datafication* and *big data* have massively increased what might be captured and recorded as prosthetic memories, as well as increasing the density and *granularity* of the data generated and retained. The development of *data infrastructures* has enabled far more data to be stored, archived, and shared. Digital technologies and infrastructure (e.g., social media *platforms*, archives and *data repositories*, the *cloud*) thus act as mnemotechnologies, storing vast quantities of data about everyday life and mediating how data about the past are selected, narrated, presented, and circulated. See also *data histories*.

Further reading
Jacobsen, B.N. and Beer, D. (2021) *Social Media and the Automatic Production of Memory*. Bristol University Press, Bristol.
Kitchin, R. (2023) *Digital Timescapes: Technology, Temporality and Society*. Polity Press, Cambridge.

metadata   Data about data that facilitates their use, such as data definitions, *provenance*, and *lineage*. Metadata can either refer to the whole dataset or individual variables. Metadata referring to a whole dataset consist of three forms: descriptive metadata, such as title, author, publisher, date created, subject, and content description, that detail lineage and aid discoverability; structural metadata that document *coverage* and how a dataset is structured; and administrative metadata that detail *ownership*, who can use the data and under what terms and conditions, and technical aspects of the dataset. Metadata about individual variables include the names and descriptions of specific fields (e.g., the column headers in a spreadsheet) and data definitions, and enable those re-using a dataset to understand what the data represent, inform analysis, and contextualise interpretation. In the case of *indexical data*, metadata facilitate datasets being joined together. Metadata also enable the more efficient archiving and sharing of data, with some *data repositories* acting as metadata aggregators that store metadata but not their associated data, thus enabling discovery.

Metadata are themselves a rich source of data and many forms of *surveillance* utilise metadata and not their associated data. For example, it is possible to gain a lot of insight from mobile phone metadata (call history, time, location, person called, duration, etc.) without knowing anything about the content of calls. Sometimes metadata are added manually, and in other cases, especially where processes are *automated*, they are added automatically. The consistency in how metadata are recorded also varies within and across datasets. As a result, the availability and the quality of metadata differ enormously across datasets, with some datasets having little to no available metadata and others having full metadata *coverage*. Metadata standards seek to improve the availability and quality of metadata and make datasets more directly comparable (see *standardisation*). Dublin Core (dublincore.org), for example, requires datasets to have fifteen accompanying metadata fields: title, creator, subject, description, publisher, contributor, date, type, format, identifier, source, language, relation, coverage, rights.

Further reading

Gartner, R. (2016) *Metadata: Shaping Knowledge from Antiquity to the Semantic Web*. Springer, Cham, Switzerland.

NISO (National Information Standards Organization) (2004) *Understanding Metadata*. Bethesda, MD, www.niso.org/publications/press/UnderstandingMetadata.pdf

method　A set of defined procedures and techniques for completing a task. In the context of conducting a study, a diverse range of methods might be applied at different stages of the project. For example, there are a wide range of methods for generating data (see *qualitative methods, quantitative methods*), analysing data (see *data analytics, data visualisation, qualitative analysis, quantitative analysis*), and performing data management (e.g., methods for *data cleaning, data wrangling,* and *data transformations*). Methods differ in their formulation based on their conceptual assumptions (see *epistemology, ontology*), *methodological* framing, the aims and purpose of the research, and the need to comply with *research ethics, data protection,* and other regulations. Each method is implemented through a set of procedural steps, applying techniques and practices in a consistent manner in line with expected norms and rules (e.g., statistical analysis of *ordinal data* must be undertaken using a *non-parametric statistical* method). Method selection is an important aspect of *research design* as it directly shapes how research questions are answered. That there are hundreds of different methods, which can be applied across the *data lifecycle,* illustrates the politics and *contingency* of data production within research.

Further reading

Bryman, A. and Bell, E. (2019) *Social Research Methods.* Fifth edition. Oxford University Press, Oxford.

methodological transparency　The publishing of detailed information on how sourced data were generated and processed. The information is specifically concerned with the techniques, instruments, and methodological approach, including *sampling* frameworks, measurement sites, and techniques of *data cleaning, data wrangling,* and *transformation.* Such information is sometimes termed paradata. Methodological transparency is important as it enables *repeatability, reproducibility, and replicability,* provides context for further processing and analysis, and aids interpretation by making it clear how data were produced and handled. Its publication establishes trust and enables *accountability* with respect to the data producer. Generally, detailed methodological transparency is not included in *metadata* and as such it is an important complement to it.

methodology   The overarching framework guiding how a research study is undertaken. Methodology translates *epistemological* and *ontological* assumptions into a practical means of formulating and implementing a *research design*. The *methods* chosen and how a study is undertaken are framed by the wider methodology, which defines the approach adopted. The *scientific method* is a methodology rooted in the epistemological ideas of *positivism*; it formulates *hypotheses*, uses a strategy of *deduction*, favours the use of factual data, prefers *quantitative methods*, and seeks to uphold *objectivity* in data generation, analysis, and interpretation. In contrast, feminist methodologies typically formulate *research questions* and use *induction*, are open to subjective, *qualitative data* and the use of *mixed methods*, reject the notion of objectivity, and acknowledge *positionality* and the creation of *situated knowledge*. Methodology then is not simply about assembling the procedures and methods for undertaking a study, but rather combines philosophical, method, and design aspects to formulate the approach being employed. The methodology adopted has a profound effect on the data produced, the analysis undertaken, and the insights produced.

metrics   Using a suite of *indicator data* to monitor a set of processes and their performance. Metrics, as with *metrology*, refers to the measurement of phenomena. The aim is to consistently measure and track the components and processes of a system. This is usually presented as indicator data. *Key performance indicators* are a form of metrics linked to measuring progress with respect to goals and targets. The use of metrics is common in business as a way of tracking and *benchmarking* company performance across all the processes and units in a company and to help guide management decisions. Since the late 1980s, management through metrics has been increasingly applied to public bodies and the delivery of public services. This has shifted the *governmentality* and governance of the public sector. Proponents of metrics argue that you cannot manage what you do not measure and that metrics promote efficiency and improve productivity. Their detractors counter that metrics have introduced a market logic and business rationale that is instrumental, technocratic, functional, over-bureaucratic, and encourages managers to game the data rather than best serve the public (see *juking the stats*).

Further reading

Beer, D. (2016) *Metric Power*. Palgrave, London.

metrology The science and practice of *accurate and precise* measurement. Metrology promotes a *standardised* means of measuring phenomena across jurisdictions, aiding shared under-standings and trade. Metrology consists of defining units of meas-urement, ensuring that these can be used in practice, and that they can be verified against reference standards. Its modern practice, centred on the decimal-based metric system, has its roots in the French Revolution and the desire to create harmonised units for measuring lengths, weights, time, and other phenomena across the country (at that time each local area had its own ways of meas-uring these). The Metre Convention of 1875 led to the found-ing of the Bureau International des Poids et Mesures (BIPM; in English, the International Bureau of Weights and Measures), with a number of countries agreeing to adopt common standards of measurement for science, trade, technology, and legal agree-ments. This led to the International System of Units, which is now used globally.

Further reading

Gyllenbok, J. (2018) *Encyclopaedia of Historical Metrology, Weights, and Measures*. Volume 1. Birkhauser, Cham, Switzerland.

Williams, J.H. (2014) *Defining and Measuring Nature: The Make of All Things*. Morgan & Claypool, San Rafael, CA.

mixed methods Combining methods from different *method-ological* approaches within a single *research design*. For example, combining the use of a *qualitative method* (e.g., *interviews*) with a *quantitative method* (e.g., *questionnaires*) to study an issue. In this case, interviews might be used to scope out an issue with a small sample of individuals, with the resulting insights being used to construct a *questionnaire* that is administered to a much larger sample. Alternatively, interviews might be used to explore in more depth the issues identified as important in a question-naire survey. The aim of using a mixed methods approach is to leverage the complementary aspects of different methods and to compensate for the limitations of specific methods when used in isolation.

Further reading

Cresswell, J.W. and Cresswell, J.D. (2018) *Research Design: Qualitative, Quantitative, and Mixed Methods Approaches.* Fifth edition. Sage, London.

mobilities, see *data mobilities*

model, see *data model, modelling*

modelling The building of a conceptual or computational model that represents the constitution and operation of a system. Models aim to represent reality in order to enhance understanding and enable *prediction*, and in so doing inform and test theory and reduce uncertainty and risk. A computational model seeks to operationalise a conceptual model by translating assumed processes into rules, parameters, and calculations that are designed to replicate how a system functions. Modelling is used for a variety of purposes, including *prediction, simulation,* and optimisation. There are a wide range of modelling approaches, which often use metaphors and associated assumptions in their workings. For example, agent-based models seek to mimic human behaviour, with agents ascribed characteristics which, along with a behaviour and environment rule-set, influence how they act in a scenario. Genetic models draw on concepts in natural selection, such as inheritance, mutation, selection, and crossover, to develop and evolve candidate solutions to a problem. Neural networking mimics how the human brain works to evaluate and solve a problem. *Big data,* with their extended *coverage,* stronger *granularity,* and increased *timeliness,* along with advances in computation and the development of *machine learning* that enable the efficient processing of extensive, complex calculations, have led to a marked increase in the extent and sophistication of modelling. In turn, this has produced large volumes of modelled data (see *synthetic data*), which can be subjected to other *data analytics.* Modelling is dependent on good *data quality* to minimise *errors* and *biases* in model results and to limit *ecological fallacies.*

Further reading
Smaldino, P.E. (2023) *Modeling Social Behavior*. Princeton University Press, Princeton, NJ.

mundane data   A focus on the ordinary, everyday, often unnoticed engagements with data. Introduced by Pink et al. (2017), the notion of mundane data calls attention to the routine, habitual, unconscious everydayness of data in individuals' lives, and how what might at first seem new or strange becomes familiar and comfortable. Encounters with data are mostly mundane, everyday occurrences that have been slotted into other life routines. Studies of the role of data in society then need to consider the mundane and the taken-for-grantedness of data practices and encounters – how they become habituated and accepted, and how they emerge through and are experienced as contingent, contextual moments. See also *affect, data habitus, datafied agency, embodiment, liveliness*.

Further reading
Pink, S., Sumartojo, S., Lupton, D., and Heyes La Bond, C. (2017) 'Mundane data: The routines, contingencies and accomplishments of digital living', *Big Data & Society*, 5(1): 1–12.

N

narratives, see *data narratives*

national statistics organisations (NSOs)   Public bodies that are responsible for the generation, harmonisation, and publication of *official statistics*. Nearly every country has an NSO that is dedicated to the production and coordination of official statistics and maintaining the national statistical system, defining *methodologies* and *data standards*. Their mandate, responsibilities, roles, and powers to request data from individuals and organisations is defined by legislation and statutes. They are responsible for *censuses* and a wide variety of social, economic, population, environment, and government statistical data, as well as maintaining historical *archives*. Increasingly, they publish their outputs as *open data* and *linked data*. Not all official statistics are produced by this agency, with other public bodies responsible for statistical outputs relating to their competence (e.g., central banks), though these are usually shared with, published by, and often overseen and *validated* by an NSO. Some countries have statistics offices at sub-national level; for example, at federal state level. There are also a number of international statistical offices and services; for example, the United Nations Statistics Division, UNESCO Institute for Statistics, and Eurostat. In some cases, a NSO's statistical methodology and policies will follow the requirements of an international body; for example, European Union countries adopt standards and procedures set by Eurostat for some statistical outputs to ensure *interoperability* and comparability across nations. See also *statistical geography*.

Further reading

Howard, C. (2020) *Government Statistical Agencies and the Politics of Credibility*. Cambridge University Press, Cambridge.

noise   Meaningless data in a dataset that reduces *accuracy and precision* and increases the rate of *error* and *uncertainty*. Noisy data have high rates of error in the measured values due to mis-recording, corruption or distortion. Noise is often the result of technical and methodological issues, such as a faulty sensor, or individuals deliberately recording false data into a survey form. The *validity* of any analysis using noisy data is reduced. Consequently, *data cleaning* employing statistical techniques is used to try to reduce the amount of noise in a dataset.

nominal data   Categorical data where each category is discrete and has no associated ordering (see *ordinal data*). Classifying people in relation to their place or form of work, *ethnicity*, nationality, or language-spoken, or classifying digital technologies in relation to their type, purpose or manufacturer, constitute nominal data. Nominal data can be analysed using *descriptive statistics* and *visualisations*, and using *non-parametric statistics*.

non-parametric statistics   *Statistics* specifically designed to analyse *nominal data* or *ordinal data*; that is, data that are classified into categories and are not measured on a fixed scale (e.g., *interval data* or *ratio data*). Non-parametric statistics make minimal assumptions about the probability distributions of the variables being analysed, and can be used as *descriptive statistics* or to make statistical *inferences*. Non-parametric statistical analysis undertaken on nominal data includes comparing two or more related or unrelated samples or categories; on ordinal data it includes comparing two rank-ordered variables.

Further reading

Corder, G.W. and Foreman, D.I. (2014) *Nonparametric Statistics: A Step-by-Step Approach*. Second edition. Wiley, Chichester.

non-rivalrous, see *data sharing*

notice   Individuals are informed about the data being generated relating to them and the purpose for which the data will be used. Notice is a core principle of the *Fair Information Practice Principles* that underpin *data protection* and *privacy* regulations in OECD countries. Notice is often presented as *end-user licence agreements* in relation to software/apps or the management of cookies on websites. A critique of notice is that it often uses legal language that is complex and obscures what users are agreeing to. As such, while technically users have been informed of the terms and conditions of using a site and what will happen with their data, in reality they are practising uninformed, rather than informed, *consent*.

O

obfuscation   The deliberate disruption of *datafication*, the generation of *personal data*, and the operations of *dataveillance* and *surveillance capitalism*. The aim is to protect *privacy* by limiting the ability of third parties to collect personal data and track digital behaviour, particularly through the use of apps and activity on websites. Obfuscation tactics include using *pseudonyms* and false identities, giving false answers, gaming responses, non-response, refusal, encryption and sabotage, and using privacy enhancement tools that block data extraction or explode it to create a fog of data to obscure the real data.

Further reading
Brunton, F. and Nissenbaum, H. (2016) *Obfuscation: A User's Guide for Privacy and Protest*. MIT Press, Cambridge, MA.

objectivity   The position that science should be practised impartially, free of values, preferences, and prejudices. That is, how data are generated, processed, analysed, and interpreted should be informed purely by reasoned logic and scientific principles (see *scientific method*). *Critical Data Studies* contends, in contrast, that knowledge production does not occur in a value-free vacuum, and that the scientific method is itself value-laden and ideological, framed by paradigmatic assumptions (that can change periodically) and particular ways of knowing and doing (see *epistemology*, *methodology*). Moreover, scientists make choices and decisions in deciding their questions, hypotheses, approach, and methods, and how they interpret data is shaped by their education and prior knowledge. In other words, it is not possible to gain an impartial, 'god's-eye view' of a phenomenon under investigation. At best, a form of mechanical objectivity can be practised that seeks to minimise personal and political influence in how data are produced and utilised by strictly following rules and procedures, though this does not erase the values underpinning them. Instead, CDS advocates for acknowledging *positionality* and the production of *situated knowledge*. See also *cooked data*.
Further reading
Porter, T.M. (1995) *Trust in Numbers: The Pursuit of Objectivity in Science and Public Life*. Princeton University Press, Princeton, NJ.

observation   A method that consists of observing behaviour and activity. The aim is to use the researcher's senses to gather information about how tasks are performed within a setting and the social relations and dynamics of a community. There are a number of forms of observation. Participant observation involves a researcher embedding themselves in a setting and engaging in the ongoing activities in order to experience firsthand what is taking place and to learn about it through informal conversations with others. Non-participation observation involves being present and observing what is taking place, but not actively performing as a participant. Indirect observation consists of drawing on the observations of others to understand a *community of practice*, or undertaking a task outside of a setting to get a sense of how systems operate (such as using a data entry system to get a sense of its associated *data practices* and affordances). Covert observation involves a researcher participating in a setting without revealing their identity to the others present. There are ethical concerns and risks with a covert approach as it is deceptive and there is no *notice* or *consent*, though there might be good reasons for adopting it (such as to research and reveal a politically extreme or illegal activity, though this also raises issues of researcher safety). While observation does provide strong empirical evidence, it also has some issues that need to be guarded against. The observer effect occurs when people change their behaviour and actions due to the knowledge that they are being observed (see *ecological fallacies*). Confirmation bias occurs when the observer orientates their view towards seeing what they expect to see. Observation is a core method used in *data ethnographies*.

Further reading

Angrosino, M. and Rosenberg, J. (2011) 'Observations and observation', in Denzin, N.K. and Lincoln, Y.S. (eds), *The Sage Handbook of Qualitative Research*. Sage, London, pp. 467–78.

Marzano, M. (2021) *Ethical Issues in Covert, Security and Surveillance Research*. Emerald, Bingley.

official statistics	Statistical data produced by public bodies in order to document the current state of play with respect to a phenomenon in a jurisdiction. Typically, official statistics relate to agriculture, business, crime and justice, economy, education, energy, environment, government, health, labour markets, population, social welfare, and transport. These statistical data provide a knowledge base for the creation and monitoring of policy, and inform public and political debate. *National statistics organisations* maintain national statistical systems and oversee the production of official statistics. However, official statistics are generated by many public bodies relating to their domain of responsibility at different jurisdictional scales (e.g., local, regional, national). In 1992, the Economic Commission for Europe adopted the Fundamental Principles of Official Statistics, which were adopted by the United Nations in 1994. These principles set out the need for appropriate, reliable, and impartial statistical data that meet professional, scientific, and ethical standards in relation to data generation, processing, storage, and presentation. There have been debates and legal cases in several countries with respect to political interference in official statistics and the degree to which they are independently produced. In recent years, the possibility of using *big data* to replace or supplement existing sources of data has been explored, though it is recognised that there are significant issues given that these data are typically *exhaust data* that have not been generated for the purpose of producing statistical outputs. See also *disclosure data*.

Further reading

Kitchin, R. (2015) 'The opportunities, challenges and risks of big data for official statistics', *Statistical Journal of the International Association of Official Statistics* 31(3): 471–81.

Prevost, J-G. (2023) *The Independence of Official Statistics: Norms, Arrangements, Instruments*. Springer, Cham, Switzerland.

ontology The philosophical study of the nature of being and existence. Ontology is a foundational component of philosophy (see also *epistemology, methodology, ethics*) and concerns what can be legitimately known. Social ontologies make claims about the nature of society and social reality. A realist social ontology holds that social reality exists independently of social actors, who all sense and experience the same reality. From this perspective, the world is directly observable and measurable independent of the observer and method of measurement (see *scientific method*). A constructivist social ontology holds that social reality is produced by social actors and how it is experienced and understood is mediated by circumstance and context. Observations of the world cannot then be independent of the observer and method, but are affected by *positionality*, and in the case of research, produce *situated knowledge*. Other ontological positions take different stances. For example, critical realism takes a middle line, contending that an independent social reality exists, but that this reality cannot be known outside of how it is subjectively experienced. A poststructuralist position contends that the nature of reality is never stable but always unfolding *contingently*, arguing for a need to shift from ontology (how things are) to ontogenesis (how things become). In relation to a *fact*, a social constructivist would contend that it is produced and is diversely understood but is nonetheless a fact, whereas a poststructuralist would argue that the fact itself has no ontological security but is always emergent. As these positions illustrate, the nature of data and facts varies between ontologies. Typically, *Critical Data Studies* adopts a constructivist, critical realist or poststructural perspective. A *data ontology* refers to how aspects of the world can be captured, named, and structured as data.

Further reading

Dodge, M. and Kitchin, R. (2005) 'Code and the transduction of space', *Annals of the Association of American Geographers*, 95(1): 162–80.

Searle, J.R. (1995) *The Construction of Social Reality*. Free Press, New York.

opacity   A situation in which it is difficult to know about or understand a phenomenon or process. It is the opposite of *transparency*. Opacity can be an inherent feature, caused by complexity, or it can be intentional, designed to limit insight. With respect to the latter, the *black-boxing* of *algorithms* and *software* is designed to protect *intellectual property rights*. *Data brokers* are also deliberately opaque and secretive with respect to their operations, in large part to hinder scrutiny of their work. Opacity limits who can know about data generation, how data are being processed, and what they are being used for, which in turn limits *accountability* and redress.

Further reading

Burrell, J. (2016) 'How the machine "thinks": Understanding opacity in machine learning algorithms', *Big Data & Society*, 3(1): 1–12.

Crain, M. (2018) 'The limits of transparency: Data brokers and commodification', *New Media and Society*, 20(1): 88–104.

open access   The outputs of research are distributed for free. The calls for open access research have generally related to print publications, though the same principles also apply to other research outputs such as data and software. The argument of proponents is that publicly funded and supported research should be made openly available for *re-use* to ensure value for investment and to realise the full worth of the research. The level of openness can vary, with libre open access seeking to implement a full open licence with respect to *copyright*, re-use, and *repurposing*. While open access print publishing is becoming more common, open access to data is lagging behind, though funding agencies are increasingly demanding its implementation (see *data hugging*).

Further reading

Eve, M.P. and Gray, J. (eds) (2020) *Reassembling Scholarly Communications: Histories, Infrastructures, and Global Politics of Open Access*. MIT Press, Cambridge, MA.

open data   Data that are free to access and use, with no or few restrictions concerning *re-use*, *repurposing*, redistribution, and the sale of *derived data*. Traditionally, data have been closed in nature, restricted by a desire to protect and exploit a valuable asset (see *intellectual property rights* and *licensing*) and to limit what the data might reveal. While business data remains mostly closed, there has been a major shift with respect to data produced by public bodies in the wake of campaigning by the *open data movement*. Despite a desire for open data with no restrictions, there are gradations in openness across open data sites; for example, data might be free to use but it cannot be reworked for profit, or its use might require attribution of the original producer. The sites also vary in the extent and quality of *metadata*, the *curation* and structuring of datasets, and the use of open *data formats* and *data standards*. Some sites are little more than uncurated data dumps, whereas others publish *linked data*, provide useful data analysis tools, and/ or have the status of a *trusted digital repository*. A number of factors continue to limit the publishing of open data. Institutions might not possess the skills or capacities to open data, which requires resources and compliance with *data regulations*. They might want to restrict access because of *data quality* issues, what the data will reveal, or the potential political uses of the data. There might also be legal concerns relating to *privacy*, *data protection*, and liabilities. While open data are free to access they are not free to prepare, curate, and host, and sustainable financial support is also a concern. See also *data hugging*.

Further reading

Robinson, P. and Scassa, T. (eds) (2022) *The Future of Open Data*. University of Ottawa Press, Ottawa.

Sieber, R.E. and Johnson, P.A. (2015) 'Civic open data at a cross-roads: Dominant models and current challenges', *Government Information Quarterly*, 32(3): 308–15.

open data movement   An international political campaign to make the data held by public bodies *open data*. Its aim is to create an evidence base for holding government to account and to democratise the ability to extract value from data produced by public institutions funded through taxes. The movement gathered strength and momentum in the 2000s, driven by a set of interlocking arguments (see *discursive regime*). Open data would: create more open and *transparent* government by providing data about its work; help improve the operations and efficiency of public bodies through the open analysis of their data; empower citizens to undertake their own analyses and produce *counter-data actions*; and create economic growth by providing a free resource from which business value could be derived. A number of international and national open data representative bodies have been founded, including the Open Government Partnership (OGP), Open Knowledge International, and the Sunlight Foundation. Since 2010, seventy-five countries have made open data commitments as part of their participation in the OGP, making tens of thousands of previous closed datasets open. Many international institutions (e.g., European Union and United Nations' bodies) have likewise created open *data repositories*. Within academia, there has been a drive for open data as part of a broader campaign for open science, wherein data produced through publicly funded science should be made available for *re-use*. While significant progress has been made, campaigning by the open data movement continues since many government datasets remain closed. See also *freedom of information, open access, right to information*.

Further reading

Baack, S. (2015) 'Datafication and empowerment: How the open data movement re-articulates notions of democracy, participation, and journalism', *Big Data & Society*, 2(2): 1–11.

Davies, T., Walker, S., Rubinstein, M., and Perini, F. (eds) (2019) *The State of Open Data: Histories and Horizons*. African Minds and International Development Research Centre, Cape Town and Ottawa.

oral history The gathering of personal testimonies about the past that is within living *memory*, or has been passed from generation to generation. An oral history is a form of biographical *interview* (or several interviews conducted over a period of time) used to record details about a person's life and their recollections of events, experiences, and views. The benefit of an oral history approach is that it produces an historical account grounded in the everyday lives and observations of individuals. Rather than trying to provide a single, coherent explanation of the past, oral history accepts that the past is remembered and interpreted differently by people and tries to understand these variances. Oral histories can be used to research the development of *data infrastructures* and *archives*, the creation and growth of data-related businesses, the activities of data activists, or other data work. There are weaknesses to the method, such as unreliable witnesses and false testimony, but these also exist for other forms of interview. See also *data histories, genealogy*.

Further reading

Brugger, N. and Goggin, G. (eds) (2022) *Oral Histories of the Internet and the Web*. Routledge, London.

Nyhan, J. and Flinn, A. (2016) *Computation and the Humanities: Toward an Oral History of Digital Humanities*. Springer Open, Cham, Switzerland.

ordinal data Categorical data that are placed in a hierarchical rank order. Data classified in terms of low, medium, and high, or weak, medium, and strong, or dislike, neutral, like, are ordinal data. Ordinal data can be analysed using *descriptive statistics* and *visualisations*, and using *non-parametric statistics*. See also *interval data, ratio data*.

ownership The exclusive right to possess, use, and dispose of property. In the context of data, ownership refers to the legal right to control and process data held by an entity. Such rights might be protected through *intellectual property rights* such as *copyright* and patents, and enforced through *digital rights management*. Given the *non-rivalrous* nature of data, in which more than one entity can possess the same data, ownership can be contested (see also *data scraping*). For example, an organisation can own data relating to an individual or community, who might claim *data sovereignty* with respect to the data. Generally, data ownership rights benefit the data producer rather than the *data subject*. However, data subjects are provided with some *data rights* to ensure *data protection* and *privacy*, as enshrined in *Fair Information Practice Principles*. There are calls for these rights to be extended by enabling people to share the financial benefits leveraged from data relating to them, and by providing greater data sovereignty to individuals and communities. For example, many Indigenous communities are seeking data sovereignty and the right to be able to control the generation and use of data about their people, culture, and territory, as set out in the *CARE principles* (see *Indigenous data, decolonising data*). See also *data commons*.

Further reading

Hummel, P., Braun, M., and Dabrock, P. (2021) 'Own data? Ethical reflections on data ownership', *Philosophy and Technology* 34(3): 545–72.

Scassa, T. (2018) 'Data ownership', CIGI Papers No. 187. Centre for International Governance Innovation. Waterloo, Canada, www.cigionline.org/static/documents/documents/Paper%20 no.187_2.pdf

P

paradata, see *methodological transparency*

parametric statistics *Statistics* designed to analyse *interval data* and *ratio data*; that is, data measured on a fixed interval scale. Parametric statistics take into account the probability distributions of the variables being tested, for example requiring that data are independent observations, are randomly drawn from a normally distributed population, and resemble approximately a normal distribution. If these conditions are not met, then either a larger, more *representative* sample of data needs to be generated, the data need to undergo some form of transformation to produce a normal distribution, or they need to be converted into nominal or ordinal data and analysed using *non-parametric statistics*. Parametric statistics are commonly used for statistical inferencing, such as testing the likelihood of a relationship between variables.

Further reading

Tokunaga, H. (2019) *Fundamental Statistics for the Social and Behavioral Sciences*. Second edition. Sage, London.

participant observation, see *observation*

participatory methods   A set of methods in which members of the public participate as co-researchers in a project. Rather than being about or for a community, research is conducted with or by community members. Citizens might be actively involved in the management of the research and participate as data generators, analysts or interpreters. A number of participatory approaches have been utilised that involve user-generated and user-analysed data. These can be divided into three types: *citizen science* (e.g., participatory sensing, volunteered geographic information, *hackathons*); civic engagement (e.g., public participation GIS, online participatory tools, serious games); and participatory action research (e.g., *counter-data actions, counter-archiving, civic hacking*). Undertaking participatory research does pose some challenges, including initiating a project, building a working relationship, retaining participation, and securing resourcing. Detractors raise concerns about the integrity and *veracity* of research produced by 'amateur' researchers, who may also have a vested interest, and potential *bias* introduced by who is participating (in terms of *representativeness*). For proponents, participatory methods help science serve local communities and enable the inclusion of grounded, lived expertise.

Further reading

Ash, J., Kitchin, R., and Leszczynski, A. (2024) *Researching Digital Life: Orientations, Methods and Practice*. Chapter 8. Sage, London.

McCosker, A., Yao, X., Albury, K., Maddox, A., Farmer, J., and Stoyanovich, J. (2022) 'Developing data capability with non-profit organisations using participatory methods', *Big Data & Society*, 9(1): 1–11.

path dependency   A trajectory of development that follows a self-reinforcing direction of travel. A condition of path dependency is said to exist when the way in which a data-driven system works and evolves is following a trajectory that is difficult to alter. Earlier decisions, initial implementation, contracts, and regulation can lock a system into a particular technology or set of data practices, with the pattern of system use becoming self-affirming. The continued use of *legacy systems* is usually illustrative of a path dependency. While a certain trajectory might be observable, its continuation is not inevitable given inherent *contingencies* in *data assemblages* and their operation. As a result, systems change incrementally and periodically a trajectory might be radically redirected through the occurrence of a critical juncture (e.g., regime change, a crisis or a 'game-changing' new innovation) that opens an opportunity to take a different path.

Further reading

Kitchin, R. (2023) *Digital Timescapes: Technology, Temporality and Society*. Polity Press, Cambridge.

pattern recognition   A process for automatically discovering regularities in a dataset and using these patterns to classify the data into categories (see *categorisation and classification*). It is undertaken using statistical analysis that is typically performed as *data mining* using *machine learning*. Labelled *training data* are usually used in order to refine pattern spotting, but if these are not available then unsupervised learning methods are applied. Patterns might be spotted in text data (e.g., to identify and isolate spam email) or in images (e.g., to identify specific features such as faces in a photograph). Pattern recognition is a key method underpinning *dataveillance* (e.g., text mining), *surveillance* (e.g., facial recognition), *surveillance capitalism*, and technologies using *artificial intelligence* (e.g., autonomous cars). Since training data can possess *biases*, these biases can be surfaced in systems using pattern recognition (e.g., predictive policing), creating data injustices.

Further reading

Beyerer, J., Richter, M., and Nagel, M. (2018) *Pattern Recognition: Introduction, Features, Classifiers and Principles*. De Gruyter, Berlin.

Buolamwini, J. and Gebru, T. (2018) 'Gender shades: Intersectional accuracy disparities in commercial gender classification', *Proceedings of Machine Learning Research*, 81(1): 1–15.

performance management, see *benchmarking, dashboards, metrics, key performance indicators*

performativity, see *data performativity*

personal data   Data that relate to an individual. Depending on jurisdiction, personal data in a legal sense are often synonymous with *personally identifiable information (PII)*; that is, data that identify a person. In the European Union, a distinction is made between PII and personal data, with the latter being any data related to a person, but which will not necessarily identify them. The scope and extent of data relating to individuals has expanded enormously in the *big data* age. Individuals leave *data footprints and shadows* through their digital interactions with government, businesses, and other organisations, with their details captured in hundreds of *databases*. These data are often sensitive in nature, concerning personal details (e.g., age, *gender, race, ethnicity, biometrics*) but also political positions, religious beliefs, health conditions, financial status, relationships and sexual activity, criminal record, and social networks. They also include personal and family stories, photographs and videos, and opinions and thoughts shared via social media. Personal data provide important information and insights about individuals, especially when they can be linked together to produce *data doubles* and be subjected to *pattern recognition* and other *data analytics*. Consequently, *privacy* and *data protection* legislation, underpinned by *Fair Information Practice Principles*, is designed to provide *data subjects* with *data rights* that limit what those holding their personal data can do with them. It is generally acknowledged that these data rights are limited, with many civil rights organisation calling for stronger legislation and for *ownership* rights and *data sovereignty*.

Further reading

Cheney-Lippold, J. (2017) *We Are Data: Algorithms and the Making of Our Digital Selves*. New York University Press, New York.

Schneier, B. (2015) *Data and Goliath: The Hidden Battles to Collect Your Data and Control Your World*. W.W. Norton, New York.

personally identifiable information (PII)   Any data that identifies an individual. One might possess personal data relating to an individual, but might not be able to identify that person. PII enables the connection of *personal data* to a *data subject*. For some, PII refers to *indexical data* that identify a data subject. Such indexical data include *biometric data*, unique ID numbers relating to social security, passports, driver licences, bank accounts, credit cards, phone numbers, and email address. Related, but not always indexical unless combined together, are name, postal address, and postcode. Other indexical data include usernames and passwords, device IDs, cookie ID, static IP addresses, and pseudonyms. These indexical data enable associated personal *attribute data* to be linked to a data subject. For others, PII constitutes all personal data associated with a data subject, data that while not indexical can be used to identify an individual by combining fields to produce a profile that matches a target and by using inference. It is these processes that allow *anonymised* data to be reidentified. The use of PII is key to the functioning of *bureaucracy* and *surveillance capitalism*.

Further reading

Narayanan, A. and Shmatikov, V. (2010) 'Privacy and security: Myths and fallacies of "personally identifiable information"', *Communications of the ACM*, 53(6): 24–6.

Solove, D. and Schwartz, P.M. (2023) *Consumer Privacy and Data Protection*. Fourth edition. Aspen Publishing, Burlington, MA.

philanthropy, see *data philanthropy*

pilot study   A study to evaluate the robustness of a *research design* and in particular the salience and effectiveness of the *method* of data generation. A pilot study is undertaken in order to assess and refine how the full study will be performed and to avoid costly mistakes. It involves a smaller sample than the full study, but in some cases pilot studies can be quite sizeable endeavours. For example, the pilot *survey* for a national *census*, undertaken to test the effects of questions in terms of response rate and error, might involve *sampling* several thousand households. Pilot study data are rarely published.

pipeline, see *data pipeline*

platform A distributed hosting architecture that supports many-to-many interactions, and facilitates social activity, and the buying, selling, and sharing of goods and services. A platform effectively acts as a host, broker or marketplace, enabling exchanges. A social media platform provides a means for people to keep in contact and share information, but also a channel for businesses to interact with customers. Transaction platforms use *profiling* and recommender systems to match customers to sellers (e.g., Airbnb matches short-term renters with hosts; Amazon sells products through its own platform, but also acts as a shopfront for thousands of other businesses). Platform companies have been able to scale quickly into global, multibillion-dollar enterprises with millions or billions of users, with data a key component of their business model. Platforms generate and process vast quantities of data relating to their users and transactions. These data can be used to produce advertising revenue, but are also a commodity that can be sold to third parties such as *data brokers*. The platforms and their owners are thus key actors in *surveillance capitalism*.

Further reading

Codagnone, C., Karatzogianni, A., and Matthews, J. (2019) *Platform Economics: Rhetoric and Reality in the 'Sharing Economy'*. Emerald, Bingley.

Kenney, M. and Zysman, J. (2016) 'The rise of the platform economy', *Issues in Science and Technology*, 32(3): 61–9.

policy, see *data policy*

political ecology of data The theorising and analysis of the relationship between the political, economic, and social dimensions of data and environmental issues that are implicated in their production and circulation. Data, and in particular *digital data*, and the devices, infrastructures and *data centres* that generate, process, analyse, store, share, and extract value from them, are dependent on the exploitation of natural resources (e.g., land, metals, rare-earth minerals, water), consume vast amounts of energy (much of it produced by fossil fuels), create pollution to water supplies and agricultural land, and produce carbon that actively contributes to climate change. Data, then, is not ecologically neutral but is a significant component of environmental issues. Such issues do not affect all communities equally, with some groups experiencing a disproportionate share of the environmental effects of *data capitalism*, usually poorer members of society. Somewhat ironically, *big data* are also seen as key to understanding and tackling environmental change and informing environmental governance. Vast networks of sensors, drones, and satellites produce *real-time data* with high *granularity* that provide a detailed, longitudinal picture of environments and human activity. Such data are far from neutral given the vested interests of many of the actors producing them and the ways in which the data and the responses stemming from them (e.g., renewable energy, conservation) have been commodified. These data inform territorial statecraft and how environments are managed and governed, while at the same time largely sidestepping how data are imbricated in environmental change. Data thus significantly contribute to unfolding socio-natures (the relationship between people and environment) and are an important site of environmental politics. A political ecology of data interrogates these socio-natures and environmental politics and their associated *data power*.

Further reading

Nost, E. and Goldstein, J.E. (eds) (2022) A Political Ecology of Data. Theme issue. *Environment and Planning E: Nature and Space*, 5(1).

political economy of data   An approach to data that places its production and use within the context of political, economic, and social relations. Political economy is a conceptual approach and field of study which focuses on the interrelationship between political institutions, the economic system, and society across scales from the local to international. Political economy holds that how an economy functions is directly shaped by politics and political ideology, and likewise the operations of politics and governance are beholden to economic aspirations and imperatives, and this relationship is the key driver of societal organisation and social relations. Data have become increasingly central to the political economy. Data-driven systems have enabled a shift in governmentality and governance, extending *bureaucracy* and deepening *surveillance*, providing an evidence base for policy, and shaping the form and operations of public services. They drive business decision-making, with data becoming an important asset and commodity in their own right, and form the basis for *data capitalism* and *surveillance capitalism* driven by the logics of *data colonialism*. A political economy of data examines the role of data in the relationship between state, economy, and society, and how the prevalent political economy modulates *data power*, *data citizenship*, and *data regulation*.

Further reading

Chandler, D. and Fuchs, C. (eds) (2019) *Digital Objects, Digital Subjects: Interdisciplinary Perspectives on Capitalism, Labour and Politics in the Age of Big Data*. University of Westminster Press, London.

Gandy Jr., O.H. (2021) *The Panoptic Sort: A Political Economy of Personal Information*. Second edition. Oxford University Press, Oxford.

politics, see *data politics*

positionality An acknowledgement and declaration of the logic, values, assumptions, and theoretic position adopted by a researcher. Positionality is expressed through an explicit setting out of how knowledge production is personally and professionally contextualised. Acknowledging positionality is a rejection of the notion of *objectivity*, recognising that all research is situated and not impartial or value-free – an argument forwarded through the feminist critique of the *scientific method* (see *situated knowledge*). By declaring their standpoint, a researcher enables those engaging with their work to contextualise and interpret the approach taken and the conclusions. Assessing the parameters of a researcher's position involves a process of *reflexivity*.

Further reading

Rose, G. (1997) 'Situating knowledges: Positionality, reflexivities and other tactics', *Progress in Human Geography*, 21(3): 305–20.

positivism A philosophical approach to knowledge production which contends that by *objectively* collecting and analysing observable data we can determine laws to predict and explain the natural and social world. Due to its *ontological* assertion that knowledge should be based on observable measurements, in its strict form positivism rejects asking normative (what should be) or metaphysical (concerning being and beliefs) questions as they are issues of faith, values, opinions, and judgements rather than facts. *Epistemologically* and *methodologically*, positivism promotes the tenets of the *scientific method* and the use of a *deductive* approach that can produce scientific findings that are *replicable, repeatable, and reproducible*. Positivist philosophy underpins research in the natural sciences and in the twentieth century its rationale and logics were also applied to the social sciences. This led to the adoption of *quantitative methods* and the use of *statistics* across the social sciences to try to determine laws that explain social and economic activity and systems. While much of this research involves analysing measured observable activity, a sizeable proportion of social, economic, and psychological studies have sought to apply the scientific method to quantifiably measure and statistically analyse thoughts, opinions, views, and values. The logics, tenets, and methodological approach of positivism are prevalent in *Data Science* and *computational social science*. However, this is not always the case, with approaches such as *feminist data science* and *critical GIS* utilising quantitative methodological approaches within a post-positivist framing. More generally, *Critical Data Studies* is post-positivist in its philosophical orientation, rejecting the ontological, epistemological, and methodological tenets of positivism in favour of the ideas and ideals of critical social theory (e.g., feminism, poststructuralism, structuralism, phenomenology, critical realism).

Further reading

Hasan, M.N. (2016) 'Positivism: To what extent does it aid our understanding of the contemporary social world?' *Quality & Quantity*, 50(1): 317–25.

postcolonialism and data   1. Data and *data politics* related to postcolonial states. 2. Using postcolonial theory to make sense of *data regimes*. These two foci are often intertwined, with postcolonial theory being used to make sense of data regimes in colonial and postcolonial states, as well as the metropoles that were the colonisers. The logics and relations of colonialism have also been used to theorise *data capitalism* and *surveillance capitalism* through the notion of *data colonialism*. The production, analysis, and interpretation of data were central to how colonial states imagined and acted with respect to their dominions. Key data projects included censuses (population), mapping (territory), and museums (culture and memory). After independence, post-colonial states inherited *data infrastructures* and *data practices* from colonial institutions, meaning that the *power/knowledge* of colonialism continued to shape social and economic relations, along with relations with metropoles and international bodies. The process of *decolonising data* and asserting *data sovereignty* has therefore been partial. Moreover, in the *big data* era, global *platform* companies are exerting *data power* within postcolonial states, along with global agencies such as the United Nations and the World Bank, and development aid agencies and organisations, reproducing colonial relations in which metropoles monitor and direct post-colonies. See also *data universalism*.

Further reading

Hoyng, R. (2020) 'From open data to "grounded openness": Recursive politics and postcolonial struggle in Hong Kong', *Television & New Media*, 22(6): 703–20.

Isin, E.F. and Ruppert, E. (2019) 'Data's empire: Postcolonial data politics', in Bigo, D., Isin, E., and Ruppert, E. (eds), *Data Politics: Worlds, Subjects, Rights*. Routledge, London, pp. 207–27.

power, see *data power*, *power/knowledge*

power/knowledge   The dyadic relationship between power and knowledge, wherein knowledge is produced and controlled through power, and power is exercised and legitimated through the appropriation and distribution of knowledge. The concept was introduced by Foucault in the 1970s to describe how power and knowledge are co-produced. Knowledge and the ability to control discourse help sustain a *discursive regime* that structures the way things are thought about and promotes certain ways of acting. *Big data* reproduce a power/knowledge nexus in which the interests of big data are reinforced through media discourses. Such discourses are sustained by a plethora of experts (business leaders, government officials, technology journalists, academics) who legitimate the claims and counter any critique or alternative views. Power/knowledge is central to the operations of *data power* and reproduces a *data doxa* (maintains the status quo) relating to *governmentality* and *data capitalism*.

Further reading
Foucault, M. (1980) *Power/Knowledge: Selected Interviews and Other Writings, 1972–1977*, ed. Gordon, C. Pantheon Books, New York.

practices, see *data practices*

pre-analytics   Preparation of data prior to the application of *data analytics*. Pre-analytics involves a number of data management processes designed to ensure data are *fit for purpose*, improve *data quality*, add value to the data, and align *data format* and *data structures* with analytic requirements. These processes include *exploratory data analysis*, data selection, *data cleaning, data wrangling, data transformation, data enrichment,* and *data fusion*. Undertaking these tasks increases the value, *validity*, and *veracity* of the data analytics performed.

precision, see *accuracy and precision*

prediction   A forecast or inference as to what might happen in the future. Predictions can be based on hunches, or experience and knowledge, or calculated using *inferential statistics* or using *modelling* and input data. Predictive modelling calculates the likelihood of an event occurring under different conditions. For example, a company might want to predict demand for a product in order to ensure it has adequate stock, or a police department might want to predict the location of future crimes in order to appropriately route patrols. Predictive *profiling* is a core task for *data brokers* seeking to identify and target segmented population groups. There are a number of different approaches that can be used to produce predictive models. In general, models are built by drawing on existing knowledge of a system's performance to construct a conceptual map of components and how they interact, with these relationships then translated into a rule and parameter set. The model is then tested and refined. If a prediction is used to direct decision-making and activity this potentially produces *predictive privacy harms* and raises ethical issues related to *data determinism* (treating people on the basis of a prediction). With the use of predictive modelling becoming ever more routine in governance, law and order, and business practices, the *ethics* of anticipatory and presumptive action is a growing concern. See also *inferred data*.

Further reading

Washington, A.L. (2023) *Ethical Data Science: Prediction in the Public Interest*. Oxford University Press, Oxford.

predictive privacy harms   Using inferences to make assumptions about a person and making decisions based on these inferences, which are potentially harmful to the individual. For example, data that reveals a person visits a gay bar might lead to the inference that they are gay, or if they are friends with known criminals that they are also involved in criminal activity (see *inferred data*), yet no data has been directly generated relating to their sexual orientation, and there is no direct evidence of them perpetrating crimes. In both cases, the inferences can cause a potential *predictive privacy harm*; for example, if targeted advertising relating to sexually-related products appears in social media on a computer used by family members, or if a personal profile that flagged suspected criminal activity was shared with a potential employer. Here, *data determinism* is taking place; that is, a person is treated on the basis of a prediction rather than concrete evidence. Many people would characterise such inferred data as *personal data* and sensitive in nature, and which should therefore be subject to *privacy* and *data protection* regulations. However, since the data are inferred rather than directly collected, they are exempt from *notice* and *consent*. Much *profiling*, predictive policing, and the work of *data brokers* uses inferencing, producing a range of predictive privacy harms through *social sorting* (see *geodemographics*, *redlining*).

Further reading

Crawford, K. and Schultz, J. (2014) 'Big data and due process: Toward a framework to redress predictive privacy harms', *Boston College Law Review*, 55(1): 93–128.

preservation   A set of practices and policies for ensuring that data and information are accessible and usable for future generations. Preservation is a formal process involving *data policies* and *data governance* to select, process, and manage material to preserve, along with associated *documentation* and *metadata*, and to plan long-term resourcing and media storage. *Archives* and libraries have long performed preservation for paper documents and other media. In recent years, many of these materials have been subject to *digitisation* to create additional copies and enable wider usage through *data sharing*. Digital data are particularly vulnerable to *data loss* and attention has turned to preserving digital media (e.g., digital documents, digital photos/video, internet webpages, datasets, *databases*, code), especially *born-digital data*.

Further reading

Brown, A. (2013) *Practical Digital Preservation: A How-to Guide for Organizations of Any Size*. Facet Publishing, London.

primary data   Data generated directly by a researcher using a *method* of their choice within a *research design* of their making. Many researchers seek to produce primary data because they have control of the process, with the data generated tailored to their specific aims and needs, whereas *secondary data* and *tertiary data* have to be accepted as they are, since they have been generated by another party for their purpose.

privacy   The right to selectively reveal oneself to the world and to protect *personal data*. Privacy enables people to control what others know about them. It is a basic human right that ensures liberty and dignity, though how it is understood varies across cultures and contexts, as does how it is legislated for through national and supranational laws. Privacy is a multifaceted concept. For example: identity privacy refers to controlling personal and confidential information; bodily privacy to protecting the integrity of the physical person; territorial privacy to protecting personal space and property; locational privacy to limiting the tracking of movement; communications privacy to blocking the surveillance of correspondence and conversations; and transactional privacy to protecting the history of purchases. Mass *datafication, surveillance, dataveillance, exhaust data*, poor *data security, data markets*, and the operations of *data capitalism* and *surveillance capitalism* have meant that all these forms of privacy have been compromised to varying degrees, and the ability of individuals to selectively reveal themselves has weakened. This weakening creates a number of privacy harms, such as surveillance, disclosure, *profiling, social* *sorting*, identity theft, shaming, and blackmail, that can affect a person's social standing, their ability to participate in society, and their emotional and physical well-being.

Protecting privacy in the *big data* age is a significant challenge as traditional laws based on *Fair Information Practice Principles* are ill-equipped to deal with the ways in which data can be shared, *re-used*, and *repurposed* in order to circumvent regulations. In the European Union, regulating privacy harms falls within General Data Protection Regulations (GDPR) that provide universal rights across all personal data. In other jurisdictions, they are tackled through privacy laws that might differ across sectors (i.e., there might be different privacy laws for health, education, and finance). In both *data protection* and privacy laws, the focus is on the rights of individuals and protecting directly captured personal data, rather than on *group privacy*, *derived data* or *inferred data*. The regulations and laws stipulate the obligations of *data controllers and processors* with respect to protecting privacy rights, and how breaches of defined practices are dealt with. See also *choice*, *consent*, *data minimisation principle*, *data rights*, *notice*, *privacy by design*.

Further reading

Cofone, I. (2024) *The Privacy Fallacy: Harm and Power in the Information Economy*. Cambridge University Press, Cambridge.

Hoepman, J-P. (2021) *Privacy is Hard and Seven Other Myths: Achieving Privacy Through Careful Design*. MIT Press, Cambridge, MA.

privacy by design An approach that promotes *privacy* as a default setting for systems that produce and process data. At present, many digital technologies and apps have the open sharing of data with the vendor as the default setting and users have to access the settings and request to keep their data private. In privacy by design, privacy is automatically protected and the user chooses whether to share data. Privacy is by design in the sense that it is built into the system architecture, rather than being added later and being reliant on regulatory enforcement. The approach was conceived by Ann Cavoukian and is actively promoted by many national *information commissioner* and *data protection* agencies.

Further reading

Cavoukian, A. (2009) *Privacy by Design: A Primer*, www.dataguidance
.com/sites/default/files/pbd-primer_1.pdf

pro-equity data initiatives   Activities that seek to benefit marginalised communities by providing digital infrastructures and producing data that can aid community members and leverage local services. The term was first introduced by Heeks and Shekhar (2019) to refer to data initiatives relating to informal settlements in India that seek to counter a legacy of 'datalessness' and to provide new data flows and *data rights* for residents. Informal settlements lie at the bottom of the *data pyramid*, are often *uncounted*, and lack access to *data services* and other services that evidence might reveal the need for and help leverage. A pro-equity data initiative aims to empower the residents of informal settlements by enabling access to data-driven systems and information, and by producing data about their communities; for example, installing community Wi-Fi or undertaking community *surveys* or *mapping*. While some benefits to informal settlements are gained by countering the injustice of invisibility, it is often external actors who benefit more through enhanced *knowledge* and ability to manage and exploit the area and its residents. Caution then is necessary when implementing such *data activism* in order to ensure *data justice* prevails. See also *counter-data action*.

Further reading

Heeks, R. and Shekhar, S. (2019) 'Datafication, development and marginalised urban communities: An applied data justice framework', *Information, Communication & Society*, 22(7): 992–1011.

profiling   Creating a description of an individual, group or area based on a selection of related data. The aim is to build a picture of target *data subjects* in order to then make an assessment in relation to them. This is undertaken by assembling and combining relevant data, then using an algorithmic formula to determine what treatment the target might receive. For example, in the case of a person, demographic, social, and economic data, along with customer history data (e.g., purchases, payments), might be assembled, with the profile then used to assess their potential worth to a retail chain, which then directs the rewards (e.g., the size of discount and for what products) that they will receive. In many cases, rather than direct, personalised profiling, individuals are assigned to a category that groups together people with a similar profile, with all those in a category treated in the same way. Consumer profiling has been used by *data brokers* since the mid-twentieth century as a means of segmenting markets to target advertising. In the *big data* age, this consumer profiling has expanded enormously and now underpins the operations of *surveillance capitalism*. Algorithmic profiling has also extended to public service provision and bureaucracy, being used to judge entitlement to government benefits and programmes, identify fraud, and conduct security checks.

Since profiling is used to perform *social sorting* it can have a profound effect on the lives of individuals (directly, as a member of a community, or as a resident of an area), affecting whether they receive finance, work, housing, safe passage, or government benefits, as well as their social status. In some cases, this can be highly exploitative; for example, profiling vulnerable individuals who might access financial schemes with abusive terms such as balloon payments, hidden fees, and high penalty clauses. Profiles always involve some level of inference (see *inferred data*), but this is extended with predictive profiling that seeks to anticipate how the future will unfold, including how individuals might act. In these cases, targets are treated based on a prediction, raising the issues of *data determinism* and *predictive privacy harms*. Another issue with profiling is that targets can be easily typecast, which might also follow institutionalised patterns of discrimination; for example, performing *racial* profiling and *redlining*. See also *geo-demographics*, *social credit scoring*.

Further reading

Cheney-Lippold, J. (2017) *We Are Data: Algorithms and the Making of Our Digital Selves*. New York University Press, New York.

Eubanks, V. (2017) *Automating Inequality: How High-Tech Tools Profile, Police, and Punish The Poor*. St Martin's Press, New York.

proprietary data Data that are the property of a company or organisation. These data are not accessible for use without permission. This means that the value of the data is restricted to those who own them. In some cases, the data might be made available under *licence* to selected researchers; for example, data owned by social media platforms or mobile phone companies. The issue for research based on such data is that, while the findings are public, the data are not, meaning that the analysis and interpretation cannot be *validated*. This raises questions of trust and integrity in research. It also raises moral questions about the *data hugging* of datasets that might be used in the public interest. At the same time, there might be good reasons for proprietary data not to become public, *open data*, such as *data protection*, *privacy*, and commercial sensitivity. See also *data philanthropy*, *data humanitarianism*.

Further reading

Callan, J. and Moffat, A. (2012) 'Panel on use of proprietary data', *ACM SIGIR Forum* 46(2): 10–18.

proprietary data format, see *data format*

protocol   A set of rules and guidelines as to how a task should be performed. With respect to data, protocol is often used to refer to the rule set for successfully communicating data between computers. For example, regarding the transfer of data across the internet, a number of protocols are used, such as TCP/IP (Transmission Control Protocol/Internet Protocol), HTTP (HyperText Transmission Protocol), and SMTP (Simple Mail Transfer Protocol). More broadly, a protocol can be formulated to *standardise* any means of processing data and might be instigated by any organisation seeking to ensure common *data management*, good *data quality*, and strong *interoperability*. Protocols enable a distributed network to function, but that does not necessarily mean a decentring of power, since control of the network (or *platform*, or *data infrastructure*, or data management or other formalised, standardised process) lies with those who control the protocols. In other words, protocols enable *data power*.

Further reading

Galloway, A.R. (2006) *Protocol: How Control Exists after Decentralization.* MIT Press, Cambridge, MA.

provenance   Information on the origins of data, and the individuals, organisations, and activities involved in producing a dataset. Provenance is important for assessing the degree to which a dataset provider might be employing robust procedures and *data management* principles and ensuring high levels of *data quality*. A dataset from a *national statistics organisation*, which has to meet international standards of data production, has a provenance that engenders trust, whereas a dataset produced by an individual not associated with any organisation, or through citizen *crowdsourcing*, might be seen as less trustworthy as there is less oversight and *accountability* in data production.

proxy data   Data relating to one phenomenon that are used to try to understand another. For example, using spend on research and development (R&D), or the number of patents registered, as a proxy measure for innovation. In this case, there is no direct measure for innovation, so it can only be measured via a proxy. An issue with using proxy data then is that it is an indirect, inferred measure that might reveal one aspect of a phenomenon but provides a limited picture. One solution is to combine a number of proxy measures together to create a *composite index*; for example, combining income, social, health, and education *indicator data* to provide a measure of social deprivation.

Further reading

Mulvin, D. (2021) *Proxies: The Cultural Work of Standing In.* MIT Press, Cambridge, MA.

pseudonym   A fictitious name or a code used to represent an individual and protect their real identity by rendering them anonymous. For example, replacing the real names of individuals in interview transcripts with fictitious names, or in a database with random codes. While a pseudonym renders an individual anonymous for third party users of a dataset, this is often not the case for the dataset owner, with pseudonymous IDs linked to real identities. Even if the dataset owner does not know the real ID, the pseudonymous code is usually unique and persistent, which means it acts as *indexical data* and can be tracked through time and space enabling a detailed profile of each individual to be built and decisions to be made based on that profile. In other words, an individual can be treated as a known persona without knowing their actual identity, rendering *anonymisation* mute.

Pseudonymisation as a means of anonymisation has also been critiqued because individuals can potentially be reidentified by combining datasets together, looking for data and profiles that match across datasets. There have been several reported cases where publicly released pseudonymised data were reidentified.

Further reading

Barocas, S. and Nissenbaum, H. (2014) 'Big data's end run around anonymity and consent', in Lane, J., Stodden, V., Bender, S., and Nissenbaum, H. (eds), *Privacy, Big Data and the Public Good*. Cambridge University Press, Cambridge, pp. 44–75.

public sector data   Data that are produced by public sector bodies. Such data can include *administrative data*, operational data used in running public services, *indicator data* used to monitor how public bodies and their programmes and policies are performing, and *official statistics*. Some of these data are *big data* and *real-time data*. A selection of these data are published as *open data*, either through individual webpages or a dedicated open data site.

Q

qualitative analysis   The preparation and analysis of qualitative data. Qualitative analysis traditionally has involved undertaking a 'close reading' of a dataset. Here, *sampling* is typically quite small and the researcher will work with these materials intensively to draw out meaning and insight. Generally, a range of different text-based (e.g., content and discourse analysis) and visual methods (e.g., compositional interpretation, iconography, semiotic analysis) are employed depending on the nature of the data. Often there is some preparation work to be undertaken, which itself forms part of the analysis; for example, coding text into a set of categories. This is an *inductive* and iterative process, the coding structure evolving as material is coded. A 'distant reading' approach is becoming more common through the development of the *digital humanities*. This approach uses *data analytics*, particularly *data mining*, to examine very large corpuses of data; perhaps millions of records or images rather than a close reading of a small sample. There is an active debate as to the merits of this approach. On the one hand, it widens the sample and allows for patterns and generalities to be observed, but on the other *algorithms* are generally poor at establishing meaning.

Further reading

Drucker, J. (2021) *The Digital Humanities Coursebook: An Introduction to Digital Methods for Research and Scholarship.* Taylor and Francis, London.

Flick, U. (ed.) (2013) *The SAGE Handbook of Qualitative Data Analysis.* Sage, London.

qualitative data   Qualitative data are non-numeric in form, such as text, images, sound, and audio-visual media, and are unstructured in nature. Generated as *primary data*, qualitative data include *interview* and *focus group* transcripts, *data ethnography* fieldnotes and photographs, and images drawn by respondents. *Secondary data* include documents, art and other images, music, radio, television and movies, and social media posts. Much social sciences and humanities research, including *Critical Data Studies*, generates and analyses qualitative data. While qualitative data can be converted into *quantitative data* and be subjected to *quantitative analysis*, given the significant abstraction this involves, much of the context, richness, and value of the original data is lost by such a process. See also *qualitative analysis*.

quality, see *data quality*

quantified self   The activity of self-monitoring and the knowledge formed through analysis of the generated data. Wearable and personal digital devices, such as smart watches, fitness trackers, and smartphones, enable their users to automatically generate *real-time data* about their activities (e.g., distance run, speed, heart rate). A range of apps aid the tracking and monitoring of these data through the use of *dashboards* and *visual analytics*. Individuals can then come to understand themselves through self-monitoring their own data, which they can use to improve their performance in relation to a specific aspect of their lives (e.g., health, work, sporting activity). For some, this interest in self-tracking has led to the formation of a quantified self community in which members share and discuss data, provide advice, and encourage each other's endeavours. See also *sousveillance*.

Further reading

Lupton, D. (2016) *The Quantified Self*. Polity Press, Cambridge.
Fors, V., Pink, S. Berg, M., and O'Dell, T. (2020) *Imagining Personal Data: Experiences of Self-Tracking*. Routledge, London.

quantitative analysis   The analysis of quantitative data. A number of different *methods* can be used to analyse *quantitative data* depending on the form of the data, the purpose of the analysis, and *epistemology* employed. Quantitative data have traditionally been analysed using the *scientific method*, usually underpinned by the tenets of *positivism*, though not exclusively so (e.g., empiricism, critical realism). Traditionally, quantitative data was analysed using *descriptive statistics, inferential statistics, modelling, data visualisation*, and *mapping*. This is still the case, but these are now undertaken computationally using *data analytics*, which can process *big data*. This has led to the development of a *computational social science* approach, with some epistemological variations (e.g., *critical GIS, feminist data science*).

Further reading

Krieg, E.J. (2019) *Statistics and Data Analysis for Social Science*. Second edition. Sage, London.
McLeavy, J. (2021) *Doing Computational Social Science: A Practical Introduction*. Sage, London.

quantitative data   Quantitative data are captured and recorded as numeric records. Generated as *primary data*, quantitative data are extensive and relate to the physical properties of phenomena (e.g., age, length, weight, height, area, volume), or are representative and relate to non-physical characteristics of phenomena (such as marriage status, social class, educational attainment). Derived quantitative data might be percentages, or statistical or model outputs (see *derived data*). Quantitative data consist of four types, which delimit how they should be processed and analysed: *nominal data, ordinal data, interval data*, and *ratio data*. Scientific research is predominately undertaken using quantitative data employing various forms of *statistics, visualisation*, and *modelling* (see *quantitative analysis*). Social science research also makes extensive use of quantitative data, especially those generated through *questionnaires* and *surveys* (e.g., *census*) and administrative processes. *Critical Data Studies*, with its interest in the social production of knowledge and issues such as *data politics*, *data power*, and *data justice*, typically uses *qualitative data* generated through *interviews*, *focus groups* or *data ethnographies*, or sourced from documents and other media (e.g., television, radio, film, social media). That is not to say that *Critical Data Studies* does not generate or use quantitative data in conducting analysis, but it does so employing an *epistemology* that is mindful of the shortcomings of quantitative approaches (see *critical GIS*, *feminist data science*, *radical statistics*).

queer data   1. Data that relates to members of the LGBTQ (lesbian, gay, bisexual, trans, queer) community. 2. The queering of data, questioning the essentialist foundations of social categories. These two aspects of queer data are interlinked through the question as to who belongs to the LGBTQ community, which is not a well-bounded category given it involves the intersection of gender, sex, and sexuality and elements of self-identification and performativity. Sex as a category, for example, can include biological characteristics (e.g., genitalia, reproductive functions, chromosomes, hormones), legal status (e.g., what is stated on a birth certificate), and lived identity (e.g., how a person self-identifies and presents themselves to others). Queer data then disrupts binaries such as male/female, heterosexual/homosexual, and cis/trans, and in so doing illustrates how all social categorisations are constructed, how they are queered and always somewhat fluid (as per queer theory). It also illustrates the epistemic violence enacted on the LGBTQ community through social *surveys*, such as a *census*, when the categories presented flatten out diversity and do not match self-identification, thus designing-out certain lives while at the same time reaffirming the heteronormative status quo. This presents LGBTQ people with a dilemma: to remain *uncounted* (which traditionally has been the case) or to be counted, though in ways that may be inaccurate. Queer *data activism* seeks to address these issues, as well as opposing the weaponising of queer data by those who spread misinformation and seek to delegitimise queer lives.

Further reading

Guyan, K. (2022) *Queer Data: Using Gender, Sex and Sexuality Data for Action*. Bloomsbury, London.

Ruberg, B. and Ruelos, S. (2020) 'Data for queer lives: How LGBTQ gender and sexuality identities challenge norms of demographics', *Big Data & Society*, 7(1): 1–12.

questionnaire   A method in which a pre-defined set of standardised questions are presented in a specific order. Questionnaires generally consist of closed questions (where there is a set choice of answers) seeking factual information (see *facts*), though there may be some open questions to enable respondents to elaborate in certain cases. Questions typically consist of selecting from categories or rating or ranking items on scales. A questionnaire might be used in a *survey*, for example as part of a *census*. A questionnaire is not a common method within *Critical Data Studies*, which is typically more interested in meaning and uses *qualitative methods*, but it might be used to sample a much larger constituency than is usually the case for a method such as *interviews*.

R

race and racist data   Data about race, and data that encodes racial biases or can be used to discriminate on the basis of race. There has long been data generated with respect to race, with people being classified into racial groupings based on skin colour, facial and bodily characteristics, parental lineage, and *ethnicity*. Although race has often been conceptualised in essentialist terms as biologically given, racial classifications have never been fully stable and may shift in their formulation, revealing the constructed nature of race. For example, the racial categories used on *censuses* have changed over time, in part in relation to prevalent racial discourses, but also as a reaction to how respondents contest the categories offered. Race data have been used extensively to perform racist discrimination through *profiling*, *social sorting*, and *redlining*. This is being perpetuated in the *big data* era through the embedding of institutionalised racism in *training* *data*, with previous generations of racist data being used to train *automated* systems, leading to racial *biases* in predictive policing and court sentencing systems, as well as in the digitally mediated provision of welfare services. The *civic hacking* initiative Data for Black Lives undertakes *counter-data actions*, seeking to enact *data justice* and to reclaim, recast, and own the notion of black data.

Further reading

Browne, S. (2015) *Dark Matters: On the Surveillance of Blackness*. Duke University Press, Durham, NC.

Hochschild, J.L. and Powell, B.M. (2008) 'Racial reorganization and the United States Census 1850–1930: Mulattoes, half-breeds, mixed parentage, Hindoos, and the Mexican race', *Studies in American Political Development*, 22(1): 59–96.

McGlotten, S. (2016) 'Black data', in Johnson, P.E. (ed.), *No Tea, No Shade: New Writings in Black Queer Studies*. Duke University Press, Durham, NC, pp. 262–86.

radical statistics   The use of statistical methods for tackling social issues. Rather than statistics serving the interests of states and corporations, radical statistics seeks to challenge hegemonic power by advocating for social responsibility in science and the use of statistics to address community needs and deliver social justice. Part of its mandate is to demystify statistics and make its assumptions, language, and findings transparent. It also aims to tackle the institutional power within statistical organisations, such as *national statistics organisations*. While radical statistics adheres *epistemologically* to the *scientific method*, it does so while practising *reflexivity* with respect to the politics of its praxis. See also *feminist data science, critical GIS*.

Further reading

Evans, J., Ruane, S., and Southall, H. (eds) (2019) *Data in Society: Challenging Statistics in an Age of Globalisation*. Policy Press, Bristol.

ratio data   *Quantitative data* ordered along a scale that has fixed intervals, an absolute zero, and where ratios hold true. Many weights and measures (e.g., mass, area, length) are ratio scales, where the difference between measures is a relative ratio (unlike *interval data*). For example, ten minutes is twice as long as five minutes, six kilograms is three times heavier than two kilograms. Ratio data can be analysed using *descriptive statistics, visualisations,* and *parametric statistics.* See also *nominal data, ordinal data.*

raw data   Directly captured *primary data* that has not yet undergone any post-capture processing. The signifier of raw denotes that the data are in their essential state and free from any *data transformations.* For some, it also signifies that the data are *objective,* neutral, and value-free in nature. However, *Critical Data Studies* holds that data are never raw, but are always cooked to some degree, shaped by the assumptions and techniques used to produce them (see *cooked data*).

Further reading
Gitelman, L. (ed.) (2013) *'Raw Data' is an Oxymoron.* MIT Press, Cambridge, MA.

real-time data   Data that are generated, shared, and acted on in the same moment or with little latency in duration. Such data are often generated continuously and thus have high *velocity.* For example, in the case of traffic management, *sensor data* in the form of inductive loop readings are captured continuously and communicated back to a control room where they are immediately analysed and acted upon to alter traffic light phasing. Real-time data enable systems to be monitored and to act in the here and now, reacting to present conditions. On social media platforms, the recording and processing of real-time data enables synchronous conversations to be undertaken. Real-time data also enable now-casting (near to the present time forecasting) to be undertaken (e.g., weather forecasting, stock market movements). In practice, real-time data are never quite immediate as there is always a small latency in capture, transmission, and processing. Even in continuous monitoring systems, there is always a small gap between data points; depending on the system this can vary from microseconds to a few minutes. In non-continuous systems, data are generated only at the point of use (e.g., clickstream data that is measured in real-time but only when a user clicks on a link to a new website). As such, there are varying forms of 'realtimeness', and thus of real-time data. See also *temporalities of data.*

Further reading

Kitchin, R. (2023) *Digital Timescapes: Technology, Temporality and Society*. Polity Press, Cambridge.

Weltevrede, E., Helmond, A.A., and Gerlitz, C. (2014) 'The politics of real-time: A device perspective on social media and search engines', *Theory, Culture and Society*, 31(6): 125–50.

redlining   A spatialised form of *social sorting* that discriminates against people living in certain areas and excludes them from goods and services. The aim of redlining is to reduce investment risk by denying services to those most likely to default or be less profitable. It therefore typically seeks to identify areas that are poor and avoid serving those living there. These areas often have high proportions of racial and ethnic minorities (see *ethnic data, race and racial data*). Typically, redlining is used to deny credit and insurance, but it can also affect decisions as to whether to upgrade infrastructure (e.g. internet provision) or whether to locate or close shops and services in an area. Beyond the effects on individuals, redlining further impoverishes an area and extends spatial divides between communities. While the practice is illegal, in that each person is meant to be judged as a potential customer on their own merits and not on where they live, it is still commonly undertaken by *data brokers* and other companies. See also *demographically identifiable information, geodemographics*.

Further reading

Aalbers, M. (2020) 'Redlining', in Kobayashi, A. (ed.), *International Encyclopedia of Human Geography*. Second edition. Elsevier, Oxford, pp. 213–19.

reflexivity   An act of self-reflection in order to become self-aware of one's *positionality* with respect to a study. Reflexivity involves critical introspection and scrutiny of the *epistemological* assumptions, *methodological* approach, ethical considerations (see *data ethics*), and the choices and decisions made while undertaking research, and considering their potential implications for the conclusions drawn and the populations the findings might affect.

regime, see *calculative regime, data regime, discursive regime*

regulation, see *data regulation*

relationality The degree to which data can be linked together across datasets. Datasets are highly relational when they can be conjoined to many other pieces of data, enabling complex queries and analyses to be undertaken. Datasets can be linked together through the use of *indexical data* and shared fundamental fields (such as *statistical geographies*). In contrast, it is difficult or impossible to usefully link weakly relational data to other data. Relationality is considered by some to be a core attribute of *big data* as fine *granularity* and the strong use of indexicality is a central feature of big data systems. See also *stranded data*.

reliability Consistency in the performance of a measuring instrument or *method* and the *repeatability, reproducibility, and replicability* of findings. Strong reliability indicates that a method is stable and that a study has a high degree of precision in its operation and outcomes (see *accuracy and precision*). Quixotic reliability concerns whether a single method of observation continually yields an unvarying measurement; diachronic reliability, the stability of an observation through time; and synchronic reliability, the similarity of observations within the same time period. Other forms of reliability include inter-method reliability, which refers to the consistency of results and findings when different methods are used to investigate the same phenomenon; and inter-personal reliability, referring to the extent to which different assessors or researchers agree in their measurements and findings (e.g., they score performance identically). It is generally accepted that the more reliable a study is, the more confidence one can have in its findings and conclusions, though validity is not ensured (a measure might be reliable but invalid).

repair, see *data maintenance and repair*

repeatability, reproducibility, and replicability Measures of precision that determine the *reliability* and *validity* of outcomes from a measurement or analysis process (see *accuracy and precision*). The three measures vary in the conditions used to establish precision and the robustness of an outcome. Repeatability is the degree of variability in an outcome when a process is repeated by the same operator using the same equipment under the same conditions. Reproducibility is whether the same level of precision in an outcome is achieved when the process is repeated by a different operator using the same techniques, equipment, and conditions. Replicability is whether the same result can be achieved by a different operator using a different setup; that is, the same outcome is produced completely independently. A consistently repeatable outcome indicates a reliable, precise process; reproducibility provides independent confirmation of repeatability; and replicability indicates a universal outcome or finding (a scientific law). These measures are foundational to the *scientific method* and important for ensuring trust in the processes used to generate and analyse data and provide reassurance with respect to *data quality* and *data integrity*. Over the past decade, a significant replicability crisis has emerged in science, undermining confidence in supposedly landmark studies.

Further reading

Andreoletti, M. (2021) 'Replicability crisis and scientific reforms: Overlooked issues and unmet challenges', *International Studies in the Philosophy of Science*, 33(3): 135–51.

Friedland, G. (2024) *Information-Driven Machine Learning: Data Science as an Engineering Discipline*. Chapter 15. Springer, Cham, Switzerland.

replicability, see *repeatability, reproducibility, and replicability*

repository, see *data repository*

representativeness   The extent to which data are representative of a population. Data are *sampled*. Even big data sets do not capture whole populations. For example, not everybody shops in a certain supermarket chain or uses a social media platform, and those not participating are not evenly spread across social groups. The extent to which findings from studies using *social media data* are representative of the wider population are then questionable. There are similar concerns relating to whether findings derived from a small group of people are representative of a larger group. Issues of poor representativeness can create *ecological fallacies*.

reproducibility, see *repeatability, reproducibility, and replicability*

repurposing   The *re-use* of data for a purpose other than was originally intended. For example, the repurposing of *big data* for producing new or replacement *official statistics*. One of the initial key arguments for promoting big data was that they had large potential to generate additional value by being used to cast light on and tackle other issues. This was particularly stated with respect to *exhaust data*, which is often a byproduct of a process and might have limited initial use. The main issue with such repurposing arises if *personal data* are involved as this breaks the *data minimisation* principle of the *Fair Information Practice Principles*. Data minimisation is a core element of *data protection* in the European Union, with repurposing requiring consent from *data subjects*. It is widely acknowledged that this principle is being worked around by *data brokers* and others through the repurposing of *derived data* and *inferred data*, rather than the original captured data. Such workaround practices enable *surveillance capitalism* and raise *data ethics* concerns. These concerns are not easily addressed through formalised re-use strategies because of the various entanglements in which they are enmeshed.

Further reading

Custers, B. and Uršič, H. (2016) 'Big data and data reuse: A taxonomy of data reuse for balancing big data benefits and personal data protection', *International Data Privacy Law* 6(1): 4–15.

Thylstrup, N. B., Hansen, K. B., Flyverbom, M., and Amoore, L. (2022) 'Politics of data reuse in machine learning systems: Theorizing reuse entanglements', *Big Data & Society*, 9(2): 1–10.

research-creation   A methodological approach that uses *arts-based methods* throughout the entire research process. Creative practices and media are used as a means to generate, analyse, and interpret data about a phenomenon (often alongside traditional social science and humanities methods) and to communicate findings and conclusions to others. The aim is to use the affordances of the arts to examine and reflect on a phenomenon through a different type of sense-making, one that is more reflexive, inventive, lively, and speculative. Producing fiction, arts, crafts, performance or media installations allows alternative questions to be asked and explored in novel ways that provide fresh insights. The approach can be practised individually or collectively. In the latter case, an artist or creative writer works collaboratively with a scholar or with a community to co-create knowledge about an issue. This collaboration might also be action-orientated, seeking to intervene through counter-narratives and dialogue to change how key actors think and act.

Research-creation has been used a number of times in *Critical Data Studies* research. This includes projects that have used creative fiction (improvisational writing, short stories, sonnets, word-play techniques) to explore issues such as smart city data, and zine's (magazine style booklets) to reflect on personal data. Other projects have created data artworks and *data physicalisations* through art practices (e.g., sculpture, weaving), with the resultant art seeking to create *visceral data*. Research-creation has been critiqued as an approach for lacking rigour, *objectivity*, and *reproducibility*, and for being overtly political in intent. However, the approach is not seeking to produce universal truths, but rather reflective insights into particular issues and phenomena that might spark action and change.

Further reading

Lupton, D. and Watson, A. (2021) 'Towards more-than-human digital data studies: Developing research-creation methods', *Qualitative Research*, 21(4): 463–80.

research design   The plan for how research objectives, *research questions*, and *hypotheses* will be operationalised and how an empirical research project will proceed. A research design includes making decisions about sources of data, *sampling* framework, and *methods* for data generation and analysis, and considering *research ethics*. These aspects of research design need to be cognisant of the philosophical framing and theoretical context of the study (see *epistemology*, *methodology*, *induction*, *deduction*). In addition, research design needs to include operational planning, such as formulating a *data management plan* and a project management plan. These need to consider practical constraints, such as available resourcing, costs, access to equipment, case and field sites, and time availability. A *pilot study* might be undertaken to test the feasibility and to refine a research design.

Further reading

Cresswell, J.W. and Cresswell, J.D. (2018) *Research Design: Qualitative, Quantitative, and Mixed Methods Approaches*. Fifth edition. Sage: London.

research ethics   Consideration of, and compliance with, moral principles, societal expectations, and legal requirements when conducting research. Research ethics seeks to ensure that research is *transparent*, fair, and does no harm to participants, *data subjects*, communities or the researchers themselves, and that there is no malpractice, such as theft or fabrication of data and analysis. Research ethics is a fundamental consideration in *research design* and involves careful assessment of the potential risks and benefits to participants and data subjects of each element of the study and of the ways in which the risks might be avoided or mitigated. In the context of university research, research ethics are usually overseen by *institutional review boards*, who are responsible for approving ethics plans. Failure to design a study that meets ethical standards can result in reputational damage and legal action.

Research ethics is underpinned by four general principles: the right to choose whether to participate; equal treatment of participants, with no group denied access to, or the benefits from, research; all risks and harms are minimised; and compliance and *accountability* with law and regulations. In addition to not harming communities, research ethics seeks to maintain public trust in research. As a rule, research ethics seeks to avoid practices such as involving people in research without their knowledge or consent, exposing them to physical or mental stress or unfair treatment, failing to protect their confidentiality or anonymity, and producing research that might negatively impact on an individual or community. With respect to data considerations, there are particular ethical aspects to consider with respect to producing *primary data* – such as covert participation, lurking, *crowdsourcing*, working with commercial or state partners, and *data sharing* – and the use of *secondary data*, such as *consent* and *data minimisation*, *privacy* and confidentiality, and the use of *data scraping*, hacked data and historical data.

Further reading

Ash, J., Kitchin, R., and Leszczynski, A. (2024) *Researching Digital Life: Orientations, Methods and Practice*. Chapter 4. Sage, London.

Markham, A.N. and Buchanan, E. (2015) 'Ethical considerations in digital research contexts', in Wright, J.D. (ed.), *Encyclopedia for Social & Behavioral Sciences*. Elsevier, Waltham, MA, pp. 606–13.

research questions   The specific questions that a research project seeks to answer. Research questions are designed to enable research objectives to be met by providing a clear operational focus for a project. Through their formulation, they provide a means of theory testing and making. In the case of *deductive* research, research questions are posed as *hypotheses*. Good research questions are clear and unambiguous. In projects that have multiple questions, these should be logically linked so that the answers to each scaffold to produce greater insight. Research questions shape the production of *primary data*. In projects using *secondary data*, research questions influence *data management* and how data are handled and processed to make them amenable to forms of analysis that answer the questions. Research questions are answered using research *methods* framed within an *epistemology* and *methodological* approach.

resolution, see *granularity*

re-use   Data are re-used to repeat a study in order to validate it, or to undertake additional analysis of the same issue or related questions, or to extract additional value from the data. Through calls for *open data* and the avoidance of *data hugging*, there is increasing pressure to make data available for re-use so that the full value of the data can be realised. In addition, data might be *repurposed* for an alternative re-use, though there may be *data protection* and *privacy* issues involved if the dataset includes *personal data*.

rights, see *copyright, data rights, digital rights management, intellectual property rights*

right to be forgotten   A legal concept that provides individuals the right to have *personally identifiable information* removed from internet searches in particular cases. The aim is to allow people to request that certain information about them be made less discoverable if it is causing unfair reputational damage or stigma (such as an accusation that is proven to be false, or links to revenge porn). This does not include removing the offending material, such as a newspaper story, but only pointers to it; it is therefore not a right to *privacy*. There has to be a legitimate reason for the material to be made less discoverable and the right is only granted through a formal process. The right is not universally recognised across jurisdictions and it has only been implemented in varying forms in the European Union and a handful of other countries. See also *forgetting*.

Further reading

Jones, M.L. (2016). *Ctrl + Z: The Right to Be Forgotten*. New York University Press, New York.

right to information A right to know how public bodies operate and how they make key decisions. The right to information is a legal right in many jurisdictions, entitling members of the public to request key documents held by public bodies at minimal charge, barring exceptions such as *personal data*, and confidential and commercially sensitive details (also known as *freedom of information* laws). This right includes being able to access key evidence used in decision-making, including being able to request *databases*.

S

sampling The process of selecting what data to generate or use from the total potential sources of data. For example, it might not be possible to canvas every person in a city, so instead a *survey* is administered to a sample of them. The means of selecting this smaller sample depends on the phenomenon being sampled and the purpose of the data production. In studies using *quantitative data* and *statistics*, the aim is usually to adopt a sampling method that will produce data that are free of *bias* and are representative of the larger source population (see *representativeness*). A representative sample is produced by using a probabilistic sampling method. Probability sampling methods include random sampling (elements selected randomly) and stratified random sampling (population is stratified into groups, with random selection within groups). A non-probabilistic sampling method is used when it is difficult to access populations or because the research is purposeful in orientation, seeking to focus on a specific rather than a representative sample. Non-probabilistic sampling frameworks include quota (e.g., the first fifty encountered), systematic (e.g., every tenth case), purposeful (selected because they have particular characteristics), convenience (selected based on ease and availability), and referral (members of the initial selected sample suggest others to be included). The generation of *qualitative data* is usually undertaken using a non-probabilistic purposeful or referral sampling strategy. In qualitative research, the sample size might be quite small. Typically, the aim is to reach a saturation point wherein no new information is being gained from the addition of new sampled data. While *big data* would claim to possess *exhaustivity*, they are nonetheless a sample and not fully representative of a population (e.g., not everyone uses a platform or system).

Further reading

Bryman, A. and Bell, E. (2019) *Social Research Methods*. Fifth edition. Oxford University Press, Oxford.

scaffolding   The choices, decisions, and material resources that are assembled together into a framework so that a process can take place. For example, building a *data infrastructure* involves creating a scaffold of data, technologies, finance, governance, and personal and institutional relationships that provides a framework that supports its construction. A suite of training courses, or on-the-job training, is a scaffold to support the development of new skills and capacities that improve ongoing operations. Scaffolding helps strengthen *articulation* work by providing a more robust framework to support its realisation. Ideally, once a framework is in place, the scaffold can be removed, although in cases where it is not well embedded its removal can make data work falter.

Further reading

Halfmann, G. (2020) 'Material origins of a data journey in Ocean Science: How sampling and scaffolding shape data practices', in Leonelli, S. and Tempini, N. (eds), *Data Journeys in the Sciences*. Springer Open, Cham, Switzerland, pp. 27–44.

scale 1. The ratio of a data measurement to the corresponding real-world phenomena, or 2. an ordered categorisation by size. With respect to *spatial data*, in the first case, scale refers to the ratio of the distance on a map corresponding to geographic distance; in the second case, scale refers to an ordering of geographic units such as street, neighbourhood, district, city, region, and nation. The scaling of data can have a significant impact on what the data reveal, and therefore how they are interpreted, because of *generalisation* effects wherein variance in the data is masked. For example, a *mapping* of *census* data at neighbourhood and district scale may produce quite different patterns (known as the modifiable areal unit problem, a form of *ecological fallacy*, which can be used to perform gerrymandering). The same effects have been shown with respect to the scaling of temporality (e.g., plotting data by second, minute, hour, day, month, quarter, annually), and other forms of *ratio data*.

Further reading

Manley, D. (2021) 'Scale, aggregation, and the modifiable areal unit problem', in Fischer, M.M. and Nijkamp, P. (eds), *Handbook of Regional Science*. Springer, Heidelberg, pp. 1711–25.

Stehle, S. (2022) 'Temporal aggregation bias and gerrymandering urban time series', *GeoInformatica* 26(1): 233–52.

scalability The extent to which a system can cope with varying data flows and changing *data models*. *Big data* systems, such as social media platforms or online purchasing sites, need to be able to cope with surges in interactions, capturing all data and maintaining operations. Some of them also need to be able to accommodate changing data models as the requirements and functionality of these systems are altered. This has been facilitated by NoSQL database solutions and distributed *cloud* storage. Scalability is seen by some as a core attribute of big data.

scientific method A methodological approach that is the predominant means of conducting research in the natural sciences, but has also been widely adopted in the social sciences. The scientific method assumes that research should progress by testing the *veracity* of theories through the *objective* measurement of directly discernible observations (empirically observed by human senses or a scientific instrument) and rigorous, impartial analysis (e.g., the use of *statistics*) that does not involve human judgement. In this sense, it is *positivistic* in orientation. If performed correctly, then the findings should exhibit *repeatability, reproducibility, and replicability*. The methodology uses a *deductive* approach in which a *hypothesis* is formulated based on existing knowledge, which is then tested to determine if it is true. If the hypothesis is proven, then the insight is used to adjust established theory, which in turn provides the basis for new hypotheses, with research progressing through a continual loop of hypothesis, experiment, analysis, findings, revision of knowledge, and new hypothesis. In the case of the scientific method applied to social issues, it similarly adopts an objective, impartial approach and a focus on measurable phenomena, rejecting an analysis of normative (ethical and political) questions. With respect to opinions and values, the scientific method seeks to capture these as *quantitative data*, using methods such as *surveys, questionnaires,* and psychology and behavioural experiments, and to analyse the resultant data statistically. Any *qualitative data* are converted into quantitative data or are analysed using *data analytics*. A variation on the scientific method in the age of *big data* is *data-driven science*, in which hypotheses might be guided by the data rather than theory. The scientific method has been widely rejected by many in the social sciences and humanities, with detractors using qualitative and other post-positivist methodologies. See also *computational social sciences, critical GIS, feminist data science*.

Further reading
Staddon, J. (2018) *Scientific Method: How Science Works, Fails to Work, and Pretends to Work*. Routledge, London.

scrubbing, see *data cleaning*

seamlessness and seamfulness The points of contact between component parts of a data system (or *data infrastructure* or *data assemblage*), which can be designed to be more or less visible to the person interacting with the system. These seams between elements enable the free movement of data rather than creating *data frictions*. Seamless design seeks to provide a clean, well-functioning system, where complexity and technical operations are non-intrusive, hidden from the user. Seamful design instead foregrounds the seams to reveal how the system's components have been patchworked together. This affords the user a form of *methodological transparency* that aids interpretation. It also enables the user to make choices about how the seams work, prompting reflection on how they might be reconfigured. Movement of data across seams is facilitated by *metadata* and *data standards* that enable *interoperability*.

Further reading

Inman, S. and Ribes, D. (2018) 'Data streams, data seams: Toward a seamful representation of data interoperability'. Paper presented at Design Research Society, University of Limerick, 25–28 September, https://dl.designresearchsociety.org/drs-conference-papers/drs2018 /researchpapers/16

Vertesi, J. (2014) 'Seamful spaces: Heterogeneous infrastructures in interaction', *Science, Technology, & Human Values*, 39(2): 264–84.

secondary data   Data that are not generated by a researcher but are sourced from elsewhere, such as a data repository (e.g., an *open data* site). Secondary data are often published as *tertiary data* in order to protect confidentiality. See also *derived data, primary data*.

security, see *data security*

semantic web   A means by which the internet is transformed from a web of documents into a web of data through encoding with semantic tagging to render the content as *semi-structured data* and *machine-readable*. The internet consists of a wealth of factual information, however this information is not identified as such and is organised in an unstructured way that makes harvesting difficult. The solution has been to use mark-up language (see *XML*) and unique identifiers to make this information visible, with the identifiers connecting to associated information stored in a RDF (Resource Description Framework) file, that enables the creation of *linked data*. Importantly, this process uses *data ontology* standards to formally represent *metadata* and relationships between entities and categories, and common exchange *protocols*, with this applied across the web. The semantic web enables the automated harvesting and processing of web data, opening it up to *re-use* and *repurposing*.

Further reading

DeWeese, K.P. and Segal, D. (2022) *Libraries and the Semantic Web*. Morgan & Claypool, San Rafael, CA.

semi-structured data   Data that have no formal, defined *data model*, but which do have some structuring that enables them to be *machine-readable* and processed using automated techniques. For example, the tagging in *XML*-encoded web pages can be treated as data which are machine-readable. Here, the data structure is not fully defined, but rather is irregular, flexible, yet reasonably consistent and often nested hierarchically. The semi-structured tagging provides a means to classify, order, and sort the data. See also *structured data*, *unstructured data*.

sensor data   Data that are generated through the use of sensors. A sensor is a technical instrument that responds to a physical phenomenon and provides a mechanical, electrical or optical signal that may be interpreted as a value with respect to a measurement scale. For example, a thermometer that measures temperature in degrees Celsius. Sensor data used to be recorded by a person reading and noting the measurement; recently, this process has become *automated* with the use of networked digital sensors continuously generating and recording *big data* and sending them to a central server. Many digital devices now have embedded sensors that produce and record data; for example, an iPhone has several sensors: accelerometer, three axis gyroscope, compass, GPS, barometer/altitude, ambient light, moisture, thermal, touch ID, Face ID, proximity to screen surface, camera, and a microphone. While sensors seemingly capture data in a neutral, technical way, decisions and choices are made with respect to the sensitivity of the sensor, its *calibration*, its siting, and how often it captures a reading, all of which can have effects on *data quality* and lead to *ecological fallacy* issues.

Further reading

McGrath, M.J. and Ní Scanaill, C. (2014) *Sensor Technologies: Healthcare, Wellness, and Environmental Applications*. Apress Open.

services, see *data services*

sharing, see *data sharing*

simulated data   Data that have been produced using a simulation model. Simulated data are an imitation of real-world data. They are useful when it is difficult to produce real-world data for reasons of access or ethics sensitivity, or because real-world data has significant *data quality* and veracity issues. They can be used as *synthetic data* in other models.

simulation   A form of *modelling* in which a computational model aims to imitate how a real-world system performs, or how an as yet unmade system might perform if created. The aim is to replicate real-world processes to simulate how these might perform under different conditions (e.g., different evacuation routes), or to simulate new processes to assess and select preferred options (e.g., what might happen to traffic on a road network if a new road is built). By constructing and running the simulation, one gains a deeper understanding of the logics of a system, of how its processes work and how different outcomes are achieved. One can also validate whether a system such as a road traffic control system is optimally configured. An interactive simulation involves the presence of a human actor; for example, a flight simulator in which a trainee pilot can practise flying in a highly realistic simulation. Well-performing simulations require good *data quality* and strong data *veracity*, and their performance might be refined through comparison to real-world outcomes. In many cases, simulations might be trained on or use *synthetic data* that mimic real-world data but provide controlled parameters and environments. Simulations can produce *simulated data* that can be used in other modelling tasks.

Further reading
Robinson, S. (2014) *Simulation: The Practice of Model Development and Use*. Second edition. Red Globe Press, London.

situated knowledge   An *epistemological* position that acknowledges that there is no *objectivity* in the production of knowledge, but rather it is *contingent* on and reflects the logics, values, assumptions, and learned behaviour of those undertaking research. That is, situated knowledge recognises that knowledge production is not impartial and value free. It advocates that a researcher practices *reflexivity* in how they conduct a study, details their *positionality* with respect to their approach and values, and makes clear the context, assumptions, and choices made. The concept of situated knowledge also makes clear that there is no one way to produce knowledge (see *scientific method*), but there are a plurality of approaches that can be legitimately adopted in undertaking research. Such a view is not, however, advocating relativism (i.e., claiming that all knowledge has equal *validity*); instead, the call for situated knowledge is for all knowledge producers to acknowledge and take responsibility for their epistemic claims.

Further reading

Haraway, D. (1988) 'Situated knowledges: The science question in feminism and the privileges of partial perspective', *Feminist Studies*, 14(3): 575–99.

slow computing An approach to digital life that uses practical and political interventions to reassert self-determination of time sovereignty (control over time) and *data sovereignty* (control over data). Drawing parallels with other slow movements, such as slow food, slow tourism, and slow scholarship, slow computing seeks balanced digital lives. Part of that balance is asserting data sovereignty: adopting personal practices that seek to limit data extraction, and collective tactics to campaign for institutional, regulatory, and legislative change and to shift societal attitudes towards mass *datafication* and *dataveillance*. Collective tactics are important as not all members of society have the same ability or power to personally assert data sovereignty. Underpinning the approach are a progressive set of *data ethics* (rooted in an *ethics of data care*) and *data justice*.

Further reading

Kitchin, R. and Fraser, A. (2020) *Slow Computing: Why We Need Balanced Digital Lives*. Bristol University Press, Bristol.

small data Data that are *sampled* and generated occasionally or in a single study. Prior to the *big data* age, small data were simply labelled as 'data'; the designation of small is a recent addition, signifying that the data have different *ontological* characteristics to big data. In the past, data were costly to produce and were generated to perform particular tasks. Due to the resources needed to capture, process, and analyse them, data were typically sampled and were narrow in *variety*. That is not to say that some small datasets do not have large *volume*. A *census*, for example, is exhaustive in terms of sampling (population = all) and will generate millions of records. However, it is undertaken once every five or ten years, only asks thirty to forty fixed questions, publication is usually a year or more after generation, and the published data are *tertiary data*. In other words, census data have no *velocity*, variety or *extensionality*, and lack high resolution *granularity*. *Primary data* generated through one-off studies have no temporal continuity and typically have weak *relationality*. Small data studies remain important because they can be tailored to answer specific questions. Additional value can be leveraged from small data by scaling them into larger datasets, ingesting them into *data repositories* for *re-use*, and analysing them using *data analytics*.

Further reading

Kitchin, R. and Lauriault, T. (2015) 'Small data in the era of big data', *GeoJournal*, 80(4): 463–75.

social credit scoring   The calculation of a score that represents the performance and reputation of individuals and companies, with that score used to practise *social sorting*. Social credit scoring is often associated with the various scores introduced in China by the state and companies to rate people and institutions, but they are also calculated elsewhere; for example, by *data brokers* to assess the relative merits of individuals with respect to creditworthiness and access to services. In the Chinese case, a plethora of social credit score systems are in operation, administered by national and municipal governments, banks, and platform companies. In the case of the state, the National Credit Information Sharing Platform pulls together 400 datasets from forty-two central agencies, thirty-two local governments, and fifty market actors with respect to public administration, law enforcement and security, social activities, and commercial activities. These data are used to calculate a score for each person and company, which represents how well they conform to expected behaviour. Achieving a high score means receiving preferential treatment with regards to government services, housing, schooling and university, travel options, financial loans, and access to work, whereas a low score leads to penalties. For companies, the score affects their access to public procurement and market permits. The Chinese government argues that social credit scoring creates a fairer society by treating people on their relative merits, as captured in the data about them, and the system eradicates bias and corruption by officials in the treatment of the population. Nonetheless, social credit scoring raises significant political and ethical concerns since it deepens state *surveillance*, reinforces the power of the state to control lives, and institutionalises pronounced *social sorting* that reproduces inequalities.

Further reading

Liang, F., Das, V., Kostyuk, N., and Hussain, M.M. (2018) 'Constructing a data-driven society: China's Social Credit System as a state surveillance infrastructure', *Policy and Internet*, 10(4): 415–53.

social media data   Data that are generated within social media platforms (e.g., Facebook, Twitter/X, Instagram, Snapchat, TikTok). Such data usually have strong *variety*, including a range of unstructured media: posts, comments, emoticons, photos, videos, likes, shares, links, click-throughs, and social connections. These data are considered particularly valuable because they combine factual *personal data* with thoughts, opinions, values, reports of offline activity, social networks, and, if geo-referenced, real-time location. Such data are highly beneficial for advertising and marketing, *profiling* and *social sorting*, and they are much sought after by academics seeking to research opinions, behaviour, and social issues. Consequently, there is a sizeable *data market* for social media data, with social media platforms acting as *data brokers* and having strong business partnerships with other brokers. It is the value of these data that has led to the large share price valuation of the platform companies.

Further reading

Sloan, L., Quan-Haase, A., and Metzler, K. (eds) (2017) *The SAGE Handbook of Social Media Research Methods*. Sage, London.

social sorting The practice of segmenting and rating populations in order to treat them differentially. *Administrative data* and commercial data have long been used to calculate who should receive services, credit, and preferential treatment and who should be penalised. In the *big data* era, social sorting has become more widespread and utilises more sophisticated methods of categorising and sorting individuals. This can include predictive *profiling*, wherein people are differentially sorted on the basis of predictions about their future performance, risk, and value. Social sorting has been critiqued for its reductionist method (judging people based solely on the data associated with them), inherent *data determinism*, weak *transparency*, *accountability* and redress, as well as for reproducing and deepening social divides. See also *demographically identifiable information, geodemographics, redlining, social credit scoring*.

Further reading

Dencik, L., Redden, J., Hintz, A., and Warne, H. (2019) 'The "golden view": Data-driven governance in the scoring society', *Internet Policy Review*, 8(2): 1–24.

socio-technical A conceptual framing that recognises that how digital systems are constituted, organised, and work is always a product of the intertwining of social relations (e.g., organisational structures, the actions of people) and technical relations (e.g., hardware and software, but also governance and law, which involve sets of rules and protocols), rather than simply the latter. This entwining is captured in the notion of a *data assemblage*, wherein a diverse set of actors, objects, and organisational and technical factors are bound and work together to produce a data-driven system.

Further reading

Bijker, W.E. and Law, J. (eds) (1994) *Shaping Technology/Building Society: Studies in Sociotechnical Change*. MIT Press, Cambridge, MA.

software Coded instructions and *algorithms* compiled as computer programs that process input commands and data to undertake tasks on digital technologies and across digital infrastructures. Software codifies the world into rules and process routines that perform complex tasks quickly and efficiently. Software varies in nature from abstract machine code to programming languages and scripts, operating systems, and a diverse set of applications (programs). Software is vital to the generation, processing, distribution, and analysis of digital data. The power of software, and the reason for its incredible growth and importance in contemporary society and economy, is its ability to do productive work in the world and generate value. Software and data are largely dyadic, with many systems created to produce and process data, and the data being the core input that shapes how software functions. As with data, a critical field of study that concentrates on understanding code and software has developed in recent years named 'Software Studies'.

Further reading

Kitchin, R. and Dodge, M. (2011) *Code/Space: Software and Everyday Life*. MIT Press, Cambridge, MA.

Marino, M.C. (2020) *Critical Code Studies*. MIT Press, Cambridge, MA.

sousveillance   Self-surveillance in which a person records and monitors their own activities, and the monitoring of state and corporate surveillance by those who are surveilled. The term was first coined by Mann et al. (2003). Whereas 'sur' in *surveillance* refers to 'above' and the monitoring at a distance, 'sous' in sousveillance refers to 'below' and the monitoring from a personal perspective. With the rise of personal digital technologies that can act as *automated* recording devices through embedded *sensors* and cameras (e.g., fitness trackers, smart watches, smartphones), it is now easy for people to closely track their own activity (e.g., number of steps, kilometres walked) and health (e.g., heart rate, blood pressure, weight) and to monitor change over time. Rigorous self-monitoring has led to what has been termed the *quantified self*: measuring one's own performance through self-selected *key performance indicators*. In addition, people can use their digital devices to 'watch the watchers': to record photos, video, and audio of the activities of state and company actors and to post these on social media and websites. In other words, surveillance is inverted to come from below and used to hold those in authority to account.

Further reading

Mann, S., Nolan, J., and Wellman, B. (2003) 'Sousveillance: Inventing and using wearable computing devices for data collection in surveillance environments', *Surveillance & Society*, 1(3): 331–55.

Special issue on 'The state of sousveillance', *Surveillance & Society* 18(2): 257–87.

sovereignty, see *data sovereignty*

spatial analysis   A set of methods and techniques for analysing *spatial data*. Because of their unique characteristics and form, referring to 2D or 3D phenomena, spatial data require the use of methods other than traditional *statistics* and *data analytics* in order to extract insight from them. The longest standing is *mapping*: visualising spatial data as a map to reveal location. Others include various spatial forms of *descriptive statistics* and *inferential statistics* that reveal and test the significance of associations and relationships within spatial data, and spatial *modelling*. More recently, a new range of spatial analytics capable of handling spatial *big data* have been developed. These include spatial *data mining*, new modelling and *simulation* techniques, and *visual analytics*.

Further reading

Rey, S. and Franklin, R. (eds) (2022) *Handbook of Spatial Analysis in the Social Sciences*. Edward Elgar Publishing, Cheltenham.

Singleton, A., Spielman, S.E., and Folch, D.C. (2017) *Urban Analytics*. Sage, London.

spatial data   Data that have location or other geographic referents. Spatial data (often termed geospatial data) can refer specifically to location and geography (e.g., latitude and longitude, addresses, postcodes, or administrative and property boundaries) or to *attribute data* that are geo-referenced through being directly tied to location data. Spatial data can have a number of forms including vector (points, lines, polygons) and raster (pixels) formats, and text (address, coordinates) in spatial databases. Large volumes of digital data are geo-referenced through the collection of addresses in administrative and online retail systems, and through the use of GPS in mobile technologies, constituting spatial *big data*. When mapped and analysed using *spatial analysis*, spatial data reveal the geographic patterns of phenomena and activities. Spatial data have therefore become an important asset and *data market*. Large concentrations of spatial data are stored within *spatial data infrastructures* and viewed and analysed within geographic information systems (GISs). With respect to *data brokers*, spatial data are used for *geodemographics*, spatial sorting, and *redlining*.

spatial data infrastructure (SDI) A framework and technical architecture for the storing, exchange, and analysis of large concentrations of *spatial data* and associated *metadata* related to an area (usually a region or nation; see *statistical geography*). For example, a SDI might store national mapping data, environmental and land cover data, remote sensing data and aerial photography, and spatial *administrative data*, and provide geographic information system (GIS) and other spatial analysis tools to map and draw insights from these data. To ensure *data quality* and enable *data fusion*, SDIs enforce a common set of *data standards*, and implement a strong regime of *data governance* and *data regulation*.

Further reading

Masser, I. (ed.) (2019) *Geographic Information Systems to Spatial Data Infrastructures: A Global Perspective*. CRC Press, London.

spatial sorting, see *redlining*, *geodemographics*

spectacle, see *data spectacle*

standardisation 1. The process of developing and implementing *data standards*. 2. A *data transformation* process to ensure that a dataset complies with a data standard. The first process involves many organisations negotiating and agreeing on the formulation of a data standard and its adoption across sectors. A number of different national and international bodies coordinate the creation and maintenance of data standards (see *metrology*). The second process is the internal application of and compliance with data standards and is a part of *data management* and *data governance*. Standardisation enables digital systems to exchange and merge data by ensuring *interoperability* (see *data fusion* and *data enrichment*) and aids the coordination and sharing of data between organisations.

standards, see *data standards*

statistical geography   The organisation of spatial boundaries that are used for publishing data geographically. For example, *census* data might be published relating to districts and counties, or other administrative boundaries. The use of a statistical geography enables areas to be compared through spatial statistics, as well as the production of choropleth maps. Importantly, the statistical geography used can significantly affect the spatial pattern shown, resulting in *ecological fallacies*. This is known as the modifiable areal unit problem, wherein increasing the *scale* of geographical areas into which data are aggregated reduces variability (a scaling effect), and altering the position of boundaries affects which areas individual data points lie within and thus the pattern of aggregation (a boundary effect). These scaling and boundary effects can be used for political purposes through gerrymandering; that is, organising constituency boundaries in a way that leads to a more favourable voting outcome. In other words, a statistical geography is never arbitrary or neutral, but has a politics to its design.

statistical significance   The probability that the result of a statistical test is true and the null hypothesis can be rejected. The intent is to determine whether the outcome of a test is real and unlikely to be the result of chance, and establish the extent to which there is confidence in the analysis. Confidence is ascertained by comparing the test result to a probability estimate of the significance level of the finding. The confidence level is expressed as a p value between 0 and 1 (e.g., p=0.05 or p=0.01, which means that there is a 95 per cent, or 99 per cent, chance that the hypothesis is true; or to put it another way, there is a 1 in 20, or a 1 in 100, chance that accepting the hypothesis is erroneous). *Parametric statistics* and *non-parametric statistics* involve significance testing. While it is a mainstay of research using statistics, significance testing has a number of issues and its merits have been subject to debate. A particular issue with *big data* is that as the size of a dataset grows the number of seemingly meaningful relationships grows, producing test results that have p-values above p=0.05 yet in reality they are *false positives* and there is no association, thus producing *ecological fallacies* in interpretation.

Further reading

Lecoutre, B. (2011) 'Significance tests: A critique', in Lovric, M. (ed.), *International Encyclopedia of Statistical Science*. Springer Science, Heidelberg, pp. 1323–5.

Taleb, N. (2013) 'Beware the big errors of "big data"', *Wired*, 2 February, www.wired.com/2013/02/big-data-means-big-errors -people

statistics   A branch of applied mathematics that uses various analytical techniques to generate, describe, organise, and analyse *quantitative data*. The term has its origins in Germany, where it meant 'the science of the state', referring to the use of applied mathematics to examine a population. Statistics are now used to make sense of every kind of phenomenon and issue. There are a wide variety of statistics, including *descriptive statistics* and *inferential statistics*, *parametric statistics* and *non-parametric statistics*. Statistics are used in *modelling* and their calculation is a core part of *data analytics*. The methods, practices, and applications of statistics are not static, but have evolved over time.

Further reading

Desrosières, A. (1998) *The Politics of Large Numbers: A History of Statistical Reasoning*. Harvard University Press, Cambridge, MA.

Stigler, S.M. (2016) *The Seven Pillars of Statistical Wisdom*. Harvard University Press, Cambridge, MA.

storage, see *data storage*

stories, see *data stories*

stranded data   Data that cannot be linked to other data because they do not share *indexical data*, *metadata*, *data standards* or *data formats*. While many datasets can be conjoined, others remain isolated in *data silos*. For example, many research projects generate *primary data* that employ their own *data ontologies*, which, while fit for answering particular research questions, cannot be conjoined with other data, thus reducing their *re-use* and *repurposing* value. Despite efforts to improve data *standardisation*, stranded data remain common for a number of reasons, including the desire to produce data tailored to solve particular issues, the embeddedness of *legacy systems*, and changing data ontologies which break the time-series run of *longitudinal data*.

strategy, see *data strategy*

structured data Data that are organised in a defined *data model*. For example, numerical data in a relational database, or text data in a table, that have a consistent format (e.g. name, age, gender, address, etc.). Such data are straightforward to process, combine, and analyse, and are *machine-readable*, enabling *automated* data management and analysis. See also *semi-structured data*, *unstructured data*.

subject, see *data subject*

surveillance The systematic monitoring of people, places, and systems, usually for the purpose of management and governance. Surveillance can be conducted through in-person monitoring or by using a technology such as video cameras; it has long been a feature of societies, being used to increase safety and security, enact law and order, and monitor the activity and productivity of workers. The level and extent of surveillance varies across states, depending on the political system and security apparatus, and across sectors, depending on types of work and workers.

The ubiquity of digital technologies and systems mediating all aspects of everyday life, mass *datafication* and the advent of *big data* have radically extended and deepened the scope of surveillance – the data produced have finer *granularity*, have *velocity* (see *real-time data*), and are *indexical* in nature (e.g., unique IDs, *biometric data*). Surveillance is also being complemented with *dataveillance*, and *data standards* are enabling *interoperability* and the interlinking of data (see *control rooms*). How surveillance data are analysed has also increased in sophistication, so that rather than a person monitoring and analysing observations, a range of *data analytics*, including *data mining* and *pattern recognition* techniques (e.g., facial recognition), are being employed, along with predictive *profiling*. In addition, surveillance data and dataveillance have been enrolled into capitalism, particularly through the *data broker* industry, creating a new mode of capital production termed *surveillance capitalism.*

There has been significant concern regarding surveillance, the *data politics* involved in its implementation and operation, and the *data power* it enables. The level of surveillance and how it is being used has raised apprehensions about its role in governance and the potential for creating a *Big Brother* society, as well as its facilitation of social and economic discrimination through practices of *data colonialism* (see *social sorting, redlining, geodemographics*). In response, civil liberty organisations have been campaigning for limits on the practices of surveillance, stronger *data protection* and *privacy* legislation, and enhanced *transparency*, oversight, *accountability*, and redress, as well as conducting *data activism* through *counter-data actions*. The field of Surveillance Studies undertakes a critical analysis of all these issues. See also *data doubles, data footprints and shadows, sousveillance.*

Further reading

Brayne, S. (2020) *Predict and Surveil: Data, Discretion, and the Future of Policing.* Oxford University Press, Oxford.

Monahan, T. and Murakami Wood, D. (eds) (2018) *Surveillance Studies: A Reader.* Oxford University Press, Oxford.

surveillance capitalism   A form of *data capitalism* that derives profit from monetising *personal data* and other data in various ways, such as *profiling, social sorting*, recommender systems, and customer relations management, to target people with ads, nudge them to act in desired ways, and to make decisions about them that produce value. Part of the value is gained by creating efficiencies in marketing and sales by increasing the likelihood of a successful transaction, and reducing overheads and potential losses due to failed investment. A key means of gaining profit is through the trading of data in a vast set of *data markets* controlled by a network of general and specialised *data brokers*. These markets allow datasets to be conjoined to produce detailed profiles and perform *data services*. The key logic and mode of capital accumulation of surveillance capitalism is *data colonialism*, in which data about people are captured for as little cost as possible (preferably for free), and as much value extracted from them without sharing profits with *data subjects*.

There are several concerns with respect to surveillance capitalism. It pays minimal heed to *privacy* and *data protection* and works by monetising surveillance and actively targeting people. Moreover, the profiling and sorting practices undertaken can profoundly affect lives by determining whether individuals receive credit, work, insurance, housing or other goods and services, raising worries with respect to equity, fairness, and social justice. Given these concerns over excessive intrusiveness, the targeting of individuals and groups, and pernicious discriminatory practices, there have been calls for greater *transparency*, tighter *data regulation* of data markets and data brokers, and stronger *data rights* for data subjects. The fact that such calls often do not extend as far as a ban or tighter restrictions on the work of data brokers reflects the power of the industry's political capital in terms of blocking wholesale changes, and highlights that the present situation constitutes a *data doxa*, being institutionalised and normalised.

Further reading

Cinnamon, J. (2017) 'Social injustice in surveillance capitalism', *Surveillance & Society*, 15(5): 609–25.

Zuboff, S. (2019) *The Age of Surveillance Capitalism: The Fight for the Future at the New Frontier of Power*. Profile Books, New York.

survey A *methodology* for capturing and evaluating the experiences and opinions of a group of people. A survey refers to the whole process of capturing and analysing data in order to investigate an issue, wherein a *sample* of people are surveyed using a set of questions designed to generate data, which when analysed collectively provide a detailed picture of a phenomenon. The questions can be closed or open in nature, but there is a consistency in their structure and order. *Questionnaire* is sometimes taken to be synonymous with 'survey'; however, a questionnaire is a list of generally closed questions which might be used to collect data about a specific individual, but is not necessarily used to investigate an issue. For example, a patient might fill out a questionnaire that is simply used to aid their doctor, rather than being combined with other questionnaire data to understand the health of a population. *Critical Data Studies* research might use a survey when it is seeking to canvas the opinions of a sampled population.

Further reading

Wolf, C., Joye, D., Smith, T.W., and Fu, Y-C. (eds) (2016) *The SAGE Handbook of Survey Methodology*. Sage, London.

synthetic data   Data that are artificially produced using statistical calculations or *simulation* modelling. The benefits of synthetic data are that they can help mitigate issues relating to *privacy* and confidentiality, they are custom designed for a task rather than being *repurposed*, they should be free of *errors* and *biases* that might be present in a real-world dataset, and they can provide a viable substitute when authentic real-world data are scarce and it is difficult to gain *data access*. It is also possible to add characteristics to the data that are absent in a real-world dataset in order to test unusual or extreme conditions. Synthetic data are used to refine models with regards to handling non-standard situations and as *training data* for *machine learning* models. The main issue with synthetic data is their *veracity* and the extent to which they successfully imitate the characteristics of authentic data. Models trained on sub-optimal synthetic data will themselves be sub-optimal, which will have negative consequences for model use.

Further reading

Nikolenko, S.I. (2021) *Synthetic Data for Deep Learning*. Springer, Cham, Switzerland.

Steinhoff, J. (2024) 'Toward a political economy of synthetic data', *New Media & Society*, 26(6), 3290–306.

T

taxonomy   A scheme for organising aspects of the world through *categorisation and classification*. A taxonomy places an order on things, segmenting them into groups or types. It is usually hierarchically structured, having a tree-like structure, with categories or classes containing nested sub-categories and subclasses that are more finely differentiated. Taxonomies are often used to structure data and *information*, acting as a way of creating organised, indexed knowledge that enables browsing and searching. See also *data ontology*.

temporalities of data The timeframes relating to the *data lifecycle* and the uses of data. Data are produced in space and time, and they possess *data geographies* and *data histories*. An analysis of the temporalities of data focuses on the temporal rhythms and cycles (e.g., lifecycles, policy and business cycles, *timeliness*), temporal relations (e.g., pace and tempo, scheduling, sequencing, latency, synchronisation, time-space compression), and temporal modalities (e.g., past, present, and future) of data. *Archives* store data about the past and contribute to *memory*. *Legacy systems* and *path dependencies* shape the constitution and operation of present systems. *Longitudinal data analysis* tracks change over time. *Small data* and *big data* possess different temporalities, with the latter possessing *velocity*, being produced in *real-time*. *Prediction* enables a prognosis of future outcomes.

Further reading

Kitchin, R. (2023) *Digital Timescapes: Technology, Temporality and Society*. Polity Press, Cambridge.

tertiary data A form of *derived data*, such as *aggregated* counts, categories, and statistical results. Data published by *national statistics organisations* are usually tertiary data, rather than the original base data generated, in order to protect confidentiality. For example, *census* data are published as tertiary data, with the base data only released as *secondary data* after a set period of time. See also *primary data*.

timeliness Data are published and shared in a timely manner. *Small data*, such as most *administrative data* and *official statistics*, are not published in real-time. Instead, the data need to be managed, transformed, and checked before they are made available. In the case of official statistics, their publication is prescribed by a timetable. For example, a consumer price index is usually published within ninety days of the data being generated. In some cases, the time between generation and publication can be significant. For example, most *censuses* are published twelve to eighteen months after generation due to the scale of the task of compiling and checking the data. In other cases, significant delays are due to inefficiencies or a deliberate tactic to avoid scrutiny. The more timely the publishing of the data, the more useful they are likely to be for informing an issue.

time-series analysis, see *longitudinal analysis*

tortured data   Data that have been subjected to *data wrangling* and/or *data dredging* so that they reveal what is desired by the analyst. The phrase originates from the Nobel Prize-winning economist Ronald Coase, who stated, 'If you torture the data long enough, it will confess.' See also *lying with statistics*.
  Further reading
  Smith, G. (2014) *Standard Deviations: Flawed Assumptions, Tortured Data, and Other Ways to Lie with Statistics*. Gerald Duckworth & Co, London.

training data   Data that are used to train *machine learning* algorithms. Machine learning seeks to learn from data in order to refine a *model* and determine how to act in relation to such data. Training data are used initially to fit the model and its parameters so that it can be used to identify and act on data in a real-world setting. For example, a database of faces might be used to train a model to be able to identify faces in *surveillance* footage. The outputs of the model might initially be compared to a target dataset to determine the success rate of the predicted identification and thus *validate* the model. The results from this process are then used to adjust the variable selection and model parameters to try to improve the model's *accuracy and precision*. Care needs to be taken in selecting the training data as they can introduce systematic *biases* into the model. There has been criticism of facial recognition systems for their high error rates in identifying Black people, largely caused by the training data consisting mainly of white faces. Similarly, predictive policing systems have been critiqued for overly targeting Black people, reproducing *bias* and perpetuating institutional racism, a result of using historical police data (in which Black people are recorded as being disproportionately stopped, searched, and arrested) as the training data. In other words, while systems using machine learning claim to be impartial and *objective* in their operation, they inherently reflect any biases or errors in their training data.

Further reading

Buolamwini, J. and Gebru, T. (2018) 'Gender shades: Intersectional accuracy disparities in commercial gender classification', *Proceedings of Machine Learning Research*, 81(1): 1–15.

transformation, see *data transformation*

transient data   Data that are never examined, processed, or stored, and are deleted shortly after use. Much of the data generated within systems reliant on *big data* are transient data. The data are generated for the purposes of performing a particular task and once this is completed the value of the data is reduced. There is little to be gained from retaining the data, which given its *volume* might require a lot of storage space. Most of the data produced within a traffic control system – the hundreds of video feeds and sensor readings – are transient data. They might be kept for a day or so and then erased, or converted into *derived data* (e.g., an aggregate form) that might have some future value, with the *primary data* deleted.

transparency   A condition that permits people to easily see the intent and actions of others and enables *accountability*. Transparency is a fundamental principle of open government; that is, the ability of citizens to view the decision-making and workings of public bodies (see *freedom of information*). The principle extends to the data and *metadata* produced and processed by the state, and transparency has been a key argument used by the *open data movement* for the publication of *open data*. Such open data also create a degree of transparency on the successes or failures of public bodies in the work they perform; for example, whether a policy has had the desired effects. Companies are usually reluctant to provide transparency with respect to their data holdings and data work in order to protect their competitive advantage and to limit scrutiny of their practices. It can therefore be difficult to assess their operations and *data power*, and to hold them to account. Transparency is a key component of *privacy by design*, wherein the operations and component parts of systems that capture *personal data* should be made transparent to *data subjects* and be open to independent verification. A component of *data quality* is *methodological transparency*, wherein the specific processes used to generate data should be made open to data users.

Further reading

Wiencierz, C. and Lünich, M. (2022) 'Trust in open data applications through transparency', *New Media & Society*, 24(8): 1751–70.

Zook, M. and Spangler, I. (2023) 'A crisis of data? Transparency practices and infrastructures of value in data broker platforms', *Annals of the American Association of Geographers*, 113(1): 110–28.

trusted digital repository   A *data repository* that is certified to meet certain standards designed to ensure sustainable, long-term *preservation* and controlled access to the data it holds. It is trusted in the sense that the degree to which depositors and users can trust the repository has been independently evaluated. To qualify for certification, a repository has to demonstrate that it: serves its constituencies and has evaluation and *accountability* mechanisms; has strong *data governance* and management processes; complies with expected conventions and standards; possesses a comprehensive set of policies regarding practices, responsibilities, and performance; has access controls and *data security* to ensure that only those with permission can access data; has stable, sustainable finances and is fiscally responsible; has a long-term strategy for storage and IT migration.

Further reading

Faundeen, J. (2017) 'Developing criteria to establish trusted digital repositories', *Data Science Journal*, 16(22): 1–13.

truth   The way things actually are. The nature of truth is an *ontology* question, concerned with what we can legitimately know. The *scientific method* seeks to establish the truth about the world, to detail how it is and how it works. Truth in these terms is the correspondence between facts and reality, evident when a study has very strong *veracity, validity,* and *repeatability, reproducibility, and replicability.* Data are the basis on which *facts* are derived and thus aid the establishment of truth. Constructivists reject the notion of truth, arguing that facts are produced rather than given, and they are open to change. That is not to say that there are no valid statements about the world – there are clearly statements with a strong weight of evidence to support them – but rather that there are no absolute truths.

U

unanticipated consequences   Unforeseen or unintended outcomes from an action designed to produce a particular outcome. An unanticipated consequence can be positive (when there is an unexpected additional benefit) or negative (the expected outcome is not achieved), or create a drawback (the expected outcome is achieved, but there is also a negative effect), or be perverse (the action makes the problem worse). Data-driven systems often produce unanticipated consequences for a variety of reasons, including *glitches*, *data quality* issues (e.g., *errors*, *biases*), human error, gaming of the system, and the issue being much more complex than the system is designed to handle. Unanticipated consequences reveal the emergent, *contingent*, and *contextual* nature of data-driven systems.

uncertainty   In statistical terms, uncertainty is the estimated degree of inaccuracy and imprecision in measured data. Since the exact degree of uncertainty is unknown it has a probabilistic basis, with the extent of uncertainty being statistically calculated using measures such as standard deviations or probability distributions. Uncertainty is a component of *data quality* and the more uncertainty there is in a dataset and associated analysis, the weaker the level of trust that can be invested in the results.

uncounted   The individuals who are omitted from datasets for various reasons. Many datasets relating to society have systematic *gaps and exclusions* as a result of individuals being uncounted or under-counted. Such groups might be hard to reach, thus making it difficult to generate data in relation to them; for example, undocumented migrants, illegal workers, and homeless people. Others might take actions to avoid their affairs being monitored, such as the super-rich who offshore their assets. In other cases, a decision is taken to exclude some individuals from a sample, such as excluding homeless people, people living in correctional facilities or residential care, the military or non-local-language speakers from mental health surveys. Excluding individuals from being counted can be a means of excluding them from political representation and service delivery. In other words, there is a politics to counting: who is counted, how they are counted, who they are counted by, and the consequences of not being counted matter.

Further reading

Cobham, A. (2020) *The Uncounted*. Polity Press, Cambridge.

Wright, E., Pagliaro, C., Page, I.S., and Diminic, S. (2023) 'A review of excluded groups and non-response in population-based mental health surveys from high-income countries', *Social Psychiatry and Psychiatric Epidemiology*, 58(9): 1265–92.

universalism, see *data universalism*

unstructured data   Data that do not have a defined *data model*, except with respect to their *metadata*. *Qualitative data* are unstructured data. While each piece of data might have a specific structure or format (such as an image or narrative text), there is no consistency across data in a dataset. The lack of structure means that each piece of data is discrete and they are not easily combined. It is possible, however, to convert unstructured data to *structured data* through *categorisation and classification*. See also *semi-structured data*.

V

validation   Checking that a process, system or service performs as intended, and produces anticipated outcomes that match requirements and have strong *accuracy and precision*. Data validation is important for ensuring that the data used within a system have *data integrity* and *data veracity*, that how a data-driven system performs can be trusted and the outcomes acted on in confidence. With respect to data produced by a system, validation is sometimes termed ground-truthing, in which the data's veracity is verified by checking them against real-world phenomena (e.g., validating remote sensing data against actual ground cover). Validation might also be assessed through *repeatability, reproducibility, and replicability* and be addressed through *calibration*.

validity The extent to which a concept, statement or conclusion is well-founded and logically appears genuine or authentic. Data have validity if their constitution is based on solid conceptual and methodological foundations, and if the interpretations and conclusions drawn from them are robust and trustworthy. While validity refers to robustness and logical founding, *veracity* refers to truth and the extent to which the data are accurate and precise representations of the real world. *Data quality* issues, along with *fake data, gamed data,* and poor *research design,* raise data validity concerns. See also *data integrity, ecological fallacies*.

variety A mixture of data types within a data system. Initial definitions of *big data* included variety as one of its three key attributes. *Small data* and big data can be *qualitative data* or *quantitative data,* and can be *structured, semi-structured* or *unstructured* in nature. In the case of small data, the data tend to be discrete and any linking of them is done through *indexical data* and common fields. The same is the case with much big data; however, it is also now possible to more easily conjoin various forms of data. For example, social media platforms enable text, emoticons, photos, videos, sound, and weblinks to be joined together and handled in a single system. In the past, database management was proficient at handling quantitative data but struggled to handle unstructured data; now new database design enables the storing and interlinking of the full range of data types.

velocity The rate at which data are created and processed by a system. Velocity is considered a key attribute of *big data*. Many data-driven systems generate, process, analyse, and act on *realtime data*. This is in contrast to the production of *small data*, which proceeds at a slower pace and is much less timely (see *timeliness*). For example, a national *census* is conducted once every ten years, the data are generated over the course of a couple of weeks, but the results can take more than a year to be published. In contrast, a post in social media is immediately recorded in the system's databases and microseconds later published on user timelines, with this occurring hundreds of thousands of times per minute across all posters and readers. The velocity of data production contributes to the *volume* of data. See also *temporalities of data, variety*.

veracity   The extent to which a dataset has adherence to the *truth*. Veracity concerns how *accurate and precise* data are, and how faithfully they represent the phenomenon they seek to measure (that is, how far they have strong fidelity). How well the data faithfully represent the true nature of a phenomenon can vary. For example, judging the fidelity of data with respect to people can be particularly problematic, especially when the data relate to values, beliefs, opinions, and reported behaviour. What people say they think and do, and what their actual thoughts and behaviour are, can be quite different. Similarly, the use of *proxy data* can be problematic. For example, using research and development (R&D) investment as a measure of innovation – just because a lot of money has been spent on research does not mean that it automatically led to successful new products, and major innovations might have cost little. There are also concerns over the extent to which *synthetic data* are representative of real-world phenomena and processes. The less veracity a dataset has the less trust that can be placed in the outputs produced from it. See also *data integrity, data quality*.

visceral data   Data that utilise multiple senses and can stimulate a visceral physical or emotional response rather than just insight or critical reflection. The term was introduced by Stark (2014) to refer to forms of data that we 'see, hear, feel, breathe, ingest', which produce an affective reaction (see *affect*). He postulates that such data are more engaging and compelling, and engender stronger reflective and behavioural responses. *Data physicalisations* that conjoin vision with touch, smell or taste offer one means of producing visceral data.

Further reading
Stark, L. (2014) 'Come on feel the data (and smell it)', *The Atlantic*, 19 May, www.theatlantic.com/technology/archive/2014/05/data-visceralization/370899

visual analytics   A form of analytical reasoning using interactive and dynamic *data visualisation* methods. Rather than simply display data, visualisation is used as an analytical tool. Visual analytics mostly consists of interactive statistical charts and graphs and interactive maps. Here, analysts can 'play' with the data, turning layers on and off, zooming in and out, altering *scales* and *categorisation and classification*, and modifying the visual form of display. A suite of interlinked visualisations might be used, where interactions with data points in one display highlight related data in another. In this way, an analyst can explore the data to reveal patterns and relationships. In addition, *data mining* and *pattern recognition*, and the visualisation of *inferential statistics* and *spatial analysis*, can be performed. Visual analytics can be used in the telling of *data stories*.

Further reading

Andrienko, N., Andrienko, G., Fuchs, G., Slingsby, A., Turkay, C., and Wrobel, S. (2020) *Visual Analytics for Data Scientists*. Springer, Cham, Switzerland.

Tominski, C. and Schumann, H. (2020) *Interactive Visual Data Analysis*. CRC Press, Baton Rouge, FL.

visualisation, see *data visualisation*

volume   The amount of data being produced by a data system. Initial definitions of *big data* included volume as one of its three key attributes. This is because, in general terms, big data are voluminous, often consisting of terabytes or petabytes of data that are generated through billions of data processes daily. For example, every minute, millions of emails and texts are sent, and hundreds of thousands of online sales transactions and social media posts are made, globally. In 2018, it was estimated that 2.5 quintillion bytes of data are produced each day, with 90 per cent of all data existing in the world having been generated in the previous two years. It is important to note, however, that not all big data are voluminous in terms of storage space. Continuously generated sensor data consists of a large volume of records, but each record is small in size requiring little storage space. As such, volume consists of three dimensions: the number of records; the storage required per record; and the total storage required (the sum of the first two). Systems that have a high volume of records which are large in size (e.g., YouTube videos) can pose a particular challenge, with the number of new records daily requiring flexible database structure and format, and the size of files requiring extensive, scalable storage. See also *velocity*, *variety*.

Further reading

Marr, B. (2018) 'How much data do we create every day?', *Forbes*, 21 May, www.forbes.com/sites/bernardmarr/2018/05/21/how-mu ch-data-do-we-create-every-day-the-mind-blowing-stats-everyone -should-read

Kitchin, R. and McArdle, G. (2016) 'What makes big data, big data? Exploring the ontological characteristics of 26 datasets', *Big Data & Society*, 3(1): 1–10.

W

walking methods, see *data walks*

wrangling, see *data wrangling*

X

XML Extensible Markup Language (XML) is a means of tagging the content of webpages so that they become *machine-readable data*. In effect, XML turns the world wide web from a set of loosely connected, unstructured texts, images, and other content into an internet of semi-structured data that are standardised within a common framework and are open to *data mining* and being assembled into datasets. As such, it produces the *semantic web* and enables the sharing of *linked data*.

Z

zombie data 1. Data that reside on storage media, digital devices, and servers that are no longer used. 2. Data whose veracity is weak or untrue, but which continue to circulate and be used. With respect to the first case, zombie data might simply be data that have been forgotten; or their original owner might have left the organisation and the data has not been deleted. Here, zombie data serve no useful purpose, yet they have never reached the end of the *data lifecycle* and *deletion*. In the case of *open data* sites, zombie data refers to datasets that are never downloaded. In theory, they could be given new life through discovery and use, but are more likely to simply be stored indefinitely. In the case of data that are used persistently despite questionable veracity (such as a false *fact* that continues to be quoted by news media or vested interests), zombie data refuse to die, being used tactically to support political or policy positions (see *lying with statistics*). Such zombie data are often resistant to challenge given their *fixation as evidence*.

Further reading

Brennan, D. (2017) 'Fighting human trafficking today: Moral panics, zombie data, and the seduction of rescue', *Wake Forest Law Review* 52(2): 477–96.

D'Ignazio, C. and Klein, L.F. (2020) *Data Feminism*. MIT Press, Cambridge, MA.

Index

Printed and bound by CPI Group (UK) Ltd, Croydon, CR0 4YY

17/12/2025

14794995-0003